No Middle Ground

Major Thomas Ward Osborn c. 1865
(Courtesy of the Jefferson County Historical Society)

Batt. D
1st NY Lt. Art.
2nd Div., 3rd Corps.
+
11th Corps. Art.

No Middle Ground

Thomas Ward Osborn's
Letters from the Field
(1862-1864)

Edited by
Herb S. Crumb
and
Katherine Dhalle

Edmonston Publishing, Inc.
Hamilton, New York

Foreword, Introduction, Index, Notes, Maps, Editing, and Volume Arrangement Copyright © 1993 by Edmonston Publishing, Inc.

All rights reserved. No part of this book may be reproduced in any form, mechanical, photographic or electronic, nor may it be stored, transmitted or otherwise copied in a retrieval system without the written permission of the publisher, except by a reviewer who may quote brief passages in a review.

These letters are part of the journals of Thomas Ward Osborn in the Colgate University Library, Hamilton, NY.

ISBN 0-9622393-4-8

Printed in the United States of America on pH neutral paper.
∞
10 9 8 7 6 5 4 3 2 1

Library of Congress Cataloging-in-Publication Data

Osborn, Thomas Ward, 1833-1898.
  No middle ground : Thomas Ward Osborn's letters from the field (1862-1864) / edited by Herb S. Crumb and Katherine Dhalle.
    p. cm.
  Includes bibliographical references (p.) and index.
  ISBN 0-9622393-4-8 (alk. paper)
  1. Osborn, Thomas Ward, 1833-1898—Correspondence. 2. United States. Army. New York Light Artillery Regiment, 1st (1861-1865). Battery D. 3. United States. Army of the Potomac. Corps, 11th. Artillery Brigade. 4. New York (State)—History—Civil War, 1861-1865—Personal narratives. 5. United States—History—Civil War, 1861-1865—Personal narratives. 6. Soldiers—New York (State)—Correspondence. 7. Osborn family—Correspondence. I. Crumb, Herb S. II. Dhalle, Katherine, 1947- . III. Title.
E523.6 1st.083 1993
973.7'447—dc20   93-8590

To

Richard Barksdale Harwell (1916-1988)

The most honest historian in America.
Allan Nevins

*If we lose in this war, the country is lost and if we win it is saved.
There is no middle ground.*

Thomas Ward Osborn
January 1, 1863

Contents

Foreword by Richard Pindell — xi

Introduction — xiii

Preface — xviii

1. Prelude — 1

2. Williamsburg — 17

3. Seven Pines/Fair Oaks — 38

4. "Planned Withdrawal" — 58

5. Fredericksburg — 83

6. After Fredericksburg — 102

7. Chancellorsville — 116

8. Chattanooga — 158

Bibliography — 191

Index — 195

Illustrations and Maps

Illustrations

Maj. Thomas Ward Osborn c. 1865	ii
Osborn's Original Title Page	xxi
Capt. George B. Winslow	5
Col. Charles S. Wainwright	23
Burying the Dead	49
Battery D on the Rappahannock	124
Maj. Gen. Hiram G. Berry	126
Hazel Grove	127
Looking down the Plank Road	130
Staying Jackson's Advance	132

Maps

Union Artillery at Fairview	122
Chattanooga Battlefield	159

Foreword

Civil War combatants, Northern and Southern alike, routinely characterized the Federal artillery as *superb*. Confederate General D. H. Hill, who was in a position to know, reportedly boasted, "Give me Confederate infantry and Federal artillery, and I will whip the world." Federal artillery officer Thomas W. Osborn was also in a position to know. At Chancellorsville and other battles the Confederate infantry fell dead and wounded in bloody windrows along his batteries' front but not before inflicting on his men and materiel terrible losses. Privy to the unspeakable horror of combat, Osborn in these letters from the field bears news known only to those touched by the fire of America's bloodiest war.

Yet if Osborn stood inside the belly of the beast, he remained outside the military gentlemen's club of power and influence. A type of the citizen soldier, an urban Cincinnatus, totally unacquainted with the art and science of warfare, he applied himself to artillery command, it almost seems, with a sword in one hand and a military manual in the other. What one of his peers at first mistook as slowness proved to be deliberateness. For even as he developed in command skills, Osborn maintained a healthy respect for what he still did not know. And develop he did. Captain of Battery D, First New York Light Artillery, in September 1861, Osborn found himself two years later the Chief of Artillery in the Federal Army of the Tennessee. But this mortar-shell-like rise in responsibility was unaccompanied by an equal elevation of rank. Incredibly, the shoulders that carried the "long arm" of an entire army bore only a major's straps. At this injustice Osborn, who practiced law before the war, must have surely smarted.

For this discrepancy, one of the Civil War's smaller mysteries (his lack of West Point or government connections only begins to explain it), this volume, with its incidental semaphoric flashes from Osborn's inner character, may provide an answer. Possessed of that scrupulous pride which, wholly untainted by vanity, verges on humility, Osborn was not of the stripe, like a Joseph Hooker or a Phil Kearny or a George Armstrong Custer, to push himself forward with jingling spurs. With unquestioned and inspiring bravery he stood fire, once being the target not only of sharpshooters, which was nearly routine, but also of an entire Rebel battery. But recklessness, particularly recklessness choreographed to catch the eye of superiors, he eschewed, out of pride and love for his men.

One of the most intriguing, if inexact, mirrors of the man himself may be his choice and deployment of words. The schoolboyishly correct grammar and syntax shadow forth, together with what can be gleaned from the content, a capacity for meticulous preparedness and strict subordination. His understatement of the horror and intimacy of combat shows at once a wariness of emotion and a delicacy of feeling. Withal, the style sketches the young gun captain of old in his reserve, his steadiness, and his cool selection of targets and distances.

Although their writing is not at all "poetic," these letters, which are set forth here for the first time under the able oversight of Civil War editor and historian Herb S. Crumb, achieve a poetic justice. They open a rare loophole on the workings of a superb and comparatively unwritten about military machine. Too, they present the third and last parcel of Osborn's war writings (the other two are *The Eleventh Corps Artillery at Gettysburg,* also edited by Herb S. Crumb, and *The Fiery Trail*, edited by Richard Harwell and Philip N. Racine). In thus completing for the public record his eyewitness opus, this volume goes some way toward burnishing the major general's stars this major never received.

Spring, 1993   Richard Pindell
Binghamton, NY

Introduction

These previously unpublished letters of Major Thomas W. Osborn record a remarkable metamorphosis, his transformation from law clerk to preeminent Union artillery commander. It is the story, too, of his first command, Battery D of the First New York Light Artillery, a battery composed of upstate New York country boys, all raw recruits who, bonded together in a common cause, became one of the star batteries in the Union Army.

Most of the junior officers serving in the Union Army during the Civil War had had no prior military training and many of them were ill-prepared to command or to organize and train civilians for combat. Some, like Thomas Osborn, who were fully committed to the task would excel in their duties and have a unique impact on the regiment in which they served and on the men they commanded. Battery D of the First New York Light Artillery Regiment thought so much of their battery Commander that on January 26, 1862, they presented Osborn "with a splendid saddle, bridle, holsters, saddle valise and housing complete for an artillery officer."[1] A feeling of mutual respect and admiration existed between the Captain and his men. Battery D remained his first love, and 25 years after Gettysburg the survivors of the battery chose their former Commander to give the principal address at the dedication of their monument in the Wheatfield.[2]

On January 21, 1863, Lieutenant Angell Matthewson, one of the battery's section chiefs, wrote his hometown newspaper that, "he [Osborn] is one of the most brave and confident officers in the service and a perfect tiger in a fight. He has been well tried in all the battles of the Peninsula, from Yorktown up and from Fair Oaks down. He has done his duty well."[3]

Osborn was extremely proud of the Battery's men and officers. In a May 7, 1863, letter, written to his mother shortly after Chancellors-

---

1 *Carthage Republican*. Carthage, NY, February 6, 1862.
2 Fox, W. F. (Ed.) (1902) *New York at Gettysburg*. Albany, NY, Vol. 3, Pp 1194-1195.
3 *Mohawk Valley Register*. Fort Plain, NY. (Fort Plain, NY Free Library, Matthewson Letters), January 21, 1863.

ville, he wrote, "I have the satisfaction of knowing I have commanded a force which have displayed the valor of true soldiers." "No troops ever exceeded them in bravery or determination."[4] Others shared Osborn's opinion of the battery and recognized its performance under fire. While commending a member of Battery D in March 1863, Major General Hiram G. Berry, Division Commander, spoke of the Battery in complimentary terms saying, "the battery to which this man belongs is one of the very best in the service and is a star battery of this Army. Captain Osborn is its chief, as well as Chief of Artillery of this division."[5]

Earlier, the Battery had been cited for its effective service on the Peninsula by its division and corps commanders, Generals Hooker and Heintzelman, and by General McClellan in their battle reports.[6] Following Fredericksburg, in order to improve the performance of the Army's artillery, General Hooker had established "acceptable standards" for the 74 batteries to meet. The results of a subsequent inspection were published on March 3, 1862, in Hooker's General Orders No. 18, which listed 14 batteries worthy of commendation. Battery D was one of the 11 volunteer batteries that were commended.

Colonel Charles S. Wainwright, in his journal, described the recruits of the First New York Light Artillery as "round-shouldered, stooping and very slack in the joints . . . and generally lacking in soldierly qualities." His comments about the officers were no more flattering, commenting that, "I have not come across more than half a dozen in the lot who can get fairly wakened up."[7] Wainwright, who was a former New York State Militia officer, viewed the men and officers as not being of the caliber from which great batteries were to be molded.

It must be assumed that Osborn was one of the half-dozen officers to have been deemed "awake" or one who awoke at a later date. A few months later, Wainwright had praise for Osborn and his men when

---

4 *Carthage Republican*, op. cit., May 19, 1863.
5 *Mohawk Valley Register*, op. cit., March 18, 1863.
6 U.S. War Department. (1880-1901) *The War of the Rebellion: A Compilation of the Union and Confederate Armies*. Washington, DC. Vol. 25, Part 1, Pp. 99, 110; Hereafter abbreviated to *OR*; McClellan, G. B. (1864) *Report on the Organization of the Army of the Potomac and of its Campaigns in Virginia and Maryland. July 26, 1861-November 7, 1862*. Washington, DC: U.S. Government Printing Office. p.134.
7 Nevins, A. (Ed.) (1962) *A Diary of Battle: The Personal Journals of Colonel Charles S. Wainwright, 1861-1865*. New York. p. vii (Introduction).

they volunteered to a man to rescue a Regular U.S. Army battery whose cannoneers had deserted their guns under enemy fire. In their first combat experience, Battery D demonstrated that they were fast learners. Osborn over and over demonstrated the qualities of leadership, the command presence that led to his phenomenal rise from battery commander to Chief of Artillery of the Army of the Tennessee, from farmer and law clerk to one of the Union's most successful civilian officers.

On May 23, 1865, at war's end, Osborn was invited to sit in the Washington reviewing stand among a group of notables that included President Johnson, General Sherman, and Secretary of War Stanton. On the same day, following the Grand Review of Sherman's Army, he wrote A. C. O. (his brother), "I have had more or less acquaintance with nearly all the prominent generals and a very agreeable acquaintance with several of them."[8]

As a forward observer to the war, he was able to view and record for his brothers many of the significant events that marked his long journey from Watertown, New York, to the Washington reviewing stand.

In his Preface, Osborn lists the criteria by which a subordinate officer's letters should be judged: "how well he guessed; how good and how bad his general conclusions were; and how justly and how unjustly, in the light of subsequent operations and of history, as now written, he judged his superior officers." On all three counts, Osborn seems to have come close to the truth with most of his conclusions.

Even as McClellan seemed to enjoy the support of most of the troops, Osborn criticized him for being overly cautious and unwilling to engage the enemy. Osborn's lack of trust of newspaper reporters and his extreme dislike of their embellished stories led him to write, "I never knew one of them [reporters] to be in sight of a battlefield. They are the greatest cowards that hang on our Army, besides being the most contemptible liars!" These opinions were quite similar to the contempt for reporters expressed by General William T. Sherman.

His letters, quite descriptive of the sights and sounds encountered on the battlefield, are addressed to his two older brothers, Spencer Coan Osborn (S. C. O.), and Abraham Coles Osborn (A. C. O.). Spencer was a lifelong farmer, who remained on the family's North Wilna farm

---

8 Harwell, R & Racine, P. N. (Eds.) (1986) *The Fiery Trail: A Union Officer's Account of Sherman's Last Campaigns*. Knoxville. p. 221.

during and after the war, until 1875 when he moved to a Nebraska farm. Abraham, like Thomas, was a graduate of Madison University (now Colgate University in Hamilton, New York), and became an ordained Baptist minister residing in St. Louis during the war. After serving as pastor of a North Adams, Massachussetts, Baptist church, he became President of Benedict College at Columbia, South Carolina, and a Colgate University trustee, before retiring to North Adams. Thomas Osborn, who never married, is buried in Abraham's family plot in Hillside Cemetery, North Adams. Born in 1833, he was the youngest of six children, three daughters and three sons born to Jonathan and Amelia Van Deursen Osborn.

The 3,194 pages of manuscript in the Osborn papers in the Colgate University Library Special Collections, all handwritten on legal size paper, represent a considerable investment of his time and labor. The letters published here for the first time cover Osborn's career with the Army of the Potomac from the recruiting of Battery D through Chattanooga. "The Journal of a Staff Officer," a copy of which was shared with General O. O. Howard, along with selected letters from August 5, 1864, to May 23, 1865, appeared in *The Fiery Trail*. In addition to "Letters from the Field, 1862-1865" and "The Journal of a Staff Officer," Osborn's Civil War writings also include a "History of Battery D" and "Experiences at Gettysburg," the latter of which was published in 1991 as *The Eleventh Corps Artillery at Gettysburg*.

Another section of his papers covers his post-war career during Reconstruction as assistant commissioner of the Bureau of Refugees and Freedmen for Florida, delegate to the Florida State Constitutional Convention, Florida state senator, and one term in the United States Senate from the state of Florida. There are also two short stories and an autobiographical sketch of the family's migration in the 1840's from Scotch Plains, New Jersey, to the North Wilna farm on the New York State northern frontier.

"I have determined to print the letters written by me to my brothers, Spencer C. Osborn and Abraham C. Osborn, during the War of the Rebellion.... Taken together these letters form a comparatively good journal of my Army experiences." The editors trust that publication of these letters will satisfy and complete what Thomas Osborn had "determined" to do nearly 100 years ago.

Minor modifications in spelling, punctuation, and syntax have been made in Osborn's handwritten manuscript. Misspelled proper names have been corrected and several long and rambling sentences have been divided into shorter sentences for clarity. Osborn organized his letters into nine different sections, the latter two dealing with his

Eleventh Corps assignments following Gettysburg and during the Chattanooga campaign. We have combined these two sections into one chapter and omitted from this chapter a few of his very brief letters which did not add substantively to the content of his papers. In addition, we have added descriptive chapter titles to the sections.

The editors are indebted to many persons for their help. Special thanks are due to Melissa McAfee and Carl Peterson of the Colgate University Library; Laura Prievo of Carthage, New York; Margaret Aldous of Gouverneur, New York; Spencer C. Osborn's great-grandson, James R. Peck, of Walnut, California; Lou Fischer of York, Pennsylvania; and Gregory A. Mertz, Supervisory Historian of the Fredericksburg-Spotsylvania National Historic Park for their research assistance. We owe credit to Michael J. Winey of the U.S. Army Military History Institute, Carlisle, Pennsylvania; Roger D. Hunt of Rockville, Maryland; Patrick Lewis-Moors of Norwich, New York; Melissa Widrick of the Jefferson County Historical Society, Watertown, New York; Thomas Paine and Diane Jones of the St. Lawrence County Historical Society, Canton, New York, for the photographs. Finally, we thank Linda Delong and Joan Briggs of Norwich, New York, for their assistance with the manuscript.

Spring, 1993
Norwich & New Hartford, NY

Herb S. Crumb
Katherine Dhalle

Preface

To My Nephews and Nieces

I have determined to print the letters written by me to my brothers, Spencer C. Osborn and Abr'm C. Osborn, during the War of the Rebellion from March 6, 1862, to August 12, 1865. I have reviewed those letters which they preserved, and rejecting all matters pertaining to the family, business, or private affairs, have retained only those parts or paragraphs relating to military matters.

Taken together these letters form a comparatively good journal of my army experiences. I regret that many of the letters have been lost, yet those preserved give a much more clear idea of army life as we saw it in the field than anything I could now write. Together they convey an idea of how little about the great military operations a subordinate officer was permitted to know on the one hand, and on the other, how much he did know, how well he guessed, how good and how bad his general conclusions were, and how justly and how unjustly, in the light of subsequent operations and of history, as now written, he judged his superior officers. Few officers of my grade had superior opportunities to be well informed and I doubt very much whether nine-tenths of the generals in the armies in the field were better informed than I. It was not for subordinate officers to know the plans and designs of the generals commanding the armies, but we drew our conclusions from what we saw and thought, and wrote what we pleased on military affairs. It is in this light only I print these letters for your information. They tell what I saw and what I thought at the time they were written. So far as they go, they are strictly truthful as I saw the military conditions and operations at the time.

As an introduction I give a brief account of enlisting the men for the company with which I went to the field, the time passed at the recruiting depot at Elmira, New York, and in the camp of instruction, at the city of Washington. I take up the letters with the first one written after leaving the camp of instruction and reporting for service in the field. There is frequently an unavoidable appearance of repetition growing out of the fact that I frequently wrote a letter to each brother on the same day and in each letter spoke of the same subject matter.

The letters written to my brother Spencer have the initials S. C. O. and those written to my brother Abr'm have the initials A. C. O.

T.W. Osborn
Brevet Colonel
First New York Light Artillery

(Title page)

Letters

Written in The Field by

T. W. Osborn,

During The War of The Rebellion

1862 - - 1865,

To his Brothers,

S. C. Osborn and A. C. Osborn.

with an

Introduction

[The photograph on the preceding page is of Thomas Ward Osborn's original, handwritten title page to his "Letters Written in the Field." Courtesy of the Colgate University Library Special Collections.]

Chapter 1

Prelude

Whenever I heard of a man who had expressed a desire to enter the Army, or who his neighbors thought might be induced to do so, I went to see him....

Osborn's account begins in August 1861 and relates his experiences in recruiting the members of Battery D, recounting his travels on horseback through St. Lawrence, Jefferson, and Lewis Counties in that part of northern New York State sometimes referred to as the "North Country." It includes the northern tier of counties bordering the St. Lawrence River and reaching to the Canadian border. This account is quite similar to the one contained in his July 2, 1888, address at Gettysburg for the dedication of Battery D's monument in the Wheatfield.[1]

The Battery left Watertown for Elmira, where it was mustered into service on September 6, 1861, and underwent basic training as one of the 12 companies (batteries) of the First New York Light Artillery Regiment. The Battery arrived in Washington on October 30th and was assigned to Camp Barry, the Union artillery training school on Capitol Hill.

On March 3, 1862, Osborn and his men joined Major General Joseph Hooker's division of the Union Third Corps on the northern bank of the Potomac River in Maryland, opposite the Confederate batteries blockading the river. After the removal of the blockade, Osborn's battery left Maryland on April 9th, moving to Fort Monroe by transports. On April 13th, Battery D joined McClellan's siege lines in front of Yorktown. After his departure from Washington, Osborn begins his lengthy correspondence to his two brothers.   *The Editors*

---

1 Fox, W. F. (Ed.) (1902) *New York at Gettysburg*. Albany, NY, Vol. 3, Pp. 1194-1195.

Introduction

From the first of August 1860 to the first of August 1861, I was a student with the law firm of Starbuck and Sawyer[2] at Watertown, Jefferson County, New York. My home was at North Wilna in the same county. At the commencement of the war I had no thought of entering the army. I took no interest in the military affairs of the country beyond that which any student would feel in the general welfare of the country. I took no interest in the military organizations then being formed. Nothing in the service had any attraction or charm for me. This feeling in no way changed until the Battle of Bull Run had been fought and lost. After this defeat I immediately determined to enter the army as a duty only. Many others shared this feeling with me.

Having determined to enter the army, the first step was to determine how to enter and what arm of the service to adopt. I had little to guide me. I had never taken sufficient interest in military affairs to have any well-defined ideas about them. I informed myself as well as a few days consideration would permit and determined to apply for service in the artillery.

It was then a question with me whether I should enlist as a private and seek promotion from the ranks or attempt to secure a commission when I entered the service. My family had no considerable influence in official circles and I was still a student; prominent professional and business men only were being commissioned as military officers, and they were being commissioned to fill all the offices from Second Lieutenant to Colonel.[3] This condition of affairs gave me substantially no opportunity to secure a commission unless I made a place for myself and to accomplish this I should need to work. Still, I determined to secure a commission by enlisting a company and applying for acceptance in the branch of the service I desired to enter. All I hoped for or planned for was a commission as Second Lieutenant.

---

2 State Senator James F. Starbuck and Judge Azariah H. Sawyer were partners of the law firm in which young Osborn served as law clerk. Starbuck was described as a brilliant man in politics, a man to be reckoned with. Sawyer was a successful corporation lawyer and county judge who played a prominent role in Jefferson County, New York, civic affairs for over 40 years.

3 Osborn had connections with Sawyer and Starbuck, men who had "considerable influence."

When I had determined upon the course I should pursue, without consulting a single person, I laid my plan before Mr. Sawyer. He then told me that his personal friend, Lieutenant Guilford A. [D.] Bailey[4] of the Regular Army had lately been authorized to enlist a regiment of light batteries, to be known as the "First New York Light Artillery" with himself as Colonel. Also, that he would write to Colonel Bailey at once, asking that I be received into that regiment. This, Mr. Sawyer did and Colonel Bailey replied accepting a company and expressing a desire that it be enlisted at the earliest possible day. I then considered how I could best and quickest accomplish my object. I desired a Second Lieutenancy, thus leaving the offices of Captain and First Lieutenant open for older and more influential men and those who could give me active and effective assistance. I learned of a prominent farmer named Kieffer,[5] living a few miles from Watertown, who had served as First Sergeant in the Regular Army and then desired to enter the service as an officer. I saw him and upon his representing that he could procure half the men required without difficulty, I proposed to him that he should take the Captaincy of the company. He accepted and promised to have half the men ready in ten days. He secured one man and for all the time I knew him after, he never ceased to talk of "my man." Having, as I supposed, provided for a Captain of my proposed company, upon the recommendation of friends, I saw Joseph Spratt,[6] a lawyer in Watertown and a nephew of the Hon. Joseph Mullen, who had been a cadet at West Point but had not graduated. Upon his assurance that he could and would secure from thirty to forty men, I proposed to him that he should take the First Lieutenancy. He accepted my proposition, but did not secure a single man for the company. Had Kieffer and Spratt been able to have fulfilled their promises, I would have had twenty-five or thirty men to provide to secure the place I sought.

This preliminary of operations having been perfected, I went home and gave out that I intended to enter the service and desired to enlist men. This proposition from a person, whom the neighbors had only known as a boy and who was still a student, was received by them

---

4 Col. Guilford D. Bailey was a native of Lewis County, New York, and personal friend of Azariah Sawyer. He graduated from West Point and served as a captain with a regular U.S. Artillery Battery. New York State Governor Edwin D. Morgan (1859-1863) appointed Bailey to organize and command a volunteer artillery regiment. He was killed at Seven Pines on May 31, 1862.

5 Luther Kieffer later served as captain in the Fourteenth New York Heavy Artillery. He was killed at North Anna on May 26, 1864.

6 Capt. Joseph Spratt who later commanded Battery H, First New York Light Artillery.

with philosophic indifference. The fact of my making this effort as in competition with men of large influence was in a measure looked upon as bravado. The substantial farmers were willing I should succeed if I could, and if I failed they could readily say, "I told you so" and dismiss the subject. I made no public demonstration, but taking one of my brother's horses, a most beautiful animal, I went on horseback to look up my men.

I rode over portions of Jefferson, Lewis, and Saint Lawrence Counties. Whenever I heard of a man who had expressed a desire to enter the Army, or who his neighbors thought might be induced to do so, I went to see him and told him I was going into the service and asked him to go with me. I used no other argument. I said nothing about the questions of right or wrong involved in the war, nor did I hold out any special inducements for him to go. I informed each man who expressed a willingness to enlist, who were to be the officers, that the company would be in the artillery. The community in these counties was intelligent on all questions of a public character. Many of them were as well informed as the public speakers who were urging them to go into the service but would not themselves enlist. At different times I visited Watertown to learn how Kieffer and Spratt were progressing. I invariably received the same report, that they had no men yet but would soon have their proportion ready.

While making the canvass of Saint Lawrence County, I met George B. Winslow[7] of Gouverneur, whom I had known while I was a student at the academy in that village. He was inclined to go into the service, but he wished a definite prospect for advancement. I consulted Kieffer and received a promise that Winslow should be made Orderly Sergeant and receive the first promotion. Winslow then undertook to aid in recruiting men for the company. He succeeded admirably. When the one hundred men for the company had been enlisted, all excepting one had been secured either by Winslow or myself.

About the 20th of August I reported my company full and received orders to take it to Elmira, where the regiment was being organized. These orders provided for the expenses of the men and transportation after they should have left their homes. On the 25th of August the men all reported at Watertown; on the evening of the 28th we left Watertown for Elmira where we arrived on the afternoon of September 4th, without one man whom we had enlisted being missing.

I had been present when several of the military organizations had left Watertown to enter the service. At no time had any demonstration

---

7 Capt. George B. Winslow who succeeded Osborn as commander of Battery D.

been made by the citizens of the place beyond that which necessarily arose by the friends of those leaving home, bidding them farewell. These several organizations had all been recruited in Watertown and its immediate vicinity, and the officers were from Watertown or nearby and were nearly all men of local prominence. My company had been enlisted among the farming communities from 20 to 40 miles distant. Less than a half dozen men were from the vicinity. Kieffer and Spratt had attracted no notice, nor had they enlisted any men excepting Kieffer's "my man." Winslow was from Gouverneur and I was from North Wilna, twenty miles distant, and only temporarily in Watertown as a student. I was therefore much surprised and greatly gratified when my company took the cars, to know that the citizens of the place had turned out almost to the last person to bid us a cordial and hearty farewell.

Captain George B. Winslow (Courtesy of U.S. Military History Institute, Carlisle, PA.)

The only unpleasant incident of the departure was that when I bade my mother[8] farewell in the depot as the train was about to leave, she fainted and I left her in the arms of Miss Mary Weeks, an old friend.

The barracks at Elmira were built for the accommodation of two regiments of one thousand men each. Half the barracks had been assigned to Colonel Bailey for his regiment and the remaining half to the 64th New York Volunteer Infantry. My company was the fourth which reported to Colonel Bailey for the 1st New York Light Artillery, and was designated as Company D. We found the quarters comfortable, the food wholesome and well cooked. The military post and recruiting depot at Elmira was commanded by Brigadier General R. B. Van Valkenburg of the state militia.

On the 6th of September the company was mustered into service. The men had not yet become accustomed to military discipline and insisted upon electing me, Captain, and Winslow, First Lieutenant.

---

8   Amelia Van Deursen Osborn, wife of Jonathan Ward Osborn.

After considerable persuasion, they elected Kieffer, Captain; myself, First Lieutenant; and Winslow, Second Lieutenant. This left Spratt out. As he had been of no assistance in enlisting the company, had given no time or money to aid in doing it, had not joined it until after it had reached Elmira, and as the men refused to elect him, no great wrong was done. If, however, it had been left to me, I should have given him the place he expected.

Colonel Bailey had known Spratt at West Point and desired to have the benefit of his military training and experience in the regiment. Spratt had none of those qualities necessary for a recruiting officer while Winslow possessed them in a marked degree. The Colonel therefore detailed Winslow to return to the northern part of the state and recruit a company for Spratt. Winslow left Elmira September 16th and enlisted about 50 men, who were then consolidated with those brought into the regiment by Mr. Mink, and the company so organized was designated as Company H. Spratt made Captain and Mink First Lieutenant.[9]

While we were at Elmira, we did all we could to make officers of ourselves and soldiers of the men. All we did was wholly new to us as we knew nothing of discipline or drill. One thing, however, we quickly realized, and that was the fact that Kieffer knew less of military matters than either Winslow or myself. Colonel Bailey was with us but little and when he was absent there were no trained officers at the post. The field officers of the regiment were Colonel Bailey, Lieut. Colonel Turner, Major Wainwright,[10] and Major Van Valkenburg.[11] Of these, Major Wainwright, excepting Colonel Bailey, was the best read in military matters, but the practical command of troops was new to him. Thus, it was necessary for each officer to prepare himself as well as he could to drill and discipline his men.

The monotony of the routine of the camp did not vary much except as it was relieved by the visits of many of our friends. We taught ourselves to drill the men and then did it. We made requisition for the uniforms of the men and what little camp equipage we required. But altogether the time wore away without marked incidents. The remaining companies for the regiment came in one by one until twelve companies were present and the regimental organization was complete.

---

9 Lt. Charles E. Mink.

10 Lt. Col. Henry E. Turner; Major Charles S. Wainwright who succeeded Bailey as the regiment's commanding officer on June 1, 1862.

11 Col. Bailey's adjutant, killed at Seven Pines.

A regiment of Light Artillery is entitled to three Majors. We had but two. Kieffer proved to be worthless as Captain. His services as an enlisted man in the Regular Army had taught him nothing of the duties or courtesies of a commissioned officer. Winslow and myself compared news concerning the situation. I wrote the facts to Mr. Starbuck and suggested he get Kieffer commissioned as Major and that would permit me to be commissioned Captain and Winslow, First Lieutenant. Mr. Starbuck secured the change at once and we were commissioned: Kieffer, Major; myself, Captain; and Winslow, First Lieutenant.[12] The Colonel and other field officers were at first pleased with the arrangement, but when it was too late learned that we had done a greater favor for Kieffer than we had for them and that the only officers who had received substantial benefits were Winslow and myself. A few weeks later Colonel Bailey insisted upon Kieffer handing in his resignation as Major, which he did. In this way he passed out of the regiment.

On the 29th of October, we left Elmira for Washington where we arrived after two days of excessively unpleasant traveling. Upon reaching Washington late in the evening of the 31st, we slept upon the floor of the freight depot. On November 1st at ten o'clock in the morning, we moved to the ground which had previously been selected for the camp of the regiment on East Capitol Hill, where the School of Instruction for Light Artillery had been established. The seat of ground, an open field, is that now embraced between Avenues C and E and Streets 11 and 13 North East in the city of Washington. The regimental camp was pitched under the immediate supervision of Colonel Bailey. The camp equipage had been sent under the instructions of the Colonel to the ground before we arrived there, and we received it upon our arrival. The day was pleasant and the men put up their tents and got into them before dark.

During the night a violent rainstorm set in, and the ground was speedily covered two or three inches in depth with water. Nothing had been provided for bedding, and the men had lain down on the ground with only their blankets. That night was a most disagreeable one for both officers and men. The former were no better prepared for the storm than the latter and were subject to the same inconveniences. In the morning the ground was ditched and bedding provided, after which the camp was comfortable while we remained in it.

---

12 Starbuck wielded considerable influence.

At the insistence of Colonel Bailey, the camp we occupied was named "Camp Barry," as a compliment to General William F. Barry,[13] who was then in charge of the artillery of the Army of the Potomac. While we were in this camp, my company received much attention from prominent persons who visited Washington from northern New York.

After the promotion of Kieffer the company had but two officers, Winslow and myself. On the 21st of November a Second Lieutenant by the name of Stolper[14] was assigned by Colonel Bailey to my company. He had been a sergeant in the Regular Army and was reported to have served with much credit. He made a fair officer. In camp he was an agreeable officer and, in managing the details of the company, was of considerable assistance. On the 11th of December, another Second Lieutenant by the name of McDonald was assigned to us. He, too, was a promoted sergeant from the Regular Army. From the day this man reported for duty, he was a nuisance. He had no comprehension of the duties of a commissioned officer. He considered his new position of value only as affording means and opportunities to lead a life of unrestrained licentiousness. A few days after he reported to me for duty, the Colonel secured the cancellation of his commission.

There is but little to speak of concerning our duties and occupation during the time we were in Washington. The Colonel and other field officers gave us all their time; very close attention to our line officers was given by the Colonel. A course of instruction was given in the evenings. For many days, the Colonel drilled the officers each afternoon at the manual of the piece. As soon as the Ordnance Bureau was able to supply the guns, the several Captains were instructed to make requisitions for them. My company was the second which procured its guns; Company B, Captain Pettit,[15] being the first. A few days after securing the battery, I made requisition for and received the horses and equipments for it. After the battery was mounted, the drill of men and horses proceeded with the same care as the men received before.

The men in this camp were hardened to camp life. They were well fed and clothed, and during the entire winter they had but few privileges, and the officers had but few more than the men. In all these particulars, my company was more rigidly commanded than any other

---

13 Maj. Gen. William F. Barry, McClellan's Chief of Artillery, who later served on Maj. Gen. William T. Sherman's staff as Chief of Artillery.
14 Augustus Stolper.
15 Capt. Rufus D. Pettit, Commander of Battery B, First New York Light Artillery.

in the regiment. Company B, Captain Pettit, was the first pronounced prepared to go to the front. Mine was the second.

From the 1st of November to the 3rd of March we passed the time in the monotonous routine of the Camp of Instruction. Aside from doing a little service as a member of a court-martial, I did nothing but look after the company. On the 26th of February I received orders to be ready to move on the 3rd of March. Major Wainwright had been assigned as Chief of Artillery on the staff of General Hooker. He had received permission to take with him his choice of the batteries of the regiment and had selected my battery.

General Hooker[16] commanded the troops on the north bank of the lower Potomac and opposite the enemy's blockade batteries. General Hooker's camp was 40 miles south of the city of Washington. We left the Camp of Instruction on the morning of the 3rd of March, 1862, at which time our service in the field commenced.

Letters from the Field

Battery D, 1 N.Y. Lt. Artillery
Hooker's Division
Lower Potomac, Md.
March 6, 1862

[To S. C. O.] At daylight on Sunday morning,[17] we broke camp in Washington and, taking steamer, came down the river 40 miles and then from the landing moved three miles inland. The roads are exceedingly bad, the mud being very deep. This was our first march with the battery and our horses gave us some trouble. We reached the ground selected for our camp at half past ten in the evening and in a severe rain and snow storm. At midnight we had sufficient tents up, so we laid down and slept comfortably till morning.

The rain fell all day on Monday, but we put up the remaining tents and got our camp in fair condition. The weather is now clear and beautiful, and our camp is in a delightful spot.

---

16 Maj. Gen. Joseph Hooker commanded the Second Division of Maj. Gen. Samuel P. Heintzelman's Third Corps.
17 This is Osborn's first letter from the "field."

Yesterday, when we had been here but two days, one section of the battery was detailed to do duty opposite the enemy's blockade batteries. Lieutenant Winslow was in command of the section which occupied a small earthwork near the bank of the river. At this point the river is about a mile and a half wide. About noon I was at the section and gave the men permission to throw a few shells into the enemy's works across the river, my object being to test the shells and the accuracy in firing by the men. The first shell exploded beyond the enemy's works and the second directly in the face of the works upon which the enemy opened on us with their heavy guns and with great vigor. The majority of their shells fell close to us, though many went very wild. They threw in all 23 shells mainly from eight and ten inch guns. We threw in all 12 shells. No one of my men was hurt. The men were cool and enjoyed this, their first little fight.

There is no sickness in the company. Kieffer has finally gone entirely out of the regiment.[18]

Battery D, 1 N. Y. Lt. Artillery
Hooker's Division
Lower Potomac, Md.
March 10, 1862

[To S. C. O.] At half past three in the afternoon yesterday, Major Wainwright brought me the information that the enemy were evacuating their blockade batteries[19] on the south bank of the river. My battery being camped a mile from the river and not in sight of it, I rode to the bank and saw that everything which could be burned in the enemy's works was on fire. Even the little steamer which they had used to capture sailing vessels attempting to run the blockade and the vessels they had captured were burning. A little later the magazines began to explode and continued to do so until all had exploded.

It was the grandest exhibition of fire and fireworks I have ever seen. I think it was about two hours after the enemy had left the river front when our gunboats landed men at the earthworks. So this blockade of the Potomac River, which has lasted six months, is now broken. But of all this you will learn more from the papers than I can write.

---

18 Kieffer had remained with the regiment after leaving Battery D.
19 The Confederate Blockade was removed when Maj. Gen. Joseph E. Johnston withdrew from the Manassas Line to the south side of the Rappahannock River.

PRELUDE 11

Just before dark last evening Lieutenant Dimmick[20] and myself crossed the river in a small boat and walked through the main works of the enemy. They are very strong.

We are told today that it is probable this division will cross to the Virginia side in a day or two. But should we do so, we will still be on the extreme left flank of the Army of the Potomac.

This company has had no mail in three weeks.[21]

Battery D, 1 N. Y. Lt. Artillery
Hooker's Division
Lower Potomac, Md.
March 20, 1862

[To S. C. O.] Yesterday we were ordered to move and, having drawn out with the battery and train on the road, were ordered into camp again. I learn this order was from General McClellan and applied to the whole division. At noon today we were ordered to move at half past one, and when we were ready the order was countermanded. So we have twice taken down our tents and loaded the train ready to move and have twice gone into camp again. I presume, however, we shall move soon.

The camp talk is that we shall be shipped across the river to Aquia Creek and march from there to Fredericksburg.

Day before yesterday, a fleet of steamers carrying, as near as we could get the information, 30,000 or 40,000 men passed here going down the river.[22] I have not been able to learn the exact destination of these troops, nor do I know whether General Hooker has the information.

I received the company mail day before yesterday having sent a man to Washington for it.

---

20 Lt. Justin E. Dimmick, Battery H, First U.S. Artillery, who was mortally wounded at Chancellorsville on May 2, 1863.
21 Osborn continues to refer to the battery as Company D, as it was called during training.
22 The first contingent of Maj. Gen. George B. McClellan's huge army left for Ft. Monroe on March 17, 1862, after the Monitor proved to be a match for the C.S.S. Virginia, formerly the U.S.S. Merrimac.

Battery D, 1 N. Y. Lt. Artillery
Hooker's Division
Lower Potomac, Md.
March 23, 1862

[To S. C. O.] We expect to move soon, but are not informed just when we shall go. A staff officer tells me that a few days ago it was expected this division would go to Fredericksburg, but information has been received that the enemy have left that city and now we will not go there.

It is understood here, I think gathered from the newspapers, that an order has been or will be issued forbidding those at the front sending letters north.

Battery D, 1 N. Y. Lt. Artillery
Hooker's Division
Lower Potomac, Md.
March 25, 1862

[To S. C. O.] We have orders now to procure and have on hand six days quartermaster and commissary stores and be prepared to leave this camp permanently.

I learn now that we are to go to the James River or near Fortress Monroe. Two or three fleets of steamers have gone down the river carrying troops to that locality. A large number of these steamers are now returning to Washington, and I presume some of them will take this division. If so, we shall soon go.

The weather is beautiful.

Battery D, 1 N. Y. Lt. Artillery
Hooker's Division
Lower Potomac, Md.
March 29, 1862

[To S. C. O.] Still we have no final orders but are kept ready to move at an hour's notice. From what I see, I shall not be surprised to move in 12 hours, nor if we remain here several days. This division belongs to the Army of the Potomac but has for a long time been separated from the main body of the Army. It may be in the plan of General McClellan to hold it as a detached division.

Today it both rains and snows.

PRELUDE 13

Battery D, 1 N. Y. Lt. Artillery
Hooker's Division
Lower Potomac, Md.
April 2, 1862

[To S. C. O.] Last evening General McClellan passed down the river with a large fleet carrying troops south. He came ashore here and had a conference with Generals Hooker and Naglee,[23] lasting some time. Of course, subordinate officers cannot know what passed, but it is generally understood we will not now remain here long.

It appears to me that this vast expedition cannot fail of being successful in whatever it may undertake. I feel confident of its future. Undoubtedly, the immediate object is the capture of Richmond and I believe we shall succeed.

Battery D, 1 N. Y. Lt. Artillery
Hooker's Division
Lower Potomac, Md.
April 4, 1862

[To S. C. O.] We are to leave our present camp tomorrow and go down the Potomac. I do not regret this change. I would much prefer to be with the main body of the Army than separated from it as we now are. Our orders indicate we will land at, or near, Fortress Monroe, but how long to remain I have no idea. My Company's health remains good.

Battery D, 1 N. Y. Lt. Artillery
Hooker's Division
Lower Potomac, Md.
April 8, 1862

[To S. C. O.] We are still in Maryland, laying at Liverpool Point, waiting for transports to carry us down the river. Our horses have been shipped but the battery is still on the wharf, as are the other batteries of this division. We shall certainly not sail before tomorrow

---

[23] Brig. Gen. Henry Naglee who commanded the First Brigade of Maj. Gen. Silas Casey's division in Maj. Gen. Erasmus D. Keyes's Fourth Corps.

evening. It is reported at General Hooker's headquarters that 97,000 men have gone down the river. This division has 14,000. Until one has seen an Army, he can form no idea of how large a force this is. The newspapers report that as large an army as this is being concentrated at Corinth, Mississippi.[24]

Snow fell yesterday, and rain is falling today.

Battery D, 1 N. Y. Lt. Artillery
In the Harbor
Near Fortress Monroe, Va.
April 11, 1862

[To S. C. O.] We left our old camp on Saturday, the Maryland shore on Wednesday, and arrived here last Thursday evening. We had a stormy, disagreeable, and very dangerous trip. For several hours, the barge on which the batteries of Bramhall[25] and myself were shipped, were in danger of foundering every minute. I am told the Captain of the steamer that had us in tow was determined to cast us off, which if he had done, our craft would have foundered in a half minute. We were saved by the senior military officer, a Colonel on the steamer, ordering the Captain not to cut us loose. Since we left our camp, the weather has been continually cold, rainy, and foggy and the same as we had when we went from Washington to Liverpool Point. Consequently, I have seen nothing of the country between Washington and here, except at our camp in Maryland. Today is clear and warm.

I have not been on shore here. We are laying in front of Fortress Monroe and about a quarter of a mile from it. It looks like a very strong work, much stronger than any I have before seen. A great number of vessels, both steamer and sailing vessels and all of which are war vessels or transports, are laying in the Harbor. I attempted to learn something of the Army in front, but have obtained but little information, except that it is some miles inland and near Yorktown.

At seven o'clock this morning the rebel ironclad steamer Merrimac steamed down the bay from Norfolk, coming to about two miles of us and a mile and a quarter from the Monitor, which lays farther up the bay than any of the other vessels. It was accompanied by several small gunboats and following it, still about two miles in the rear, were two or three large bay steamers covered with people evidently expecting

---

24 The report of Union and Confederate troop concentrations just prior to the Battle of Shiloh on April 6-7, 1862.
25 Capt. Walter M. Bramhall, Battery H, First U.S. Regiment.

PRELUDE   15

to see a fight. Each of the ironclads fired two or three shots but for some reason which I do not know, neither of them made any further movement for a direct attack. One of the small gunboats captured and took in tow two schooners which lay well up the bay and took them into Norfolk. The Merrimac lay facing the Monitor about an hour and then steamed back to Norfolk.[26]

I can give you no better description of the Monitor and Merrimac than to say the pictures representing them look wonderfully like them.

Since I commenced this letter, the barge on which we are has been taken in tow by a steamer, and we are now on our way to the York River.

Battery D, 1 N. Y. Lt. Artillery
2 Division, 3 Corps
Before Yorktown, Va.
April 14, 1862

[To S. C. O.] Yesterday we unshipped our battery and horses in a little bay just below the mouth of the York River and this morning moved inland about two miles where we are now in camp. We were one week on shipboard and, excepting a few hours while we were at Fortress Monroe, the weather has been bad and disagreeable.

I have seen and talked with many officers, and they are nearly all of the opinion that Yorktown will be taken without a battle.

Battery D, 1 N. Y. Lt. Artillery
2 Division, 3 Corps
Before Yorktown, Va.
April 18, 1862

[To S. C. O.] We are now with the advanced line of the Army and two and a half miles from Yorktown.

At nine o'clock yesterday morning the artillery of General Hooker's division was reviewed and this afternoon will be reviewed again by other officers. These reviews are an annoyance to me, but the reviewing officers appear to enjoy them greatly. The Artillery of this division

---

26 Osborn describes the events of April 11, 1862. The C.S.S. Virginia steamed out of Norfolk but returned when the Monitor failed to appear.

when drawn up for review has a quarter of mile front and is one-fifteenth of the Light Artillery of the Army. In other words, the Light Artillery of the Army, if drawn up for review together, would cover three and three quarters miles front. There is also a regiment of heavy artillery here, having the siege train of the Army, embracing eighty guns, diverse but all of larger caliber than the guns of the light batteries. This regiment is reported to contain 1,400 men. There are other detachments also assigned to the artillery service during these siege operations. At General Hooker's Headquarters, I am told there are 100,000 infantry here. I have learned nothing about the Cavalry.

The enemy's works begin at Yorktown on the York River and extend unbroken across the peninsula to the James River, a distance of about seven miles. The Army of the Potomac is distributed along and in front of these works. The bulk of the Army, however, is in front of Yorktown. It is expected now to get control of these works by a regular siege and that it will require about four weeks to accomplish it. At all events, this is the opinion of officers who should know.

Day before yesterday—Wednesday—our troops mounted the first siege guns. Since then, the artillery firing has been almost continuous both day and night. The monotony of this firing has been varied by sharp skirmishes taking place at intervals of about 12 hours. At one o'clock last night, very heavy firing commenced and continued for 15 minutes, artillery and infantry firing rapidly. The artillery engaged in this little affair was of all sizes and calibers, from rifled field pieces to the heaviest guns mounted on the works at Yorktown.

Chapter 2

Williamsburg

*I think we have a great deal of fighting to do
before Richmond is taken.*

The battle of Williamsburg on May 5, 1862, was the opening engagement of the Peninsular Campaign and followed the Confederate withdrawal from Yorktown on May 3rd. Facing superior Union manpower and firepower, Major General Joseph E. Johnston, the Confederate commander, had concluded that his position was untenable. In retrospect, Johnston viewed Williamsburg as a rearguard action to protect his baggage trains threatened by the Union advance. He preferred to oppose the larger Union army nearer Richmond, farther from its Fort Monroe haven.[1]

Hooker's division of Brigidier General Samuel P. Heintzelman's Third Corps led the Union advance from Yorktown and, with a timely assist from Heintzelman's other division—that of Brigadier General Philip Kearny—bore the brunt of the fighting at Williamsburg and sustained 1,575 of the total 2,283 Union casualties.

Commanding the Confederate defense was Major General James Longstreet's division of six brigades. The Confederate losses numbered 1,700, and at the end of the bitterly contested, all day (ten-hour) engagement, the Confederates held the field. On May 6th they continued their unhurried retreat toward Richmond. The approach to the old colonial capital was protected by a series of 13 earthen fortifications, constructed by slave labor, that crossed the narrow peninsula between the York and James Rivers.

---

1 Johnson, R. V. & Buel, C. C. (Eds.) (1956) *Battles and Leaders of the Civil War*. New York. Vol. 1, p. 203.

The principal work, Fort Magruder, named for Confederate Brigadier General John B. Magruder who had commanded the Confederate forces prior to Johnston's arrival from northern Virginia, stood astride the Williamsburg Road. Most of the action occurred in the vicinity of Fort Magruder and the adjacent redoubts. In their efforts to silence Confederate artillery and to stem repeated Confederate infantry assaults, Hooker's four batteries, commanded by Major Charles Wainwright, played a key role and suffered serious casualties. Osborn and his men distinguished themselves when they answered Wainwright's call for volunteers to man Webber's Regular U.S. battery after most of its gunners had taken flight in the face of enemy fire.[2]

Poor visibility hampered the gunners, and torrential rains turned the ground into what Wainwright called knee-deep "soft mortar," making it impossible to move the guns. Sometime after noon, Confederate infantry overran Osborn's position forcing his men to abandon Webber's guns mired in the mud. They then returned to Battery D's guns farther to the rear.

Williamsburg does not rank as a major battle, but for Osborn and his men it was a major experience. Their baptismal battle had been no gradual, gentle sprinkling affair. Their introduction to conflict had been more like a sudden encounter with a tidal wave that had threatened to overwhelm them. They emerged from their ordeal as combat veterans.

Having borne the brunt of the Williamsburg fighting, Hooker's maimed division and its crippled artillery were the last Federal forces to leave Williamsburg. No longer the vanguard of the Union advance, the division resumed the advance to Richmond on May 8th.

Osborn felt that Hancock had received unearned praise for his part in the recent battles and that the praise heaped on Hancock by McClellan and the press belonged instead to Hooker's division. After Williamsburg McClellan, in referring to Brigadier General Winfield Hancock's flanking movement against Fort Magruder, had described Hancock and his maneuver as "superb." In his report to Secretary of War Edwin M. Stanton, McClellan stated that, "This was one of the most brilliant engagements of the war...."[3] Osborn disagreed, as did Wainwright, who commented that "Hancock did very little fighting."[4]

---

2 Nevins, A. (Ed.) (1962) *A Diary of Battle: The Personal Journals of Colonel Charles S. Wainwright, 1861-1865*. New York. p. 58.

3 McClellan, G. B. (1864) *Report on the Organization of the Army of the Potomac and of its Campaigns in Virginia and Maryland. July 26, 1861-November 7, 1862*. Washington, DC: p. 91.

4 Nevins, *op. cit.*, p. 60.

Hancock's one-hour battle produced 31 Union casualties. He had seized two unoccupied redoubts on the Confederate left flank and positioned Charles E. Wheeler's Battery E, First New York Light Artillery, so as to threaten Fort Magruder. Brigadier General Jubal Early's Confederate brigade had responded to this threat and had attacked Hancock, who held his position and later withdrew. If Hancock had been reinforced, his move might have resulted in a Union victory, but his action had no major impact on the outcome of the battle. Johnston described Hancock's effort as "a detached affair, unimportant because it had, and could have, no influence upon the real event."[5]

McClellan's estimate of Hancock's contribution seems overblown. Some 14 months later at Gettysburg, Hancock would earn the sobriquet "superb." *The Editors*

Battery D, 1 N. Y. Lt. Artillery
2 Division, 3 Corps
Before Yorktown, Va.
April 22, 1862

[To S. C. O.] We are occupying the same ground which Washington and Lafayette occupied 81 years ago. The magnitude of the then and the present Army differs widely. Washington captured the Army then in Yorktown. Shall we capture the one now in it? We shall see.

It is evident now that General McClellan considers the works in front of him too strong to be carried by direct assault and has settled down to a regular siege. I have seen but little of our siege works, but what I have seen are very strongly built. I am told at Division Headquarters that 6,000 men are now working on the approaches. This afternoon I visited one of the new works upon which 100- and 200-pounder guns were being mounted.

This evening I have received instructions to make my camp as healthy and pleasant as possible. It is thought we shall remain here at least two weeks unless some unforeseen contingency should arise. The enemy can, of course, bring on a general battle any hour, but I do not think they will do it.

Captain Derbey is in camp near us.

5 Johnson & Buel, *op. cit.*, p. 205.

Battery D, 1 N. Y. Lt. Artillery
2 Division, 3 Corps
Before Yorktown, Va.
April 25, 1862

[To S. C. O.] There has been no material change here since I last wrote you. We have the same routine of constructing siege works, making roads, building bridges, mounting heavy guns, etc. We are having less skirmishing than a few days ago since the firing is now being confined to sharpshooting and an occasional shell from the enemy's heavy guns. At first our men did most of the firing; now it is done principally by the enemy. As the light batteries have had no picket duty, my men are not exposed to the sharpshooters' fire.

Deserters come in from the enemy's lines everyday. They are mostly privates; yet, a few officers have come in.

Battery D, 1 N. Y. Lt. Artillery
2 Division, 3 Corps
Before Yorktown, Va.
April 28, 1862

[To S. C. O.] No change in the general routine of the siege since I wrote last. I am told that from 10,000 to 25,000 men are at work day and night on the approaches to the enemy's works, preparatory to the final assault. When this is to take place, no one outside of General McClellan's Headquarters can know.

April 29

I was interrupted in writing last evening. We are now so thoroughly entrenched that the enemy, if they should attack, would necessarily fail. They must understand this, and an attack upon our position is not to be expected.

As I understand the present situation, from talking with prominent officers and by gathering all I can from the newspapers, the armies cooperating and bearing on Richmond are as follows: General McClellan, here; General McDowell, south of Fredericksburg; General Banks, in the neighborhood of Gordonsville; General Fremont, in the mountains of Virginia; and General Burnside, on the coast of North Carolina or moving north.[6]

---

6 Maj. Gen. Irvin McDowell, Maj. Gen. Nathaniel P. Banks, Maj. Gen. John C. Fremont, Maj. Gen. Ambrose E. Burnside.

It would appear this combination of forces, if this information is correct, should eventually destroy the army in our front. I am each day more of the opinion the enemy will leave here either before or when an assault is made, but will not fight a general battle here. This is my personal opinion only.

I hear indirectly that General Butler[7] has taken New Orleans and hope this is so. The loss of New Orleans to the South is what the loss of New York would be to the North. The reports we get from the Battle of Pittsburg Landing represent it to have been a drawn battle.[8] This is the only conclusion I can draw from the newspapers and from what I hear.

There is a little fighting done here every night, but I conclude no material damage is done the enemy.

We are not getting full rations for the men nor a full allowance of forage for the horses. Still, we get sufficient to be comfortable and the health of the company continues perfect.

Battery D, 1 N. Y. Lt. Artillery
2 Division, 3 Corps
Before Yorktown, Va.
May 4, 1862

[To S. C. O.] The enemy evacuated Yorktown last night without fighting. This Army will leave here at once in pursuit.[9]

Battery D, 1 N. Y. Lt. Artillery
2 Division, 3 Corps
Williamsburg, Va.
May 8, 1862

[To S. C. O.] I passed through the battle of May 5th safely. We became engaged at half past six in the morning and I remained in the fight until the end, that is thirteen and a half hours. My men behaved admirably. I lost one killed and eight wounded. It rained all day.

This is my first opportunity to drop you a line.

---

7 Maj. Gen. Benjamin F. Butler.
8 Pittsburg Landing or Shiloh on April 6-7, 1862.
9 Maj. Gen. Joseph E. Johnston, after a 30 day siege, evacuated Yorktown on May 4, 1862.

Battery D, 1 N. Y. Lt. Artillery
2 Division, 3 Corps
Williamsburg, Va.
May 9, 1862

[To A. C. O.] You have asked that whenever we should be engaged in a battle I should write you such particulars concerning it as might be of special interest. We have been engaged in a battle and a very severe one and I will undertake the task you set me, though if I should consult my own feelings, I should leave this letter unwritten.

In the morning of the 4th inst. we were notified through General Hooker's Headquarters that the enemy had evacuated their works in our front and had fallen back. At eleven o'clock in the forenoon the battery was drawn out on the road ready to move. At a quarter past one in the afternoon, we began the trials of a forced march after a retreating enemy. Eighty-five thousand men, cavalry, infantry, artillery and baggage trains were ordered to move on two roads.[10]

At nine in the morning a body of cavalry with two mounted batteries had overtaken the enemy four miles east of Williamsburg and in a skirmish had been repulsed. They reported, however, that the enemy was in no great force when they struck them.[11]

While passing Yorktown, I gave a half hour while the battery was halted to inspecting the works. I found them very strong and well mounted with heavy guns, most of which, however, were old, but there were a few new and very fine ones. As I was about to ride inside the works, an officer stationed at the entrance told me the enemy had planted many torpedoes[12] there and six men had already been killed by an explosion. One dead horse, badly mangled, lay there and the cavity in the ground where the explosion took place was seen. From Yorktown, the column moved slowly and heavily and with long and tedious halts. The battery had been on picket the previous night and the men and horses were worn and tired. Between five and ten o'clock in the evening we did not make more than a half mile. At ten the rain

---

10 Hooker's division followed the Hampton Road and Maj. Gen. William F. "Baldy" Smith's Sixth Corps division the Yorktown Road.
11 Osborn refers to the rearguard clash between Maj. Gen. George Stoneman's Union cavalry and Maj. Gen. J. E. B. Stuart's Confederate cavalry.
12 The Confederate "torpedoes" used in the defense of Yorktown resembled the modern land mine. Mortar or columbiad shells filled with powder buried a few inches below the surface of the ground were set to detonate when stepped on. Confederate Gen. G. J. Rains is credited with their invention. Their further use was discouraged by the Confederate High Command after Lt. Gen. James Longstreet termed their use as "improper."

was falling and we were ordered to cross a creek having a quicksand bottom and go into camp. As the last carriage was crossing, the team gave out, and as I was bringing up a fresher team, it dropped over a bank thirty feet high and into the mud of the creek but was not seriously injured. The night was absolutely dark. One hindrance after another detained us until half past two in the morning when we went into camp for the remainder of the night. Neither the men nor horses had had anything to eat after eleven o'clock the previous day.

We knew the enemy had been holding our advance all day and that we should probably be engaged in the morning, yet I felt no uneasiness or anxiety on that account. Without food or shelter in a drenching rain, I lay down on three fence rails to keep me out of the water and in two minutes was fast asleep, and did not wake until morning to receive orders to go to the front. I speak of my feelings at this time to answer your inquiry upon that subject. It was comparatively certain when we went into camp that we should be engaged early in the morning.

Colonel Charles S. Wainwright
(Printed with permission from the collection of Roger D. Hunt.)

Between daylight and sunrise, Major Wainwright, General Hooker's Chief of Artillery, gave me orders to move at once to the front without waiting to feed the horses or for the men to eat their breakfast. He said we could not be engaged before eleven o'clock and the men and horses would have abundant time to eat. He said the enemy were two miles ahead of us and then left us to move on. After I had moved a mile, we were met by an aide of General Hooker, who directed me to bring in the battery at once. I moved forward at a rapid trot and with what I thought was good speed, until Major Wainwright again met us with orders to bring in the battery with all possible dispatch.[13] The battery quickened its pace making the best time it was able to do over what appeared to me to be the worst road in America. It was logs, mud, water, quicksand

---

13 Wainwright mentions this incident in his *Diary*, saying "Osborn was slow (as I expected), but did capital service."

in the road, and obtuse right and acute angles, all of which were gone over and passed for a distance of two miles at a pace which threatened to wreck every carriage before we reached the line of battle.

This, Hooker's division, has four batteries which had been moving in rear of the infantry and in the following order: Captain Webber, H, 1st U.S. Artillery; Captain Osborn, D, 1st New York Light Artillery; Captain Bramhall, 9th New York Independent Battery; and Captain Smith, 4th New York Independent Battery.[14]

Before I reached the field, General Hooker had ordered Captain Webber's battery in upon the right flank of the infantry to draw the fire of the enemy's artillery to and upon itself. It took position in a small open field with the Rebel earthwork Fort Magruder 800 yards in its front and in plain view, the ground in front all being open and nearly level fields. Fort Magruder, together with a smaller earthwork on its left and all the light batteries of the enemy, promptly turned their fire on Captain Webber's battery. While Captain Webber was going into position, I had halted in a slight ravine in the edge of the timber waiting for further orders from the General.[15] I was 200 or 300 yards from Captain Webber's position. In ten minutes after Captain Webber went in, his first Lieutenant, Eakin, was led to the rear with a musket ball in his breast.[16] A few minutes later Second Lieutenant Mason[17] was carried past us with his foot carried away by a solid shot. This certainly was not encouraging for so brief an experience.

Immediately following the wounding of Lieutenant Mason, Major Wainwright rode into the battery much excited and shouted, as nearly as I can remember his words, "Who of the men of the First New York Artillery will go and work the guns of a regular battery deserted without firing a shot?" In answer to which, some profane youth in the same tone of voice replied, "Every G— D— man of us."

After getting a little additional information from the Major, I ordered the cannoneers to come forward which they readily did. We found Captain Webber's guns in good position but upon treacherous quicksand ground. The Captain was the only officer of his battery left and he was coolly walking about among his guns, but his men had left the guns and sought cover wherever they could find it.[18]

---

14 Capt. Charles H. Webber, Capt. Walter M. Bramhall, Capt. James E. Smith.
15 Osborn's guns remained here for the rest of the day while he and his cannoneers served the guns of Webber's battery.
16 Lt. Chandler P. Eakin of Battery H, First U.S. Artillery.
17 Lt. Philip D. Mason.
18 For Wainwright's account, see: Nevins, *op. cit.,* Pp. 50-51.

I manned four of these guns (he had six) with my own cannoneers and opened fire at half past six in the morning. Remaining with the men, I ordered them on and encouraged them as occasion required. They were cool, obeyed orders readily, and fought splendidly. The guns, on account of the recoil, continually sank in the quicksand and were handled with great difficulty and caused the men great labor.

In twenty minutes after we opened fire, Corporal Conant was wounded by having his thumb carried away by a musket ball, and a few minutes later E. E. Garrison[19] was killed by a six-pound shot passing through his body. Three or four spare men carried Garrison to the rear and buried him. Harrison Dike, whom you know, a private in the company and by profession a Baptist preacher, offered a prayer at the grave and this while the fighting was very hot. Garrison was the first man of my company killed. Some of my wounded are severely injured.

I will take up the details of the battle again in another letter.

We have orders to move at half past eight tomorrow morning. Since the battle, I have been kept very busy getting my battery into good working order again.

General McClellan's report to the Secretary of War has caused a feeling of intense disappointment among the officers and men of this corps. He may have made this report, as published, through a misunderstanding or on account of personal hostility to General Hooker.[20] At all events, the report is absurd and shamefully unjust. I understand today, from what I suppose to be good authority, that at General McClellan's Headquarters it is conceded an injustice has been done General Hooker and his command and that the error will be corrected.

In killed, wounded, and missing, General Hooker lost 1,580 men of whom 450 were killed. The division took 200 prisoners.

Scouts say they have been 20 miles in advance of our columns and found no enemy, but sufficient evidence of a very hasty retreat.

We are to move tomorrow to New Kent Court House, 15 miles west. This is a lovely country.

---

19 Emmanuel E. Garrison and Frederick W. Conant of Battery D.
20 Osborn refers to McClellan's praise of Hancock's role at Williamsburg.

Battery D, 1 N. Y. Lt. Artillery
2 Division, 3 Corps
Williamsburg, Va.
May 9, 1862

[To S. C. O.] Since the morning of the 6th until now, I have been very busy preparing the battery for the field again. This division has lain still until all of the Army moving on this road has passed us, leaving this division in the rear and in reserve. From Yorktown we were in the advance and had the fighting to do at Williamsburg. If only one corps is to be fought at a time, some other one will come in for its turn next and get battered to pieces as we were.

The two batteries at the front at the battle—Bramhall's,[21] which went into position on my right and about an hour later, and my own—had in addition to the musketry and sharpshooting turned against them, the artillery of the two forts in our front and of the two light batteries. Three times during the day we completely silenced the two forts and one light battery. The other light battery throwing six-pound round shot and shell we could not persuade to keep quiet. It was the best handled artillery the enemy had on the field.

Yesterday, General Hooker paid the battery through me an especially high compliment. Taking me by the hand, he said, "I am rejoiced to see you as I did not expect to see you come off the field alive, and it is a marvel how you did so. Every man you have is a hero, and you have reason to be proud of them all as I am proud of them." These are nearly his exact words, as nearly so as I can remember them.

My saddle horse was killed by a twelve-pound shot striking him just behind or back of the head and decapitating him. The roads on which we moved the day of the battle and the ground on which we fought were bad beyond imagination. The enemy lost more men than we.

Battery D, 1 N. Y. Lt. Artillery
2 Division, 3 Corps
Near West Point, Va.
May 12, 1862

[To A. C. O.] On the 10th, we moved 12 miles from Williamsburg west and yesterday three miles to the place where we are now in camp.

---

21 Battery H, First U. S. Artillery.

I will now continue my story of the battle of Williamsburg, commencing as nearly as I can remember where I left off in my last.

General Hooker during the battle made his headquarters on the main road a couple of hundred yards in rear of his line of battle, but eventually changed his position from near my battery to 500 yards to the rear. He rode a white horse and remained mounted all day. His horse was struck by a musket ball in his hindquarter but not seriously injured; the blood, however, showed plainly on his white hair. The General at no time tried in the least to screen himself or went off the road.

I had been engaged an hour when Captain Bramhall brought in his battery and took position on my right. As I was going to the front with my men, I passed General Hooker and stopped to speak to him. He greeted me cordially and frankly told me the position of affairs, saying: he had sent out two regiments as skirmishers to feel the position of the enemy; that the conditions then looked like a severe fight, but that he could not determine the enemy's exact position as the ground was strange to him, and his scouts had not returned; that his artillery must engage the artillery of the enemy and draw its fire away from the infantry. Then as I was about to leave him, he laid his hand gently on my arm and said, "Osborn I send you in there to sacrifice you, but it is necessary to save the infantry."

He may have made this remark to test my nerves; but if this was his object, there was neither in his face nor voice any indication that such was his object. When I took charge of the regular battery, I had only my cannoneers with me, the sergeants and drivers remaining in the rear with my own guns. The 5th New Jersey Infantry had been ordered in to the support of the battery and took position on our right and in the edge of the woods just to the right of the position afterward taken by Captain Bramhall.

Until half past eight no fighting had been done except sharpshooting, skirmishing, and artillery firing. At that hour the two lines of battle came together near the Revolutionary earthworks thrown up by Washington in the siege of Yorktown, which at this point cross the Williamsburg road and are still easily traced. The Excelsior,[22] or Sickles' Brigade, was moved forward 300 or 400 yards where they were met by a superior force of the enemy's infantry. General Sickles' Brigade numbered about 4,000 men. The musketry fire opened as the two lines of battle approached each other by a dropping of irregular fire, the report of each musket being readily distinguished and from

---

22 The brigade named for the New York State motto and recruited by Brig. Gen. Daniel E. Sickles and composed of five New York regiments.

the first shots, rapidly increasing or running together until separate reports could not be distinguished and increasing in rapidity. Both lines of battle fired rapidly until the sound from the musketry was a volume of sound—round, full, and smooth, like the full bass tones of a church organ. This lasted from five to six minutes and then fell off and ended as it had begun. In this short time the work done was terrible, but General Sickles held his ground and the enemy fell back temporarily out of range.

Upon inquiry after the battle, I learned that during the day there were nine of these severe collisions.

The timber immediately in front of our line and between the two lines of battle had been felled by the enemy in anticipation of a battle on that ground. About 400 yards of timber had been so cut, extending across the whole field on which the fighting was done. After the collision above mentioned, the space between the lines was quiet for say a half hour when the enemy's skirmishers commenced driving in our pickets. This indicated the enemy's line of battle was approaching, and General Hooker met it by advancing another brigade. This brigade moved by the flank down the Williamsburg road until opposite the fallen timber, and then filed to the left into this timber and by brigade front moved to meet the enemy.

The brigade kept its alignment very well until the lines came together when the firing commenced, continued, and died away in the same manner as the first contact had done, except it was a little more prolonged by reason of the partial cover afforded by the fallen timber enabling the men to hold on longer. In the end our men again drove the enemy from the fallen timber and held the ground. I need not keep up these details longer. Each attack until the two last was the almost exact counterpart of the one preceding it. All the fighting until near the close of the day was done on nearly the same ground, the different collisions differing in locality perhaps 300 yards.

I was surprised at the fact that Captain Bramhall's and my own battery were able to silence the enemy's artillery as we did three times during the day, securing each time a rest of a half hour before they again opened. The light six-pound battery was the only exception. This we could not silence. The occasion of my surprise was that two of the enemy's batteries were in strong earthworks, Fort Magruder and a smaller work. Not less than three out of five of their shots fell in or near the two batteries and yet our men showed no disposition to give way. Our guns could not have done much better work, and yet we stopped the working of their guns. They threw round shot and shell from six- and twelve-pound field guns, thirty-pound shot, shell and cannister from heavy guns, and grapeshot from cannonades in Fort Magruder. Doubtless, our guns were more accurate and ammunition better than that used by the enemy. Fort Magruder could be plainly seen, notwithstanding a slight fog and the rain which fell almost continuously through the day. Our guns sank to the axles in the quicksand and necessitated excessively hard work by the men. Yet when most pressed, we fired two and three shots per minute from each gun. The principal part of the injury done my men was that in the morning, Lieutenant Stolper[23] was injured by a solid shot striking near him and driving a quantity of sand in his face. The injury is only temporary.

From about one o'clock in the afternoon the phases of the battle changed rapidly. No reinforcements had arrived. Our division had not had a minute's rest and the men were thoroughly worn out, and yet they held on even beyond the range of endurance.

About this hour I went to the rear[24] to give some order regarding my own battery and men, to be absent less than a half hour; Lieutenant Winslow remained with the battery at the front. I had been absent but a few minutes when the guns of the two batteries at the front were turned upon our own troops and our infantry line was broken and was being driven back. I attempted to get back to the front and going as fast as possible reached Captain Smith's[25] battery where it had been held in position, about 500 yards in rear of our main line ready for an emergency.

The enemy's line had been heavily reinforced and extended so as to overlap each of our flanks and was driving our line back, but the men were rallied a little in rear of Smith's battery without difficulty. Captain Smith held his position until our men had fallen back and had passed him and the enemy, in following, were coming into the road from the open field where our batteries were and from the fallen timber in which most of the infantry fighting was done. They rushed into the road as into a funnel and without order. When the head of the enemy's column was about 200 yards from his battery, Captain Smith opened upon it with cannister, firing with great rapidity. The fire was very effective and the enemy was driven back as rapidly as it was possible for them to go.

Our line was reformed in rear of Captain Smith's battery, and moving to the front held the enemy in check. About two o'clock, or perhaps a little earlier, General Kearny[26] arrived with his division

---

23 Lt. Augustus Stolper.
24 During Osborn's absence the Confederates overran and captured Webber's guns. He had gone to check Battery D's guns where they had been left as the men went to serve Webber's guns.
25 Capt. James E. Smith, Fourth New York Independent Battery.
26 Brig. Gen. Philip Kearny commanded the Third Division of Heintzelman's corps.

and reinforced our line by extending the flanks so as to extend beyond the enemy's flanks. A forward movement was then made, and after a severe fight the enemy was pushed back beyond the ground where all of the fighting had been done. Night had come and the two armies lay down to sleep on precisely the same ground where the battle had commenced in the morning and upon which we had been fighting thirteen and a half hours.

For four days the four batteries were entirely crippled, having lost 150 horses and being much damaged otherwise. Three of the batteries were made seviceable again, and Captain Webber's battery will return to Washington to be refitted.

You will notice that this account differs in many respects from the newspaper reports, but upon all the points I have written I have had a much better opportunity to know and be informed than any newspaper reporter could have had.

A word in reply to your questions regarding my feelings while under fire: at Yorktown I received orders to move, prepared to become engaged at any minute. I knew it was General Hooker's plan to take his command into battle at the first opportunity. In this way we were prepared mentally to go into an engagement at any moment. When we went into the battle, it was under very disadvantageous circumstances and on the field we were under very trying conditions, but from the commencement of the march from Yorktown until the close of the battle, I felt no inclination to screen myself when my men were exposed as indeed they were every minute. There was not a single moment when I lost my usual self-possession or power of command. I have yet to feel the sickening anxiety so often spoken of as affecting men going into battle. I may feel it yet. I cannot tell that now.

Battery D, 1 N. Y. Lt. Artillery
2 Division, 3 Corps
Near West Point, Va.
May 13, 1862

[To S. C. O.] It is a pity the newspapers lie so in regard to the part General Hancock took in the battle of Williamsburg. He did no fighting worth speaking of, and his "brilliant bayonet charge" made that day was on an earthwork without guns or garrison. A few sick men were in it but they made no resistance whatever. The amount of fighting done is shown comparatively by the fact that General Hooker was engaged thirteen and a half hours and lost 1,580 men, while General Hancock was engaged less than two hours and lost less than 30 men.

We have moved 15 miles since we left Williamsburg. The general movement is up the peninsula and towards Richmond. I do not look for any great end to be accomplished before the middle of June unless the enemy offers a general battle. If they should do so, we may accomplish something of note—not even then, however, if General McClellan lets one corps get pounded to death while the others look on and then telegraphs the Secretary of War that some brigade which did nothing was brilliant and entitled to all the glory and he had heard the corps which did all the fighting had had a skirmish.

Battery D, 1 N. Y. Lt. Artillery
2 Division, 3 Corps
Brahamsville, Va.
May 14, 1862

[To A. C. O.] There was much connected with the battle of Williamsburg and its surrounding incidents which no one will ever know save General McClellan and the officers immediately about him. But there are other things which the more intelligent subordinate officers know but which the country does not and I presume never will know.

As compared with what might have been, the battle was an abortion. General McClellan and the newspapers—to the 10th inst.—have, by the official report of the former and the reporters of the latter, conveyed a gross falsehood to the country. If this has in any way been corrected, I am not aware of it. Unquestionably, the wrong was done through the favoritism of General McClellan. I have no sufficient cause to doubt his ability as a General; but that he made a gross blunder at Williamsburg, either intentionally or through incompetency, is beyond question; and judging from his dispatch concerning General Hancock to the Secretary of War and the failure up to this time to correct it, I cannot but conclude he will stoop below the parallel of a gentleman to favor his personal friend[27] even at the cost of those who are not his personal favorites.

What I write is drawn either from my own observation or from conversations I have had with those who are in position to know more than I and of whom I have made inquiry.

---

27 McClellan was later accused of showing Generals William B. Franklin and Fitz John Porter favors.

Battery D, 1 N. Y. Lt. Artillery
2 Division, 3 Corps
New Kent Court House, Va.
May 16, 1862

[To A. C. O.] We have moved 12 miles further west, and as we had orders not to move to the Court House until General Sumner's corps[28] had passed, we are now in camp a little east of the Court House. We went into camp here at noon yesterday. A violent rainstorm has made the road almost impassable.

I have learned nothing to change my mind in regard to the battle of Williamsburg. It appears when we left Yorktown General Sumner took the wrong road and he and General Heintzelman ran into each other with their columns. General Hooker, who was in advance, sent back for orders and was directed to move to the left and engage the enemy if found. This threw the 3rd Corps on the extreme left, General Hooker's division in advance, and General Kearny's division following. General McClellan was eight miles in the rear.[29]

After the battle had fairly opened and General Hooker found the enemy was in too strong force to be pushed back by one division, he asked for reinforcements which were not sent to him. At nine o'clock we had silenced the enemy's artillery and General Hooker reported the fact and requested that a force be sent in from the right, occupy Fort Magruder, and cut off that portion of the enemy then engaged in his front and capture it. I am firmly convinced one corps and probably one division could have accomplished this. No natural or artificial obstacle except Fort Magruder, which was large but of little account, intervened to have prevented or even retarded a rapid and vigorous movement to this end. The enemy's force engaged in our front was detached necessarily some space from the main body of the enemy and could have been cut off with comparative ease. General Sumner's entire corps was next on our right and was readily available for that use. But, the request for troops and these suggestions as to cutting off that detachment of the enemy were disregarded.

General Heintzelman[30] arrived at the front somewhere near noon; at least I saw him just about one o'clock. A little incident happened at this meeting with the General which may interest you; I will tell it

---

28 Maj. Gen. Edwin V. Sumner, Second Corps Commander.
29 Following the Battle of Seven Pines (Fair Oaks), McClellan visited the front line, one of the few occasions that he did.
30 Gen. Heintzelman, Third Corps commander. Gen. Sumner had overall command of his Second Corps and the Third Corps at Williamsburg.

here. The General wore a citizen's overcoat and, as I had never seen him, I did not know his rank. He was on horseback a little in rear of General Hooker. Riding out to him, I addressed him in an offhand bluff manner asking some question which he answered very quietly, and I rode on. For some inexplicable reason I thought him an assistant surgeon. The next day I met him in Williamsburg, and he, instantly recognizing me, related the incident to the officers about him and laughed heartily over it. So you see, in military life a man's face does not count for as much as his shoulder strap.

General Kearny's division reached us between one and two o'clock and at the moment our line had broken and was falling to the rear, and the enemy was checked by the fire of Captain Smith's battery. As I have before written, he went into line of battle with General Hooker's division, strengthening and extending the line and then crowding the enemy back to their original position.

About one or two o'clock in the afternoon we heard firing three-fourths of a mile or a mile to our right, and as the fog had raised at the time we could see the smoke from the guns. As near as I could judge, this was at about the center of General Sumner's line. As we saw the smoke and heard the firing, it appeared to be a sharp skirmish, nothing more, and in comparison with the fighting on our front, it was of very little moment. This was the movement of General Hancock's brigade. On the second day after the battle I called on Colonel Bailey of our regiment, who was with that part of the Army. He spoke of the advance of the brigade as a skirmish and commented on the work done by Batteries E and M of our regiment. I then saw Captain Wheeler[31] of Battery E who said they had a smart little fight, but spoke disparagingly of the infantry and remarked that all they did amounted to nothing. So you can readily imagine with what surprise General McClellan's dispatch was received by both wings of the Army. "Hancock's brilliant bayonet charge" was as great a surprise to General Hancock's men as it was to General Hooker's men. All reports agree that there were none but sick men in the fort taken by General Hancock and that no resistance whatever was offered to the occupation of the fort. After the occupation of the redoubt, Hancock had a little fight with a rebel brigade which attempted to head him off in his advance. But he was recalled, and if there were any possibilities in this little affair nothing came of it, not even a respectable skirmish.

After the battle, as I understand, General Sumner was suspended for disobedience of orders in moving his column from Yorktown to

---

31 Capt. Charles C. Wheeler commanded Battery E, First New York Light Artillery.

Williamsburg by taking a wrong road. I think he has since been restored even if the reason is correct.

You may think I am bitter because this division has not been sufficiently lauded. I am sure I have no such feeling. The facts show a great injustice was done and an injustice, too, that any man with the impulses of a gentleman, to say nothing of the high military rank of this one, would not have done.

I have learned a few more of the particulars of our losses in the battle. General Hooker lost in killed, wounded, and missing, 2,200 men; General Hancock, all told, 26. On our part of the field, the number of the enemy's dead exceeded the number of our dead. The day after the battle we found 1,500 of the enemy's dead and wounded in Williamsburg, and two miles west of the city we found a large number of new-made graves while all or nearly all of those slightly wounded must have gone forward with the enemy towards Richmond. It is now conceded by all with whom I have talked that if General Hooker's suggestion had been acted on and the force operating immediately on General Hooker's front had been attacked on the flank by General Sumner, they would all or nearly all have been captured. Instead of this, however, they were permitted to hold our entire Army in check by fighting one division and holding our Army quiet while the main Army of General Johnston and his trains moved west. Having by the fighting secured the day and night for this purpose, before the morning of the sixth the force in General Hooker's front, and which had fought him on the fifth, withdrew; and the country in front of us for several miles was open and clear of the enemy. Every article appertaining to Johnston's Army was moved back and saved. The only loss to the enemy was the loss of the men in the battle, and the loss inflicted on our Army was but little less than they had themselves suffered.

Three days after the battle Secretary Stanton was here and received certain officers. As this fact has not been mentioned by the papers, I presume it is contraband of war.

I have not spoken of the fight near West Point,[32] of which I only know by talking with officers who were in it. It appears to have been more serious than reported as our loss was more than 550 men and the enemy's loss quite as great or even greater. Captain M. McCurtis,[33]

---

32 After an amphibious landing near West Point, Franklin's division had been driven back to its beachhead by Confederate forces.

33 Capt. McCurtis apparently belonged to Franklin's division which had joined McClellan on April 22nd from McDowell's corps. Gouverneur, NY, is in St. Lawrence County.

who was at the Academy with me in Gouverneur, was shot through the breast.

The citizens of Williamsburg say General Johnston made a speech to them the day before the battle in which he said he would probably be repulsed but that they should all remain at their homes and that no violence would be done to anyone by our troops.

The Engineer Corps went forward yesterday with orders to bridge the Chickahominy River as quickly as possible. A large body of troops also moved yesterday from Cumberland to the White House,[34] or Custis Estate, on the Pamunkey River. This division is now in the rear of the Army.

Our armies do not appear yet to meet with reverses East or West, and I do not much fear that they will do so. The report comes from one of General McClellan's staff that there are 26 miles of fortifications around Richmond.

Mr. Starbuck told me that Mr. Brainard[35] of Watertown, a brother-in-law of General Hooker, had written the General concerning me and of the knowledge the Watertown people had of me and asking the General to keep an eye on me. I presume it was this left-handed introduction which has caused the General to show me more personal attention than he has shown most officers of my grade.

Battery D, 1 N. Y. Lt. Artillery
2 Division, 3 Corps
New Kent Court House, Va.
May 20, 1862

[To S. C. O.] What I have written you about the Battle of Williamsburg was as near correct as I can get at the facts. I do not believe we shall see much more severe fighting anywhere than we had in our front. No one with whom you are acquainted was either killed or wounded except Fred Conant of Antwerp, who was wounded in the hand. George Wood, Lester Duly, Marvin Hill, and Harrison Dike you

---

34 Formerly the property of Col. William Henry Fitzhugh ("Rooney") Lee, Gen. Robert E. Lee's son, this estate became the main Union supply depot until after the Battle of Gaines' Mill. It was located on the Pamunkey River on the Richmond and York River Railroad.

35 Orville V. Brainard, successful businessman and Watertown, NY, civic leader had married the General's sister, Mary Seymour Hooker, in 1857.

know.[36] They all did well and are brave soldiers. Indeed, all my men behaved well under fire.

We are in camp, 21 miles from Richmond, this corps being in reserve. Tomorrow we move again further west. There is a rumor running through camp and the Army that Richmond is being evacuated. This I do not believe, but many do. I think we have a great deal of fighting to do before Richmond is taken.

Battery D, 1 N. Y. Lt. Artillery
2 Division, 3 Corps
Baltimore Cross Roads, Va.
May 23, 1862

[To S. C. O.] We are in camp about three miles east of the Chickahominy River and swamp, of which the papers have said so much and know so little. On the 21st, I rode to the front and found the river and bottomlands much narrower than I had been led to believe. Some of our troops were in position on the eastern bank of the river and were attempting to develop the enemy's position on the western side by throwing shells where they supposed the enemy were. The enemy, however, refused to develop their position or else were not there in any considerable force, and nothing came of it except a feeble reply from a single field battery. My impression is the enemy have fallen back and there is nothing immediately in front of us excepting a rear guard. The ground these troops are supposed to hold and do hold, at least to the extent of a rear guard on the west bank of the Chickahominy, would be an ugly field to fight upon; but I do not think they will fight here. The river is narrow and the ground near it is swamp, steep hills, and ravines, all of which are covered either with swamp timber or pine, accordingly as the land is wet or dry. Our experience at Williamsburg has led me to the conclusion that I would much prefer to fight our next battle in the open field rather than in the forest and fallen timber.

I have just learned that one or more divisions crossed the Chickahominy yesterday[37] and have entrenched their position; probably, more have crossed today. I have studied the maps and made many

---

36 All known to S. C. O. and apparently from the Watertown-Carthage area of Jefferson County, NY.

37 Maj. Gen. Darius N. Couch's and Casey's divisions of Keyes's Fourth Corps crossed the Chickahominy River at Bottom's Bridge on May 23rd.

inquiries concerning the country in front of us and as far as Richmond, from which we are now 15 miles. I do not believe the enemy will fight a general battle until they are within six miles of Richmond. This Army is kept ready to fight any hour, which condition is very trying on the men. Yet, it appears to be necessary.

The corps is still in reserve and in rear.

Chapter 3

Seven Pines/Fair Oaks

... a stream the size of and possessing the uncertain character of the Chickahominy cutting the Army in two ... is not altogether desirable.

On May 7, 1862, four Union divisions were moved up the York River by transports and disembarked at Eltham's Landing on the Pamunkey River near West Point, the terminus of the Richmond and York River Railroad and where the Pamunkey joins the Mattaponi River to form the York. Franklin's division of McDowell's corps, which had joined McClellan on April 22nd, landed and attempted to move inland but was contained at its beachhead by a Confederate force responding to this threat to Johnston's supply trains and line of withdrawal toward Richmond. McClellan proceeded to establish his main supply base at White House close to the railroad and the Pamunkey, which would serve as the Union supply line for his army in front of Richmond until the Union withdrawal to the south bank of the Chickahominy following the Battle of Gaines' Mill.

The Union advance on Richmond was hindered by heavy rains that made the poor roads nearly impassable. It was not until May 20th that McClellan's advance units reached the Chickahominy River east of Richmond. It may never have been the Union Commander's intent to strike a quick blow at Richmond, but following his Yorktown strategy, he preferred to follow a slower, safer approach that allowed time for moving his heavy siege guns within range of the Richmond defenses to support a slow step-by-step Union advance.

Unfortunately for McClellan, the defenders of Richmond did not choose to remain passive observers to this strategy. The Confederate command had been given time to strengthen the Richmond defenses, and there was no guarantee that even Johnston, who was a conservative and defense-minded opponent, would willingly serve as a stationary target for McClellan's siege guns. Johnston's successor, Robert E.

Lee, would be even more unwilling to serve as a pawn on "Little Mac's" chessboard.

Fearing the threat to his flanks posed by Union control of the York and James Rivers, Johnston had withdrawn to the south bank of the Chickahominy,[1] a river that was readily fordable except during periods of heavy rainfall when it overflowed its banks, inundating the adjacent lowlands and becoming, in Osborn's words, "a large river" and a barrier to an advancing army. The Chickahominy under such circumstances was quite capable of washing away its bridges and flooding their approaches.

On May 23rd, the Union Fourth Corps (Keyes) crossed to the south side of the Chickahominy and advanced a little beyond Seven Pines on the Williamsburg Road, six miles from Richmond. Heintzelman's Third Corps followed on May 25th and camped five miles to the rear of Keyes. The three Union corps of Sumner, Franklin, and Porter on Keyes's right remained north of the river. Porter was on the extreme right near Mechanicsville, Franklin on his left, and Sumner to Franklin's left. Sumner was six miles from Keyes's right flank and separated from him by the Chickahominy. Heavy rains on the 30th caused the stream to flood its banks threatening the bridges that connected the corps of Sumner and Keyes.

By placing two of his corps south of the Chickahominy, McClellan had divided his army leaving the two separated units an inviting target for a Confederate attack. A rampaging Chickahominy could make support by the Union forces on the opposite bank most difficult if not impossible. McClellan faced a difficult situation. As long as he remained north of the river, he could not effect the long-promised advance against Richmond. Yet, if he were to effect a union with McDowell's force, he would still require a strong force north of the river to keep open the land approach from the north and to protect his White House supply line. Added to McClellan's dilemma was the threatened approach of Jackson's forces from the Shenandoah Valley and their threat to his right flank. Confederate initiatives would resolve this dilemma for McClellan and force him to make decisions of a defensive nature as he surrendered the initiative to Johnston and later to Lee.

The swampy wilderness near Seven Pines, in which the two divisions of Keyes's corps (Casey and Couch) found themselves, was unsuited for maneuver or defense. Johnston was quick to see the opportunity that McClellan's move had provided and attacked at Seven Pines on May 31st. The two Union defense lines stretching from

---

1 Johnson, R. V. & Buel, C. C. (Eds.) (1956) *Battles and Leaders of the Civil War, Vol. 2*. New York. p. 207.

the Williamsburg Road to the Richmond and York Railroad were only partially completed and not adequately defended. Casey occupied the first line west of Seven Pines and Couch a second line to the rear at Seven Pines. Near the road the Union positions were located in relatively small clearings and surrounded by dense forest with thick undergrowth that limited the defender's view and ability to defend.

The first line, known as Casey's Redoubt, contained a small earthwork that accommodated six artillery pieces. Rifle pits had been constructed for a short distance on both sides of the road and were protected by an abatis of felled timber. The left flanks of both lines were protected by the White Oak Swamp, but extending to the right neither line was fortified and lay wide open to an attack down the Nine Mile Road. Casey's men made a valiant defense but were eventually overwhelmed and driven from their position.

Faulty Confederate execution and coordination of the attack plan probably saved Keyes's corps from disaster. Longstreet failed to arrive in time to attack the vulnerable Union right flank in cooperation with D. H. Hill's frontal assault on the Williamsburg Road. Union reinforcements, Major General John Sedgwick's division from Sumner's corps, barely managed to cross the flooded upper Grapevine Bridge and to arrive in time to repel Longstreet's belated attack. Kearny's division of Heintzelman's corps, slow to learn of Hill's attack, arrived in time to save Casey's second line. The Confederates resumed their attack on June 1st with Brigadier General William Henry Chase Whiting and Major General Benjamin Huger's divisions; but Union reinforcements, Richardson's division of Sumner's corps and Hooker's division of Heintzelman's corps, turned back the Confederates now under the command of Major General Gustavus Smith following the wounding of Johnston on May 31st.

Osborn arrived on the field on June 1st with Hooker's division, but because of the impassable mud was unable to deploy any of his guns. Battery D reoccupied the redoubt in Casey's line that had been defended by Battery A, First New York Light Artillery, on May 31st. Battery A had lost all its guns and was never to fight another battle.

Colonel Guilford Bailey, commanding officer of the First New York Light Artillery Regiment, was mortally wounded and his adjutant, Major David Van Valkenburg, killed. Major Wainwright was promoted to Colonel on June 1, 1862, to replace Bailey as the regiment's commanding officer. Osborn's graphic description of the first day's field, the burial of the dead, and the cremation of the horses leaves a vivid picture of the dismal scene.

Seven Pines/Fair Oaks had cost the Confederates 6,134 casualties. Union casualties were 5,031. The wounding of Johnston, leading to his ultimate replacement by Lee, may have been the most important result of the battle. McClellan, however, was appalled at his losses and may have become less willing to commit his men to a general assault against Richmond. McClellan with a force of approximately 120,000 men continued to imagine, on the basis of Allan Pinkerton's intelligence, that he faced a Confederate force of 200,000.

Franklin's Sixth Corps moved to the south side of the Chickahominy on June 19th, leaving only Porter's Fifth Corps north of the river. McCall's division of McDowell's corps had joined Franklin's corps on June 12th and 13th.

The Editors

Battery D, 1 N.Y. Lt. Artillery
2 Division, 3 Corps
Near White Oak Swamp, Va.
May 28, 1862

[To S. C. O.] Before this division crossed the Chickahominy, we were ordered out to support a reconnoitering party and aid it in the event of its becoming engaged. We left our camp at noon and returned at eight in the evening. All the time we were in a drenching rain and the roads were bad beyond description.

We crossed the river three days ago and are now in camp three miles from Bottoms Bridge—[2] one mile from the river and one mile from White Oak Swamp. By the way, White Oak Swamp is a sluggish creek with swamp bottomlands on either side. Our corps crossed with no more serious occurrences than some skirmishing as the enemy's rear guard were driven ahead of us. There are at least two full corps on this side of the river now. The Chickahominy River, as it appears now, is a large creek with bottomlands a quarter of a mile wide or thereabouts. At present it has not the appearance of being a serious obstacle in military operations, but I am told that after storms the water rises to the top of the outer banks and not infrequently overflows even there. If this statement is correct, at such times it is a large river.

I am informed that the army is now so camped that it can be moved into an unbroken line of battle at very short notice.[3] It may be that right here we shall fight for Richmond. If the enemy chooses to do so, they can compel us to fight here, but should they do it, I feel confident we shall be successful.

---

2 The Williamsburg Road leading to Richmond crossed the Chickahominy at Bottom's Bridge.

3 He apparently assumes that the Chickahominy presents no problem for this movement.

Division Headquarters reports that it is said at Army Headquarters that General McDowell, with 50,000 men will make a final union with this army very soon.[4] I am also told he should have been here yesterday. At best an army moves slowly. It is also reported that General Wool[5] is somewhere near us on the south side of the James River with a considerable force, but how large I have not heard. Doubtless, the enemy has a large army in front of us, and the report comes from Army Headquarters that nearby the entire active army of the Confederacy is in our front.

Our generals do not speak of the falling back of General Banks as a necessarily serious matter.[6]

Battery D, 1 N.Y. Lt. Artillery
2 Division, 3 Corps
Seven Pines, Va.
June 11, 1862

[To A. C. O.] As I have passed through and participated somewhat in the great battle which will probably be known as the battle of the "Seven Pines" or "Fair Oaks,"[7] as very heavy fighting was done at both the localities known by these names and in the same general engagement, I will write you this letter about it.

On the afternoon of the 31st, ult., I was at a social gathering of officers at our camp near White Oak Swamp. While with this company I noticed that heavy firing was going on at the front. This, however, made no decided impression on me as it is not an unusual thing for the pickets to be advanced by one or the other army and, when the skirmishing becomes sharp, for the artillery to take up the quarrel and heavy firing follows. But while we were yet together, an orderly notified us the division had been ordered to the front and was then moving and without knapsacks. One of my lieutenants had moved the battery with the column, and I rode two miles before I overtook it. We moved about three miles from our camp, and when we were about two

---

4 Two of McDowell's divisions, Franklin and McCall, had joined McClellan.
5 Maj. Gen. John Ellis Wool
6 Banks's defeat at Winchester by Lt. Gen. Thomas J. (Stonewall) Jackson and his subsequent retreat to Harpers Ferry prevented the balance of McDowell's corps from joining McClellan.
7 Fair Oaks was a station on the Richmond and York River Railroad; Seven Pines, a short distance south on the Williamsburg Road, was named for a nearby plantation.

SEVEN PINES/FAIR OAKS

miles from General Casey's camp[8] we met a good many stragglers going to the rear. These men reported that General Casey's division of the 4th Corps, General Keyes, had been cut to pieces and destroyed.

Among others going to the rear was Captain Bates[9] of Battery A of my regiment. Most of his men were with him. He told me his battery—six brass guns—together with all its appurtenances including horses was lost. Also that Colonel Bailey and Major Van Valkenburg of the regiment were both killed, that Captain Spratt[10] of battery H of the regiment and one of his lieutenants were badly wounded. Captain Spratt, you will remember, is from Watertown. Lieutenant Rumsey,[11] adjutant of the regiment, was also wounded. Colonel Bailey and Major Van Valkenburg were both most excellent officers and their loss will be most seriously felt by the regiment.

The men falling back increased rapidly in number. The division halted at five o'clock, and immediately a line of cavalry was formed across the road and all men going to the rear were stopped and ordered to go into camp at that point. The division also went into camp for the night. This was about one and a half miles in rear of what had been General Casey's line of battle when the fighting commenced. During the night a stampede occurred among the stragglers' camp which was just in front of us, and many managed to get to the rear. There were some very funny incidents connected with this stampede, and I will endeavor to call them up and write about them some other time.

General Casey's division occupied the extreme left flank of the army, was more advanced than any other troops, and was about five miles from Richmond. What is called the State Road, running from Williamsburg to Richmond, is the principal road in this part of the country. General Casey's division lay across it on the plantation known as the Seven Pines. Fair Oaks is about a mile or a little less to the right of the Seven Pines plantation houses and is a station on the York River Railroad.

The left flank of General Casey's division was in an open field containing, say from 100 to 150 acres. The timber line about the field is very irregular, the timber dense, and the undergrowth so close that a person can see but a few yards in it. The open field does not extend more than 200 yards in front of the line of General Casey's earthworks

---

8 Named for Maj. Gen. Silas Casey, Commander of the Second Division of the Fourth Corps, and the area occupied by his men while building a defensive position west of Seven Pines known as Casey's Redoubt.
9 Capt. Thomas H. Bates, Battery A Commander.
10 Capt. Joseph Spratt, Battery H Commander and Osborn's former fellow recruiter.
11 Lt. William Rumsey.

and the redoubt, in which Captain Bates' battery was, is a part of the line of earthworks and, consequently, in the easiest possible range of the enemy's infantry in the dense timber. I am told the pickets had been thrown out only to the edge of the timber, that is 200 yards in advance of the line. I hardly think this can be correct but if it is true, that fact would account for General Casey having no notice of the movements of the enemy in his front on the morning of the attack. If it is true he was unable to force his pickets farther to the front, then his lack of knowledge concerning the enemy's movements was unavoidable. At all events, the enemy were able to get so close to General Casey's line before he had notice that their impetuous attack in great force was irresistible and carried their line upon and over his works before it could be checked.

As the battle is described to us by those who were in it, the enemy moved to the edge of the timber in full line of battle and drove our pickets in almost without resistance. The enemy opened fire with a full volley at short range upon our troops before they had time to fall in, many of them being killed or wounded before they could pick up their muskets. The attack was made upon General Casey's extreme left flank so that his line, or rather his camp, received the first volley on its front, flank, and rear at the same instant. No line of battle could stand under such a fire and especially so under these circumstances where the troops were new and no time given to form lines of battle.

Immediately following this attack on the flank, another was made covering the entire front of the division. Of course, the division gave way but our line falling back from the trenches was very far from being a rout, nor were the enemy successful in dislodging our men from their general line and position before a most desperate fight had been made. Our men fought to the extent of their ability to hold the field, having been driven off of it again in the effort to recover it. The large number of the enemy's dead on the ground over which they fought is positive proof of the quality and extent of the fighting. Our own dead prove how violent the enemy's attack was, and the enemy's dead prove how stubborn the resistance. The artillery is said to have fought magnificently and to have gone down and been destroyed without flinching. The effects of the enemy's fire upon the battery shows this was so. The two batteries, Bates' and Spratt's, are said to have held the enemy's line in check until General Couch's[12] division was brought up to the support of General Casey's division. Judging from the enemy's dead on the field, General Couch's division must have done superb fighting.

---

12 Maj. Gen. Darius Couch commanded the First Division of the Fourth Corps.

The 4th Corps comprising the divisions of Generals Casey and Couch were the newest and least disciplined troops in the army, and this fact was, of course, known to the enemy. I have no doubt but the largest part of the enemy's force was in this movement and far outnumbered the 4th Corps and, as with General Hooker at Williamsburg, General McClellan let General Keyes fight it out alone. No available force was at hand, and none was sent to aid in this desperate fight of one corps against half an army. So far as I know, there was no supporting force nearer than our corps and by the utmost exertion we could not reach the field early enough to be of assistance. Had we been in striking distance, General Heintzelman would have saved the 4th Corps from being as cut to pieces as it was.

At four o'clock in the afternoon, General Kearny, who was in advance of General Hooker, arrived on the field and engaged the enemy. At that time our advanced line had been pushed back to the ground occupied by General Couch's camp to the right and a little to the rear of General Casey's camp. General Keyes, upon the arrival of General Kearny, developed a force of the enemy sufficiently large to account for the repulse of General Casey's division at the first assault. When General Hooker reached the field at five o'clock in the afternoon, General Casey with his division fell back and in rear of General Hooker while Generals Couch and Kearny had also fallen back to and along the railroad, this being to the right and rear of General Couch's camp.

As I draw my conclusions, the worst features of this engagement were the facts that General Casey did not, or could not, get his pickets far enough to the front to give him sufficient warning of the approach of the enemy to enable him to resist the attack, and also, General McClellan putting so new a corps so far to the front and so much exposed with no strong supporting force in easy and immediate reach in the event of an attack.

But to go back to Sunday morning when I became personally more interested in the fight. We were ready to move at daylight; the firing in a moderate degree commenced at a quarter before five and became heavy at half-past six. The open field we were in was about a half mile in width and General Hooker formed General Sickles' brigade with two regiments of General Patterson's brigade[13] in the open field and moved into the timber where the enemy was believed to be in force. I was with the General when he formed his line, and I put the battery in position where it could be employed to the best advantage. I had

---

13 Gen. Sickles commanded the Second Brigade in Hooker's division; Brig. Gen. Francis E. Patterson.

the only battery on this part of the field, the others being sent to guard the left flank and rear in the event the enemy attempted to turn our position. In this first advance of General Hooker I rendered what assistance I could, but the movements were not favorable to the employment of artillery. During the day I maneuvered with the infantry, but at no time did the battery fall under the enemy infantry fire though we were much annoyed by the enemy's sharpshooters and were exposed to their artillery fire.

The infantry became engaged at seven o'clock, and the fighting was almost continuous for two hours when General Hooker ordered General Sickles to charge with the bayonet, which he did, dislodging the enemy and driving them off the field. Early in the forenoon the enemy in our front and in General Sumner's[14] front had been driven from the position they held in the morning, but they still held General Keyes' camp and the position General Keyes had when the battle opened. General Sumner's line connected with the right of General Keyes' line. That is, he was on General Keyes' right, and now as the 3rd Corps had taken the place of the 4th, he was on our right. During the day I became acquainted with General Sickles and I have found him an agreeable gentleman.

In the afternoon it was reported to us that an abandoned gun was in the road midway between the lines. I went after it and succeeded in bringing it out. It was half buried in the mud and it took the men several minutes to pry it up so the horses could start it. We had no mishap though the sharpshooters did their best to pick some of us off. The gun belonged to Captain Spratt's battery.

After the fighting in the morning the day passed quietly with the exception of considerable severe shelling by the enemy. Sunday night the corps was kept ready to resist an attack any minute, so we got but little rest.

Early on Monday morning the corps was ordered forward to reoccupy the position the 4th Corps held at the opening of the fight even if it should be done at the cost of a general battle. In this movement General Hooker had the advance. This was new work for me. The line moved with the utmost caution going only so fast as the skirmishers were able to force the enemy's picket line back. Thus, sometimes the line moved only a few yards before halting. The enemy developed no considerable strength, the field having been abandoned except by a strong picket line and a small rear guard. Pushing these back, the 3rd

---

14 Sumner's timely arrival over the upper Grapevine Bridge saved Couch's division.

SEVEN PINES/FAIR OAKS

Corps occupied the line and earthworks from which the 4th Corps had been driven.

I placed my battery in the redoubt where Captain Bates had lost his. The pickets were thrown much farther to the front than those of the 4th Corps had been, but in all other respects the line of General Keyes was reestablished. General Kearny was on the extreme left. General Keyes had gone to the rear to reorganize his corps and set it into marching condition again. Nothing has been lost or gained in this battle by either army except the loss of materiel and men. In these the enemy lost more than we.

It is here at the Seven Pines that we see how great the battle was and how severe the loss of life. We found the dead scattered over the field as if they had been sown broadcast. No place ten rods square was fewer than one or more of the dead, while in some places a dozen lay in a space ten yards square. Where the dead lay the thickest, they were all of the enemy's men and on no spot did I find ours laying so thick on the ground as were theirs. As we found them, they lay in the proportion of about three of the enemy's dead to two of ours—not less and probably more. I speak of what I have seen and place but little belief in what the newspapermen say. I have ridden over the entire field and examined it carefully.

Before we occupied the field, the enemy had had one whole day unmolested to carry off their wounded and bury their dead, and our wounded found on the field say they worked very earnestly in doing it. Of course, this would be so. Our seriously wounded were found on the field, while the slightly wounded had been removed by the enemy to their rear as prisoners. We found very few of the enemy's wounded and comparatively few of their dead officers. The latter had most all been carried to the rear or buried. Many of the enemy's men had also been buried. Immediately in front of the redoubt I occupy and where I am now writing and within a few yards of me is one grave containing 65 men belonging to the N.C. infantry. Another with 15 men of an Alabama regiment and still another with 24 men of a Louisiana regiment, etc., etc. In addition to the enemy dead laying in the open field and of which I have spoken, large numbers are in the woods both in front and on the left flank of General Casey's line. None of our men were found in the woods.

I have only spoken of the dead and wounded of Saturday or the first day's fight. I have not seen those where General Sumner fought on Saturday and Sunday, nor where General Hooker was engaged Sunday morning. The enemy made a very severe attack on General Sumner's line Sunday morning and after a severe fight were repulsed, after which General Richardson took the offensive and drove the enemy off the field.

After General Richardson[15] had driven the enemy back, they made no further attacks. As in the worst of the fighting done by General Sumner on Sunday morning, his line was covered by earthworks. It is certain the enemy lost far more heavily than we.

Large parties were detailed on Monday to bring in the wounded and worked all day without getting them all. Many were brought in Tuesday morning. The sun was broiling hot and the ground wet. Many of these wounded were parched with thirst and starving, their wounds inflamed beyond description. Their wounds were filled with maggots.

I buried a dozen men to get them out from under the carriage wheels and the horses feet, and yet there were 40 dead men and 80 dead horses within a radius of 25 yards from the center of the redoubt where I am. By Tuesday morning the stench was fearful, as up to that time the burying detachments had done nothing in our vicinity. My own were not permitted to leave their several stations for any purpose, not even to bury the dead laying almost under their feet. The infantry, except the hospital and burying detachments, had no more privileges than my men. Tuesday evening and Wednesday morning the air was thick with the stench but on Wednesday forenoon the burying parties reached our part of the field and the dead were soon out of sight. Wednesday afternoon the dead horses of Captain Bates' battery, about 80 of them, were covered with dry pine cordwood, of which there was an abundance near, and then burned. It was a quick way to dispose of them, but I will leave it to your imagination to comprehend what the air was when 80 putrid horses were burning, all within 100 yards of us.

From General McClellan down to the brigade commanders, every General every minute expected an attack on this flank to dislodge this wing of the Army. The enemy's skirmishers and artillery every moment threatened this movement, and every man was held to his position in the line to repulse an attack if made. This continued until the works were so strengthened as to give perfect confidence that any attempted assault could be warded off with comparative ease.

By Wednesday evening my men began to give out and show strong symptoms of serious sickness. Lieutenant Winslow gave way, but my own general health withstood the pestilence surrounding. When the dead had been buried and the horses burned, I had my camp thoroughly policed, since which the health of my men has improved and most of them are now comfortable.

---

15 Maj. Gen. Israel B. Richardson commanded the First Division of Sumner's corps.

Burying the Dead and Burning Horses at the Twin Houses near Casey's Redoubt after the Second Day's Fight. (From *Battles and Leaders of the Civil War*, Vol. 2, p. 216.)

At division headquarters I have been told that our loss in this engagement was 800 killed and 3,100 wounded, very few missing. Whole loss between 5,000 and 6,000 men, while from all the information we can gather the enemy is believed to have lost in the neighborhood of 10,000 men.[16] On Saturday the enemy might have claimed a victory. On Sunday we were certainly entitled to it; on Tuesday both armies occupied the same ground they occupied on Friday before the fight. In the two days fighting we did the enemy more damage than they did us. It was Williamsburg over again, but on a larger scale.

During the week commencing Sunday morning, the second day of the fight, my horses were released from the guns just 24 hours. At one time they were 36 hours without an ounce of food. I worked several of them to death and another will die. The men were very short of rations and had but little sleep. Towards the last of the week the men gave out rapidly but most of them rallied where they could rest and get rations; some, however, will have to be sent north to the hospitals. Circumstances after the first day's fight appeared to work together to throw the heaviest work on this battery, the other batteries having lighter work to do. General Sickles' brigade has suffered the same hardships and been worked the same as we to an hour.

By the way, I like General Sickles. He appears to be a good man and is a good officer. This battery appears to be a favorite with both him and General Hooker. Either of them are willing to do anything for us, even to working us to death.

Battery D, 1 N. Y. Lt. Artillery
2 Division, 3 Corps
Seven Pines, Va.
June 13, 1862

[To S. C. O.] This Division was not in the battle of Saturday the 31st, but moved from our camp to the edge of the battlefield. On Sunday June 1 the battery was engaged, being nearly the entire day with General Sickles' brigade. During the heavy fighting in the morning the infantry lines were so near together during the fighting that the artillery could not be extensively used to advantage on account of the danger of injuring our own men. On Monday morning when General

---

16 According to Livermore, T. (1900) *Numbers and Losses in the Civil War in America 1861-65*. Boston & New York, Union losses were 5,031 and Confederate casualties were 6,134.

SEVEN PINES/FAIR OAKS 51

Hooker occupied the field on which General Casey fought, I had the only battery moving with the division. The others were on duty elsewhere.

You ask me to write in full of the battle. This I have already done to A. C. and if you desire you can send for that letter as I have not the opportunity now to duplicate it, or you can depend on the newspapermen for the information. But there is so much falsehood in their reports that they are a poor dependence.

For instance, just now they are saying a great deal about the groans and shrieks of the wounded and dying. This is nonsense. As a rule, a wounded man makes no noise whether he is seriously or slightly wounded.[17] The exceptions are rare, so rare as to be scarcely worth mentioning. Certainly, no newspaperman was ever near enough to a battlefield to hear a wounded man if he shrieked as loud as the whistle of a locomotive.

The enemy had removed nearly all their wounded and many of their dead before we reoccupied the field, and even then their dead largely outnumbered ours. The battlefield extended about one mile east and west along the Williamsburg road and about one mile and a half north and south. All the fighting on Saturday and Sunday was done within that space. The enemy were too severely repulsed to attack us after Sunday morning, but it is not too late for them to make another effort to permanently dislodge us from this position. However, I do not think their entire army could break this line by direct assault in front. At all events, I hope our next battle may have better results follow it than have followed this or the battle of Williamsburg.

After the battle the burying of the dead went on slowly for many reasons, and we were three days in position among the decaying men and horses before they were disposed of. On this part of the field where we are, they had lain two days before they were buried, and the weather is as hot as any you ever experienced.

Battery D, 1 N. Y. Lt. Artillery
2 Division, 3 Corps
Seven Pines, Va.
June 16, 1862

[To A. C. O.] With this battery there has been no particular change since I last wrote. We are frequently on picket and much more

---

17 Osborn makes an inaccurate generalization that he later modified.

frequently called upon to meet a supposed attack or supposed attempted surprise. So far, these have resulted only in sharp skirmishes with one or two killed and a few wounded. Yesterday at four in the afternoon our cavalry and infantry were driven in rapidly by the enemy who came within 600 or 700 yards of our works when a sharp skirmish along our picket line commenced. General Sickles, who was at the time at my battery, sent his aide, Captain Palmer, to the front to see what the disturbance amounted to. The Captain with a few mounted men rode rapidly down the road and ran into an ambush and was fired upon by the enemy, and the Captain was instantly killed, several bullets passing through him. The Captain was an accomplished gentleman, a genial and gallant officer and a general favorite.

In 15 minutes after the volley was fired which killed the Captain, 50,000 men were standing ready to receive an attack as all supposed one would be made by the mass of the enemy's force. But this proved to be only a reconnoitering party and it immediately fell back. These affrays are frequent and are usually carried out by the infantry alone.

As it looks to us officers of smaller rank, we have again settled down to siege operations in much the same way as we did at Yorktown. We are thoroughly entrenched, and the enemy is quite as thoroughly so, a mile and a half from us in our front and parallel to us. In our front, that is the left of the Army, the country intervening between the two armies is mostly swamp covered with timber, underbrush, and water; the water in many places being half-leg deep. As matters stand now, it is a serious question and one upon which we may well have our doubts whether it is the enemy's army or our army being besieged. This depends very much on which army is the largest and best handled. This much we can see. Our line of battle is firmly entrenched where it is in position and has also a very substantial line of works in the rear, where it could make a stand if it should be compelled to fall back from its present position.

June 17

I was not able to finish this letter last evening. Today the gunboats on the James River have been engaged with the enemy's batteries on the banks of the river. The results I do not know.

The enemy's losses in the battle of May 31st and June 1st post up larger than I knew when I wrote last. The official report at Headquarters shows 2,840 of their dead were buried by our men. I know the enemy buried many before they abandoned the field; many were buried by our troops to get them out of the trenches where our line was re-established. I buried several to get them out of the way of the battery. None so buried were reported. I, therefore, conclude the enemy loss in killed alone posted up little if any less than 3,500 men.

SEVEN PINES/FAIR OAKS 53

The exact positions of General Porter's[18] and Franklin's corps I do not know. They are beyond the Chickahominy and form the right of the Army. It appears to me that a stream the size of and possessing the uncertain character of the Chickahominy cutting the Army in two and only passable by long bridges is not altogether desirable. In fact, it makes two armies half the size of the one we nominally have. If this stream is not more easily passable, when even half of the Army is forced to cross it in a general battle, than Bottom's Bridge or the Railroad Bridge were when we crossed them, then when necessity shall arise, one wing of the army will not be able to render the other much assistance.[19] If I were not so closely confined to the battery by the continuous threatening of the enemy in our front, I would make a scout along the whole line of the Army and satisfy my own curiosity by studying grand tactics by personal observation. So far, no control has been exercised over my personal movements by any superior officer. Still, I do not like to leave the battery while so great an uncertainty exists as to what the enemy will do.

N.B.[20] The numbers given in this letter, as to the number of dead of the enemy's troops buried at Seven Pines and Fair Oaks differs very widely from those which have been officially published. I am positive in my own mind that future investigation will show that the number was much greater than that given officially, 1,129 officers and men killed. The number given above in the letter was written immediately after an inquiry at headquarters as to the facts.

Battery D, 1 N. Y. Lt. Artillery
2 Division, 3 Corps
Seven Pines, Va.
June 22, 1862

[To S. C. O.] We are still on the same ground we occupied immediately after the battle. In fact, we are doing now apparently just what we did at Yorktown, that is attempting to take Richmond by siege. So

---

18 Maj. Gen. Porter commanded the Fifth Corps near Mechanicsville. Maj. Gen. Franklin, Sixth Corps Commander, was on Porter's left. Both were north of the Chickahominy.
19 Osborn apparently recognizes the Union Army's perilous position.
20 Osborn apparently added this note to his letters at a later date when he was preparing the letters for publication.

far as we can see, it is the same except it is being carried on on a larger scale. General McClellan compelled the enemy to leave Yorktown without fighting, and perhaps he may succeed by the same tactics here. If he should accomplish this he will be much longer about it. In every movement he makes, he moves with the utmost caution, but so far he has gained a little at each move.

The enemy is commanded by men educated at the same school as those who command this Army, and many of the generals of the opposing armies are personal friends. General McClellan may think he has sufficient reason through his knowledge of his opponents to be cautious in all his movements. Personally, I am satisfied with this slow movement and would be equally well satisfied if a far more vigorous and active campaign was in progress, or would be entirely willing to take the chances of success in a general engagement fought out to the bitter end.

My own health has continued good, but Lieutenant Winslow and about one-quarter of my men became sick within a few days after we went into these works. The air and the water were both so filthy the men became sick from their use. The infantry, of course, suffered the same as we.

Whenever this line is advanced to occupy and entrench in a new position, we shall have heavy work to do. The enemy must be pushed back and held while we establish and entrench on a new line.

Battery D, 1 N. Y. Lt. Artillery
2 Division, 3 Corps
Seven Pines, Va.
June 22, 1862

[To A. C. O.] It is shown more conclusively each day that my conclusions in regard to the last battle were in the main correct. The losses were about as I have stated before. We claimed a victory because the enemy attacked us in order to prevent our holding this position and constructing our earthworks.[21] They were repulsed and lost heavier than we. They held the field one day, were pushed off of it the next, and these works reoccupied and completed.

---

21 The Confederate attack aimed to destroy or capture the two Union corps south of the Chickahominy. Osborn does not seem to appreciate or will not admit that the two corps narrowly escaped disaster.

In all these fights there has been one noticeable feature, that of the enemy massing their troops in an attack and thereby being at the time and point of attack in much greater force than our troops. This plan of attack gives the assaulting force an excessive advantage. In the two engagements we have had, General McClellan has shown marked slowness or great timidity in moving fresh troops rapidly to the support of those engaged.

The earthworks on our present line are completed and very strong. A large area of timber has been felled in our front to open the field and act as an abatis in case of an attack. The Generals are talking of an approaching battle, but based on what facts I am not informed. If we are to have a general engagement, it appears to me we are as well prepared now as we shall be. If such a thing is possible as getting ready, we are now ready. I do not know whether this rumor or information or whatever it is of a coming battle comes from General McClellan's headquarters or not.

Battery D, 1 N. Y. Lt. Artillery
2 Division, 3 Corps
Seven Pines, Va.
June 26, 1862

[To A. C. O.] Doubtless the newspapers have reported that General Heintzelman's corps was engaged yesterday and fearing you might feel some uneasiness about me, I write at the first opportunity.

Yesterday morning General Heintzelman was ordered to advance his corps and engage the enemy in his front, that is on the left of the Army. This he did and had a sharp fight at a plantation known as Oak Grove. The infantry only was engaged. I took no part in it. At three o'clock in the afternoon another advance was ordered and made. I was then directed to put the battery in position 500 yards in advance of the works and aid our line by firing over it at the enemy's line or columns. A large body of timber intervening between my position and the enemy, I fired by the telegraphics signals of one of the signal corps posted in the top of a high pine tree. I threw about 250 shells, and the flagman reports did good service by breaking up the enemy's columns as they were moving to the front.[22]

---

22 Oak Grove engagement.

Our infantry passed through the swamp in our front and upon the high ground beyond, a full mile from our line of works. There were three collisions between the enemy's lines and our own, and in each the enemy was forced back. General McClellan was on the field a little while in the afternoon. Early in the evening General Heintzelman was ordered to fall back to his works, against which he and his two division commanders protested earnestly.

This evening I was told at division headquarters that while operations were going on in our front, General Porter advanced his lines two miles nearer Richmond and suffered but little loss in doing so. To me this information is indefinite as I am not well informed as to what General Porter's position was or now is.

Today everything has been quiet along the line until a little after three o'clock when we heard heavy cannonading on the extreme right and north of the Chickahominy, and now an hour after dark we can hear it distinctly. It is a good way off and I have not been able to hear any musketry, but the sound of the artillery is much like that of a heavy battle—yet it may be heavy firing in progress to cover some movements of the troops.[23] No report has reached Division headquarters of what is going on at the right.

9 p.m.

No cessation of the heavy firing on the right and no report received at Division headquarters of what is being done north of the Chickahominy.

Battery D, 1 N. Y. Lt. Artillery
2 Division, 3 Corps
Seven Pines, Va.
June 27, 1862

[To A. C. O.] It is now after dark. A battle has been in progress at some point on our line since the morning of the 25th, though but little of it has been on our line since that day. It is reported at Division Headquarters that General Porter gained a fine advantage last night.

We know by the sound of the artillery that the battle opened this morning at daylight and slackened away at half past nine in the morning, at noon began again and is still in progress, now at fifteen

---

23 On June 26th, the Confederates attacked Porter at Beaver Dam Creek. Gaines' Mill was fought on June 27th which accounts for the heavy firing heard by Osborn.

SEVEN PINES/FAIR OAKS 57

minutes past eight. The firing has been but little interrupted and is on the extreme right. The distance is so great we can but occasionally hear the musketry and then but lightly. Today we have no information from that wing of the Army. General Hooker thinks General Sumner will be attacked tomorrow, and he is being rapidly reinforced. It would seem the enemy have determined to fight it out now.

Current rumor has it that Stonewall Jackson and Beauregard[24] are with the army in our front and are now engaged in this fight.

Battery D, 1 N. Y. Lt. Artillery
2 Division, 3 Corps
Harrison's Landing, Va.
July 4, 1862

[To S. C. O.] I send you this to say I have passed through all the fighting and changes this Army has undergone in the last ten days without personal injury and with my general health remaining good.

We are now on the bank of the James River. Our position is in the nature of a fortress and we are able here to resist any possible attack, but I have no idea the enemy will attack us here. Each assault the enemy made on any part of the Army while changing from the works in front of Richmond to this place was repulsed.

This whole movement is a mystery to me. The Army is in as good condition today as it has ever been and there is no symptom of demoralization in it. I don't believe as much can be said of the General commanding it.

---

24 Gen. Pierre Gustave Toutant Beauregard; Jackson had arrived, but Beauregard's arrival was a rumor apparently encouraged by McClellan to justify his demand for more troops.

Chapter 4

"Planned Withdrawal" or Hasty Retreat

*... General McClellan was driven off that field and sought shelter here.
...and our flank movement to the James was a bonafide retreat.*

Although Osborn's letters appear in chronological order, he frequently writes about events that occurred several weeks earlier. He reviews the events of the Seven Days Campaign from Harrison's Landing and describes the Savage Station affair after his return to the Washington area. As a battery commander there were apparently more pressing duties that demanded his attention.

On June 25, 1862, Heintzelman's Third Corps moved forward in a limited offense at Oak Grove, mentioned by Osborn. This was the beginning of McClellan's long-promised offense against Richmond. On the next day Lee began his own offense and sent Lieutenant General Ambrose P. (A. P.) Hill's division against Porter's Fifth Corps at Mechanicsville, the right flank of the Union corps and the only Union corps remaining north of the Chickahominy. Porter withdrew to a strong defensive position along Beaver Dam Creek and repulsed Hill's attack inflicting heavy losses on the Confederates. Hill was supposed to have been supported by Jackson's corps, recently arrived from the Shenandoah Valley, but Jackson failed to appear. Porter withdrew to Gaines' Mill where on the 27th after a number of costly Confederate assaults, the Fifth Corps was forced to retreat across the Chickahominy and join the other four Union corps on the south bank. Jackson was late joining the Confederate attack, and McClellan was late in sending reinforcements to the hard-pressed Fifth Corps. Failed Confederate cooperation again helped to save Porter's corps. Meanwhile, Magruder's slim Confederate force, standing between Richmond and the other four Union corps, had maneuvered skillfully so as to deter any Union move against the city.

"PLANNED WITHDRAWAL" OR HASTY RETREAT 59

On the evening of the 27th, McClellan officially announced his plans to move his supply base to the James river, a plan he probably had contemplated since Stuart's ride around his army in mid-June and more recently upon Jackson's arrival from the Shenandoah Valley.[1] Union corps commanders were given orders for a general retreat to the new base.

Keyes's corps, on the extreme Union left, was to withdraw first and to secure the White Oak Swamp Crossing. Porter was to follow Keyes while Heintzelman, Sumner, and Franklin were to hold their lines so that the supply trains could escape Confederate efforts to intercept their movement south. Union supplies not readily movable were to be destroyed. On the 29th, the Third Corps rear guard left their entrenchments to take a new position in the rear to protect the White Oak Swamp Crossing. In an effort to cut off McClellan's retreat, Lee ordered Magruder to pursue by the Williamsburg Road while Jackson crossed the Chickahominy from the north and attacked the Union right flank near Savage Station on the Richmond and York River Railroad.

Magruder, fearful of a Union attack,[2] waited for Jackson, who spent the day repairing the lower Grapevine Bridge over the Chickahominy. Finally, at 4 p.m., Magruder attacked with two and a half brigades on a narrow front between the railroad and the Williamsburg Road. Four Union brigades of Sumner's corps and three Union batteries, including Osborn, turned back Magruder's attack.

Jackson continued to manifest the behavior that had marked his two earlier failures at Beaver Dam Creek and Gaines' Mill, behavior quite uncharacteristic for him. E. Porter Alexander suggested it may have been Jackson's regard for the Sabbath that prevented his 25,000-man force from fighting on Sunday.[3]

It was a combination of unusual and confusing events that caused Osborn's participation with Sumner's Second Corps at Savage Station. His corps commander, Heintzelman, had crossed the swamp leaving Sumner and Franklin to cover the crossing. And then, when Smith's Second Division of Franklin's corps, to whom Osborn's battery had been temporarily assigned, crossed the swamp without informing Osborn, the latter found himself left to serve under Sumner. Osborn describes the action at Savage Station after which the Union rear guard withdrew safely across the White Oak Swamp.

---

1   Sears, S. W. (1988) *George B. McClellan: The Young Napoleon*. New York. p.202.
2   Freeman, D. S. (1944) *Lee's Lieutenants*. Vol. 1. New York. p. 544.
3   Alexander, E. P. (1977) *Military Memoirs of a Confederate*. Dayton. p. 145.

After crossing the White Oak Swamp Bridge, Osborn reported to Hooker who ordered him to proceed to Malvern Hill and to report to any commanding officer there. Consequently, Osborn did not participate the following day at Glendale or Frayser's Farm.

Jackson again played a spectator role on June 30th. After arriving at the White Oak Swamp Bridge and opening fire with his artillery upon a Union force on the opposite bank, he apparently decided not to contest the crossing even failing to reconnoiter Brackett's Ford, a nearby alternate crossing. His idleness cost A. P. Hill and Longstreet the needed support for their attack against the Union position at Glendale and frustrated what may have been Lee's last best chance to cut off McClellan's retreat.

On July 1st, Osborn's battery joined the mass of Union artillery at Malvern Hill and helped neutralize the efforts of the outgunned Confederate artillery to silence the Union guns. In late afternoon, the ill-advised and poorly coordinated infantry assaults by Brigidier General Daniel Harvey (D. H.) Hill and Magruder against the Union fortress resulted in what Lee's biographer, Douglas Freeman, called "mass murder"[4] on this the final day of the Seven Days' Campaign.

For the Army of the Potomac, those seven days posed a most serious threat to its continued existence as a fighting force. The retreat to the James River was a perilous one as Lee and his lieutenants planned and attempted to execute several attacks that if accomplished, would have captured or destroyed one or more of the five Union corps. Lee's plans required coordination, cooperation, and staff work that his inexperienced officer corps was unable to accomplish. Jackson's performance was most disappointing to his fellow officers who, after his Valley successes, had expected him to perform miracles.

Credit goes to McClellan for planning what turned out to be a masterful withdrawal helped by Confederate ineptitude. McClellan was absent from the front lines during much of the retreat, so much of the credit for the execution of the plan must go to the Union corps commanders.

Richmond had been saved and the Yankees driven from the gates of the city back to their gunboats on the James River at Harrison's Landing. It had been a costly victory, seven days that had claimed 20,000 Confederate casualties added to another 6,000 at Seven Pines. The Union rank and file seemed to believe that they had fought their adversaries to a standoff and may have concluded that it was their commanding general who had been defeated. *The Editors*

---

4 Freeman, *op. cit.*, p. 602.

"PLANNED WITHDRAWAL" OR HASTY RETREAT   61

Battery D, 1 N. Y. Lt. Artillery
2 Division, 3 Corps
Harrison's Landing, Va.
July 8, 1862

[To S. C. O.] I have just received 20 horses to replace that number lost in the movements from Seven Pines here. Together with putting the battery into condition to take the field again, sending my sick to hospital, and much other necessary work I have been very busy and am very tired.

The history of our march from the works in front of Richmond to this place would make too long a story to write now, and with the conveniences at my disposal I can give you only an outline. June 25th, we were engaged with General Hooker's division on the extreme left of the army and had a sharp fight at Oak Grove.[5] On the 30th, at Peach Orchard[6] at ten o'clock in the morning and in the evening at Savage Station under General Sumner. I opened that fight at five o'clock in the afternoon and continued in the fight till its close after dark. It was a severe and splendidly conducted battle. July 1st I was engaged at Malvern Cliff near Malvern Hill in General Morell's line. July 2nd at seven in the morning on Malvern Hill in General Sykes' line.[7] The same afternoon on another part of the line with General Hooker's division in the main battle of Malvern Hill. Many of my men gave out before and when we reached here. They were completely exhausted.

From the morning of the 25th of June until we reached here, fighting was continually going on on some part of the field of operations or, say more properly, along our line of retreat as we were falling back or retreating or whatever history may call this movement. The enemy were able to mass their troops in every attack they made. Whenever we crossed a road perpendicular or comparatively so to the one on which we were moving, the enemy would strike our moving column with their troops massed and with the belief each time they struck us that their attacking column was heavy enough to cut our moving column in two. Each time they struck us, they did so with more men than we had at the point attacked, and yet at each assault we repulsed them. Judging each fight independently and upon the field when we

---

5   The beginning of McClellan's offense against Richmond resulted in an inconclusive engagement with Huger's Confederate division.

6   Peach Orchard or Allen's Farm on the morning of the 30th as Magruder attacked Sumner's corps retiring from Fair Oaks.

7   Brig. Gen. George W. Morell, First Division, Fifth Corps; Brig. Gen. George Sykes, Second Division, Fifth Corps.

fought, we whipped them, with the single exception perhaps of the attack on General Porter on the 27th June.[8] But the results of the last ten days, taken as a whole, are most decidedly against us, if I can judge correctly. Yet it is continually dinned into our ears that the changing of base or the transferring of the army from sitting astride of the Chickahominy River to the bank of the James is a great and successful military exploit. At all events, the army is together and not split in halves by an impassable river.

July 10

The finishing of this letter has unavoidably been delayed two days.

I have seen the Richmond papers, and the Confederates do not appear to be jubilant and speak of the late ten days fighting as a "drawn game."

It is now stated to us that General McClellan fell back from before Richmond because of the overwhelming force the enemy had concentrated there, that a movement was about to be made by the enemy to cut our line of supplies at the York River, that if the enemy had cut our line of supplies this army would have been compelled to surrender, and General McClellan took time by the forelock and fell back, and that he moved to this point where the gunboats could aid in keeping the line of supplies open.[9]

The officers who are more intimate with Army Headquarters are continually explaining that this last movement of General McClellan's was a most excellent one from a military point of view. Perhaps so, but how in fact it is all to be accounted for or how it all happened is a difficult matter for a volunteer Captain to reason out. It cannot all be accounted for by what has transpired in the last 20 days. It covers the whole campaign from the day it was determined to transfer the army from Washington to the Peninsula, then to the time it was split in two in the middle by the Chickahominy River, making two little armies of what should have been one great army for the enemy to fight. Also, leaving the country open between the little armies and our base of supplies in such a manner as to coax the enemy to turn us and get possession of our general depot of supplies. It is all very queer. But here we are and are told it is all right; perhaps it is.[10]

I see much is said in the newspapers about the gunboats aiding the army while it was falling back. This is all gammon. They threw a few

8 Gaines' Mill.
9 Osborn echoes McClellan's explanation of the Seven Days Campaign.
10 Osborn asks relevant and critical questions.

shells here and there, but with no knowledge where either army was and with no beneficial results. Our troops feared them quite as much as the enemy, and as a fact I think they injured our troops more than they did the enemy. A single shell from one of the gunboats fell in the center of a battery on the afternoon of July 1st and exploded, absolutely ruining the battery.[11] That battery was in position on Malvern Hill, not more than 300 yards of my own. I saw this and was with the battery inside of two minutes after the explosion. I do not believe that, all told, these gunboats injured the enemy as much as the injury to that single battery.

The position occupied by the army is very strong by nature and has been made more strong by the skill of the military engineers. Troops are coming to us everyday, and probably after a little while we shall move out again. There has been and is no demoralization in the army. It can do as good or better fighting now than ever before. It is more of a veteran army today than it was ten days before it arrived here.

N.B.[12] By some official oversight the affair in General Sykes' line on the morning of July 2nd has no official notice in the records. It was a sharp little affair with one brigade of the enemy's infantry and was repulsed mainly by a crossfire secured by Bramhall's battery and my own. It should have been recognized officially.[13]

Battery D, 1 N. Y. Lt. Artillery
2 Division, 3 Corps
Harrison's Landing, Va.
July 11, 1862

[To A. C. O.] Reinforcements continue to come to the Army, and to us subordinates it appears we are nearly ready to move again. New troops are being raised and organized all over the country, and I presume before the next general movement will be put in with and among the old troops in the Army and in this way can be made of

---

11 Col. Robert O. Tyler's First Connecticut Heavy Artillery Battery.
12 Osborn apparently added this note to his letters at a later date when he was preparing the letters for publication.
13 An engagement Osborn mentions in his report. The batteries commanded by Winslow and Bramhall repelled a Confederate infantry attack. It was known as Malvern Cliff.

practical use.[14] I hardly think we shall move until near or after the first of September.

This Army may now be considered thoroughly veteran. The prospect of future battles does not cause that anxiety among officers and men they experienced a few months or even a few weeks ago. The morale of the Army is excellent. My own company is in good condition and excellent spirits. It has been weakened somewhat by men being killed, wounded, sick, and worn out by hard labor; still, it is strong enough to do good and effective work.

Battery D, 1 N. Y. Lt. Artillery
2 Division, 3 Corps
Harrison's Landing, Va.
July 15, 1862

[To S. C. O.] This country looks more barren than Egypt after the raid of the locusts. The passing of the Army through the country does not much change its appearance, but wherever the Army stops and occupies it for a few days only, it looks as if no green thing had ever grown upon it lower than the leaves of the trees.

It is a pity you cannot depend more on the newspaper reports from the Army. You speak of the report of the battle of Savage Station. I have read it. The man who wrote that report had never even seen the field where the battle was fought. The only thing in the article to be recognized as relating to that battle is his speaking of Captain Pettit's battery.[15] Otherwise there is no reference to anything happening on that field. This is only a sample of hundreds of pages of bosh you get from the papers and from the reporters who gather news at the "cannon's mouth."

Everything here moves on slowly and quietly. So far as we subordinate officers can see, we are waiting for some plan of campaign for the future to be developed and matured.

I shall be glad if the Negroes are called into service in any way. Their lives are worth no more to themselves or the country than the lives of white men. There is no good reason why their services should not be made available. I have changed my mind since I have been in the service on this point. I think they should be put to such use as will be of most value to the country.

14 Osborn's recommendation was later adopted.
15 Capt. Rufus D. Pettit, Battery B, First New York Light Artillery.

"PLANNED WITHDRAWAL" OR HASTY RETREAT 65

I am also in favor of a draft and if sufficient men for the Army do not volunteer, I hope a draft will be authorized and made. I do not fear drafted men will not fight. They will fight whether they wish to do so or not.[16]

Battery D, 1 N. Y. Lt. Artillery
2 Division, 3 Corps.
Harrison's Landing, Va.
July 23, 1862

[To S. C. O.] For some time past, each day has been precisely what the preceding day was. But today General McClellan reviewed this corps and we have had a hard day's work. So far as I can see, there is no indication of an immediate movement. There are five corps in the Army, and I understand one is to be reviewed each day until the five have been looked over by the Commanding General.

If current reports are true, General Pope[17] will soon have occasion to test his skill and ground tactics in fighting Stonewall Jackson, by far the ablest fighting general the enemy has.

The information is given out here from some source, I don't know how it comes, that General Pope's army has received more reinforcements than any other army. Also, that a large force is being concentrated at Fortress Monroe under General Burnside, and that General Buell[18] is moving this way through Cumberland Gap. Some troops have been sent here.

I think the health of the Army has improved since we arrived here. It is the healthiest locality we have been in since we left Fortress Monroe, but that is not saying much for this locality. We are now having the only rest since leaving Yorktown.

---

16 An enlightened attitude not generally shared.
17 Maj. Gen. John Pope
18 Maj. Gen. Don Carlos Buell

Battery D, 1 N. Y. Lt. Artillery
2 Division, 3 Corps
Harrison's Landing, Va.
July 26, 1862

[To S. C. O.] General Hooker this morning showed me his report of the fighting by his division on the Peninsula. He speaks in very complimentary terms of my battery.[19]

Battery D, 1 N. Y. Lt. Artillery
2 Division, 3 Corps
Harrison's Landing, Va.
August 4, 1862

[To S. C. O.] Until now there has been no change of importance since the Army reached this point, but tonight this division will move out to Malvern Hill and learn what force the enemy has in our front. Today General Hooker told me that this battery had been so much overworked he should not take it with him.

There was, or has been till now, a very general feeling in the Army that the movement from in front of Richmond was a simple change of base with the intention of operating against Richmond along the James River. This belief has now given way to one quite as general, that General McClellan was driven off that field and sought shelter here. In other words, he was compelled to fall back and this was the safest place to which he could go, and our flank movement to the James was a bonafide retreat. But even now, the morale of the Army is perfect and in every way it is in complete condition to assume the offensive. I hope the government will give the General all the men he may think necessary to do the work he has planned to do, and whether the men sent here are volunteers or drafted men is not material. It is plain an invading Army must be larger than the home Army operating on the defensive, and there is no doubt but the General commanding an Army should have a force which in his opinion is strong enough to accomplish the work he has planned for it.

A few days ago General Hooker received his commission as Major General. He gave his officers a reception and considering we are in the field, it was a very elegant affair.

19 *OR*. Vol. 25, Part 1, Pp. 110.

"PLANNED WITHDRAWAL" OR HASTY RETREAT 67

Battery D, 1 N. Y. Lt. Artillery
2 Division, 3 Corps
Harrison's Landing, Va.
August 7, 1862

[To A. C. O.] You ask me to write an account of the retreat from our lines before Richmond to this place, of "what we learned, what we saw, and what we did." The comparatively little the commander of a single battery saw and experienced in the late movement, if written in full and well told, would fill a volume, but I will only pass from point to point and mention each incident which occurs to me briefly.

The operations on the 26th and 27th of June I did not see, and all I can tell is what I have gathered from officers who took part in them. I wrote you of the 25th of June but am not sure whether I wrote you later. The battle of the 26th and 27th of June is called here, Gaines' Mill.

A little before noon on the 26th of June, the enemy attacked General McCall's[20] division of General Porter's corps, the 5th, and after a very severe fight were driven back about two miles. I did not learn of other of our troops being engaged unless General Morell's Division was engaged a part of the time in assisting General McCall. The enemy was commanded on the field by General Lee in person, and Hill was in immediate command. I was on picket duty that evening, and about nine o'clock we heard enthusiastic cheering and the bands playing quick tunes to our right. The cheering passed along the line at ten o'clock and reached us. General McClellan sent a courier along the line to announce at each brigade headquarters that General McCall had driven the enemy halfway to Richmond.

General McClellan ordered General McCall to fall back from his advanced position to his original position at Beaver Dam Creek which he did in the night. At ten o'clock on the morning of the 27th, the enemy again attacked the same division. Meanwhile, strong reinforcements were sent from our center north of the Chickahominy to strengthen the extreme right. General Franklin's corps was engaged part of the day, but General Porter's corps had the weight of the battle to bear.

The enemy attacked in heavy force, and as one brigade or division became exhausted, it was relieved by a fresh one. In this way the enemy were able to maintain the attack with very little interruption and all the time with a force superior to our troops at the point of attack. General Porter soon commenced to fall back fighting, and he

---

20 Brig. Gen. George A. McCall commanded the Third Division of the Fifth Corps.

maintained his line well while doing so. His falling back was by instruction of McClellan, and we do not know whether in a square fight he could have whipped the enemy in his front or not. The retreat, of which this was the beginning, was so timed as to enable General McClellan to pass his troops then on the north side of the Chickahominy to the south side before night, but too late for the enemy to make a lodgment that evening on the south side of the river. The fighting by both armies was very severe and great courage was shown by both. Many acts of great bravery and gallantry by both officers and men are spoken of.

The retiring of General Porter from the front of the enemy was in compliance with a general plan of withdrawing the Army from its position before Richmond. It is affirmed that our line was not broken or pushed back by the enemy and in so far as the fighting went on the field, our line maintained its ground and was able to continue to hold it.

On the afternoon of the 27th, one brigade each from Generals Kearny's and Hooker's divisions and all the batteries of the corps except two were sent to reinforce the right. In consequence, this corps was weak At two o'clock I rode along the line to look up the situation and talk with the Generals whom I knew, for my own gratification. All the officers looked worn and anxious, and the men partook of the feelings of their officers. The line was noticeably weak, and both men and officers knew that it was so. It was easy to be seen that the situation was far from satisfactory to all that part of the Army I saw.

The 28th was a comparatively quiet day along the entire front in so far as actual fighting went. Both armies had apparently stopped to take breath. The 28th should hardly be counted as one of the series of days on which a battle was fought. At eleven in the morning the enemy opened with artillery upon General Sumner's corps and caused him considerable annoyance. The enemy's infantry did not attack but the artillery fire was very severe.

About noon I learned from Captain de Russey,[21] Chief of Artillery of the 3rd Corps, of the proposed movement to the rear, and who gave me the particulars, so far as he knew them, of the situation. At dark I was ordered to move my battery a mile to the rear and make myself comfortable for the night. At the time I moved, it was raining lightly and the evening was very dark. I had but just gone into camp and the men were comfortable when the Captain again came to my tent and directed me to prepare my baggage train to move at once, to load it

---

21 Capt. Gustavus A. de Russey.

chiefly with provisions and forage, and see that the mechanics and sick were ready to go with it. After getting the train ready, I was to destroy all materiel including camp equipage not loaded on the wagons and then to put my train into the corps baggage train at that time passing and let it take its chances. These chances he said were not worth a cent. However, the train was sent forward and we have it now. The Quartermaster Sergeant, Darius Chapin of Russell,[22] took charge of it and brought it through.

The train had but fairly got off and I was left with nothing but my men and battery when the Captain again came to me, this time to give me my final instructions for the retreat. These were certainly a little remarkable and briefly were in substance as follows.

The Army would be moved from its present position to the rear in the morning and as rapidly as so large a body of troops could be moved. That General Hooker's division was to be the rear guard of this wing of the Army, General Sickles' brigade the last brigade, and my battery to follow this brigade, and the battery would be guarded by a very small detachment of infantry. He stated it was expected the baggage train would be troublesome and hinder the march of the Army and that the enemy would follow in force and attack us. If they should do so our infantry would fall back and protect us, but that I must be ready to commence an engagement at my own discretion, not waiting for orders. But an important feature in regard to these instructions was in regard to our baggage train. He said it was believed the road would become blocked and that a large number of wagons might fall into the hands of the enemy. In case of the train blocking the road and an attack by the enemy being made, I was to see such impediment was cleared from the road at once so no one wagon should hinder another; that I should make such disposition of them as I saw fit even to blow up one wagon or a whole train if it appeared best to do so, or to burn any part of a train necessary to prevent its falling into the hands of the enemy. And if it should be necessary to prevent the enemy getting possession of any portion of the train, to turn my guns on the train itself and destroy it together with the horses and whatever might be with it, including men who could not get out of the way.

Fortunately, circumstances did not make it necessary for me to execute any portion of these orders. I have no doubt now I should have carried them, or any portion of them, out to the letter if occasion had made it necessary, regardless how distasteful it may have been. I believe, too, that at Headquarters it was firmly believed I could be

---

22 Russell, a small village in St. Lawrence County, NY.

relied upon to execute this order, and it is not unlikely that I was the only artillery officer who would do it.

The few remaining hours of the night I did not enjoy. We had nothing left of our camp conveniences, and it was late when I laid down on the ground for a little sleep. At half past two in the morning, orders were received from Headquarters to prepare to move instantly, and in five minutes we were ready. But it was morning before we moved and the last hours of the night dragged heavily.

I will take up this narrative again when I can find the time and have the disposition to write.[23]

Battery D, 1 N. Y. Lt. Artillery
2 Division, 3 Corps
Harrison's Landing, Va.
August 10, 1862

[To S. C. O.] The entire Army is ordered to be ready to move at two o'clock tomorrow afternoon and to be ready for action at a moment's notice. The baggage and supplies are now being sent down the river on transports. If I do not guess wrongly, we are to go to Fortress Monroe on our way to Washington and so to report to General Pope whose Army is operating south of Washington.[24] I have been expecting such a movement for some days.

Lieutenant Winslow goes north for his health as he has an attack of scurvy and on duty tomorrow.

Battery D, 1 N. Y. Lt. Artillery
2 Division, 3 Corps
Harrison's Landing, Va.
August 10, 1862

[To A. C. O.] Another great change is in progress here. A large proportion of the heavy artillery has already been shipped, together with a vast amount of stores and supplies, all of which have gone down the river. I understand General Porter's corps was shipped today,

---

23 In his letter of September 5, Osborn describes the Savage Station engagement.
24 Gen. Pope's recently organized Army of Virginia.

destined for some distant point.[25] The orders already issued virtually order the Army to be ready to move tomorrow, but this corps has no specific orders yet, but doubtless it and in fact the entire Army will move to some post on the coast very soon, probably tomorrow. We have not much information of what is being done or to be done, except at Division Headquarters it is stated General Lee's Army is moving on Washington or to the west of it going farther north and that this Army is to go to Washington and fight the enemy somewhere in that vicinity.

Have I ever written you that a few days ago I was ordered to turn in my rifled, three-inch iron guns and take a brass, 12-pound battery?[26] This exchange was given or made as a special and marked compliment to the battery for the service it had performed. One Napoleon battery was given to each division of the Army to be issued to the battery which had the best record. I received the one for this division.

Battery D, 1 N. Y. Lt. Artillery
2 Division, 3 Corps
On the Potomac River
August 29, 1862

[To S. C. O.] Yesterday morning we left Yorktown for Alexandria where we shall arrive this evening.[27]

I learn from the paper this morning that General Hooker with the infantry was engaged yesterday at Bull Run and that the division did well.

One year ago yesterday I left Watertown with the company. It has been a year full of changes.

---

25 To join Pope's army.
26 The 12-pound Napoleon became popular as the war progressed. Although not capable of matching the range or accuracy of the 3-inch rifled pieces, its cannister contained larger balls that dispersed more widely, making the 12-pound Napoleon a more effective weapon against massed infantry. In wooded terrain, target ranges were within the reach of the Napoleons. The 3-inch range advantage became less relevant.
27 Hooker's artillery arrived too late to participate at Second Bull Run (Manassas).

Battery D, 1 N. Y. Lt. Artillery
2 Division, 3 Corps
Alexandria, Va.
September 1, 1862

[To S. C. O.] The battery did not reach Alexandria early enough to take part in the battles under General Pope. We are notified that if the Army remains where it is we are to go to it tomorrow, but our immediate superiors do not know whether it is to remain or to return to the vicinity of. It is hard to determine today, from all we can learn, which army was whipped.

I have replaced the horses lost and worn out since we left Harrison's Landing, and the battery is in good condition for the field.

Battery D, 1 N. Y. Lt. Artillery
2 Division, 3 Corps
Arlington Heights, Va.
September 5, 1862

[To A. C. O.] I will now, so far as I can, call up the incidents of the battle of Savage Station fought on June 29th and give them to you.

We were turned out by orders from Headquarters at half past two in the morning and occupied ourselves as best we could till daylight when we saw our infantry falling back from our front line of works, which we had occupied since June 2nd on our supposed approach to Richmond. At daylight, the second line of trenches, about one mile in rear of the advanced and main line, was occupied by a line of battle. The troops not occupying this second line of works were falling back very slowly and waiting for an attack, should the enemy see fit to make one as soon as they had learned the advanced works had been abandoned. I also went into position in the second line of works, and everything was ready for a fight by or before sunrise. In this second line, the troops were in the same order as they had been at the front. That is, General Heintzelman occupied the left with his corps, General Kearny being the left division and General Hooker the right. General Sumner with the 2nd Corps was on the right of the 3rd Corps, but a little separated from it.

The field remained quiet until half past nine when skirmishing commenced both on Generals Sumner's and Heintzelman's fronts, and at ten o'clock the enemy opened with artillery on the front of both corps. General Sumner replied, and General Heintzelman did not. This drew the attention of the enemy to General Sumner, and in a half hour the infantry became engaged, and a sharp skirmish or a little

"PLANNED WITHDRAWAL" OR HASTY RETREAT 73

battle followed.[28] A few regiments on each side became engaged. I do not think more. These several forces in their maneuvering came together so as to test their strength three times in a little more than an hour. General Sumner's artillery became hotly engaged with the enemy's artillery and suffered some damage. Several shells fell among our men and some in my battery, but General Heintzelman would not permit a reply. One shell passed within a few inches of Lieutenant Winslow's head and through an infantryman near him. Another struck one of my men sitting on the ground with his hands clasped around his knees cutting off both his legs and arms. He died in a few seconds. He screamed at the top of his voice while he lived. I speak of this as it is very unusual for a man fatally wounded to make any noise.

The above is all there was of what is known as the Battle of Peach Orchard and which gets its name from a peach orchard where part of General Sumner's troops were.

While this fighting was going on, General Sumner's artillery got the range of the road by which the enemy were crossing our abandoned works and did them considerable damage. However, all this part of the fighting was over before noon. From my position the entire battle was in plain view.

A little after noon we received orders to continue our movement to the rear by a newly cut road on the south of the Williamsburg road. As in the retreat our front had changed, and we were going east; General Heintzelman's corps was on the right of the Army. This new road struck White Oak Swamp Creek a half mile west of the bridge on the main road and was cut for the sole use of the 3rd Corps. This was the shortest road, and by occupying it the 3rd Corps covered the remainder of the Army from an attack from our extreme right.

When the corps was fairly in motion, a staff officer of General C. [W.] F. Smith[29] of General Franklin's corps requested General Heintzelman to loan General Smith two batteries to report to him at Savage Station. General Heintzelman was very short and crabbed and said emphatically he did not wish his batteries cut to pieces fighting with other commands, but wound up by telling me to take my own and the 4th New York Independent Battery and report to General Smith, which I did.

The day was intensely hot, and I found General Smith's division lying in the woods side of the Williamburg road and a quarter of a mile from the station. We laid here till half past three when General Smith

---

28 Peach Orchard or Allen's Farm.
29 Maj. Gen. William F. "Baldy" Smith commanded the Second Division of Franklin's Sixth Corps.

commenced to move on towards the James River without giving me orders. But upon my asking for orders, he told me to report back to General Heintzelman. For a Division Commander to borrow two batteries to aid him in a fight and then moving off without giving them orders is as good an example of first class stupidity as one can often see.

As General Smith was moving off, General Sumner's corps was occupying the ground between the Williamsburg road and the station. I had no orders to report to him nor did I desire to do so but determined to get back to General Hooker's division as quickly as I could. To do this, I was compelled to follow the main road back a mile to strike the new road taken by the 3rd Corps, but the space between where I was and this junction of roads had been entirely abandoned by our troops, and I did not feel safe in taking the two batteries back over so exposed a situation. With only an orderly I rode back and when near the junction of the roads I wished to find, I saw the enemy's skirmishers moving in splendid style over our second line of works. As a skirmish line they were moving very rapidly. I was within easy musket range of them when I first saw them, but for some reason they did not fire. I turned to go back and while passing the timber on the north side of the wood where I had no thought of the enemy being, a full battery opened fire upon me at a distance not more than 200 or 300 yards. The fire was at me and the orderly only, and the shells passed uncomfortably near our heads. Had cannister been used we could not have escaped. I had often been a target for infantry sharpshooters, but to be a target for sharpshooting with a whole battery was new to me.

Upon reaching my battery, I found it had been ordered into position by General Sumner as his attention was attracted by the firing at me. My battery had been ordered in while his own batteries had not. So you see, borrowed artillery like other borrowed property is to be used up before the borrower uses his own.

General Sumner and staff were upon a rise of ground just in front of his own infantry and a little way in rear of my battery as it then stood ready for action. They had no intimation of the enemy's approach excepting the artillery fire spoken of. My military mode of address had been acquired in my service under Generals Heintzelman and Hooker, neither of whom could be forced to express surprise or excitement under any circumstances. Regardless of what the conditions or surroundings might be or how great the momentary pressure, the voice was not raised or any personal anxiety shown. The quiet address and conversation of gentlemen was always observed.

Being about to address a new commander, I was exceptionally on my guard. Riding up to the General, I raised my cap and said, "General I am just from the front and the enemy are moving against you in force." The old man looked at me with astonishment for an instant and with apparently the greatest excitement shouted at the top of his voice, "What do you say? How do you know? Who are you?" With the same manner and tone as before, I explained in as few words as possible. Again, with the same manner and tone as before, he shouted at me, "Where is Heintzelman? Where has he gone? Where did he get his orders to move off and leave me exposed? Why did he not give me notice? If there is a reverse to our Army this evening there will be a fearful responsibility resting on someone," meaning General Heintzelman. And so he ran on not waiting for a reply. But this conversation, if it could be called such, was cut square in two in the middle of a sentence by a shell dropping within a few yards of us, when he said to me, "Silence that battery."

Of course I opened fire on it, and I have since seen accounts in the Richmond papers stating the first shell fired by us that evening killed Brigadier General Griffith[30] of Mississippi commanding the brigade which opened the fight. If this report is correct, he was killed by the first shot I fired after this remarkable exhibition by General Sumner. It is stated General Griffith's brigade was supporting the battery which opened fire on us. This battery opened fire from the open field on the right, or north, of the railroad. We forced it back into the timber, but it soon reappeared and fought very stubbornly. By the time the battery had made its second appearance, the batteries of Captains Pettit, Hazzard, and Smith[31] had gotten into position forming an extension of the line of my battery on my left, Captain Smith's left resting on the Williamsburg road. Meanwhile, our skirmishers were advanced and extended well across the field which was open land the entire distance between the two armies or lines of battle and slightly undulating. The enemy formed line in the woods at the edge of the field.

Before our line of battle was advanced, a flat car with a heavy siege gun mounted on it was run down the railroad into range, and the gun opened fire. A half a dozen shots from my battery, which had an easy range on it, caused it to disappear more rapidly than it had approached. I notice the Richmond papers speak of the car and gun, calling it "The Railroad Merrimac," as a considerable factor in the fight. It was of no account whatever. I do not know how it was propelled, whether by men, a mule, or an engine. No engine came in sight.

---

30 Brig. Gen. Richard Griffith commanded the Third Brigade of Magruder's division. He was the only Confederate general killed during the Seven Days campaign.
31 Capt. George W. Hazzard, Fourth U.S. Artillery Regiment, Batteries A and C; Capt. James E. Smith, Fourth New York Independent Battery.

The enemy had two light batteries, one of which we drove off easily while the other was very stubborn. We turned sixteen guns on that battery and gave it the best of our work and soon silenced it. Later we learned we had absolutely destroyed it before it ceased firing. Our infantry found the wreck of it where it had fought. The infantry became engaged a few minutes after six o'clock. As the enemy's line was in the edge of the timber and had taken position there, our line had to move across the open field to the attack. When within musket range both lines opened fire, the artillery assisting our men all it could which proved to be a great deal.

The grand tactics displayed by General Sumner in fighting this battle were very fine. After the first outburst of passion while talking to me and growing out of his surprise at being so unexpectedly attacked, for until that moment he doubtless thought General Heintzelman was between him and the enemy, I saw no more of it. In fact, he conducted the fight with remarkable coolness. The fight was in brief about as follows: The field is open and clear of all obstructions. The front of the battlefield, that is the distance between the Williamsburg Road and railroad, is about 700 yards. The distance from where General Sumner's troops laid to the enemy's line, between a half and three-quarters of a mile. The ground was such as to make the movement of troops very easy.

When the artillery were fairly at work, the General ordered a skirmish line forward covering the space between the Williamsburg Road and the railroad. All our maneuvers were in plain view by the enemy, and the skirmish line was halted by a counter skirmish line. The General then ordered forward a full line of battle covering the same space as did each successive line. This first full line had a very serious collision with the enemy's line in position but, of course, broke it. The General knew this would be the result, and another full line was half across the field when the first line gave way.

The first line permitted the second to pass through it, and when it came into collision with the enemy the same result followed. A third line of battle was again half across the field and this same passing by the third, of the second line. This third line dislodged the enemy from their position and had them on the move. But before the third line had reached the enemy, General Meagher's brigade (Irish) was well on its way towards the enemy's line. As soon as the enemy began to give way, General Sumner ordered General Meagher[32] to give them the bayonet

---

32 Brig. Gen. Thomas F. Meagher commanded the Second Brigade, First Division of the Second Corps.

and drive them from the field. This order was carried out literally, and the enemy were driven off the field.

The time the infantry was engaged was an hour and a quarter and including the time the artillery was engaged just two hours. The enemy's force consisted of a South Carolina division and detached troops from other divisions—in all, as prisoners reported, between 8,000 and 10,000 men. A small detachment, probably two or three regiments, crossed to the south of the Williamsburg Road and were held in check by a like detachment of our troops and fell back when the main line gave way.

General Sumner had all the troops he wanted and adopted the tactics of the enemy of breaking the opposing line by putting in column after column of fresh troops until the line was broken. The enemy having been driven off the field, the troops which had been engaged were brought back to the main body and laid down to sleep. The detachments sent out to gather the wounded carried them to the general field hospital, which had before been established at the station and, in fact, on a part of this battlefield. I have not learned how great our loss was.

At ten o'clock in the evening we were ordered to move with the corps towards the James River. It so happened we were very near or at the rear of the corps. I had at no time received any orders to report to General Sumner, and I determined to get away from him and back to my own corps as quickly as possible. When I left the 3rd Corps, I knew the general direction it was to follow. That was all. It was a night march, and I could find no road leading in the direction General Heintzelman had taken. At one o'clock we crossed the White Oak Swamp and Creek. There was a bridge over this creek and a long corduroy road on each side.

As we were about to reach the creek, I found myself unable to longer remain awake. I was absolutely overcome with weariness and want of sleep. No effort would keep me awake. I, therefore, lay down upon the rear ammunition chests of one of the caissons, and two of my men held me from falling off and I slept soundly while we were on this corduroy road. In a half hour I was refreshed and again mounted my horse. To think of it now, it seems impossible one could sleep under such circumstances, as the pounding of a caisson over a log road is fearful. Three miles from the creek I drew out to the side of the road and went into camp. As rapidly as it could be done, the horses were fed and the men laid down to sleep. In the morning troops were still moving past us. I let the men sleep as long as they would and then gave them ample time to get their breakfast and feed and groom the horses. At nine o'clock in the morning we moved on. No troops passed us in the morning with whom we had any acquaintance, and all inquiring to learn where the Third Corps was, failed to give us any information.

The night before I had determined to separate from General Sumner and find General Heintzelman. The former I had accomplished; the latter I had not. But this is writing of another day from what I intended.

After we crossed the Chickahominy in going west in May, Savage Station was the chief depot for the left half of the Army, and quantities of supplies had accumulated there before the retreat was undertaken. When I reported to General Smith, the destruction of this property by fire was in progress. Great piles of ammunition and of quartermasters and of commissary stores were burning. The explosion of loaded shells and small ammunition sounded like a heavy battle. Long lines of freight cars were on fire. A train loaded with blank cartridges was run a little way east of us and set on fire. The smoke from the explosion of this powder was wonderfully beautiful. There was not a motion of the atmosphere nor a cloud to be seen, and the white smoke rose like a dense white cloud and remained stationary for a very considerable time then rolled away in the distance. All who saw it expressed their appreciation of its beauty.

The day was intensely hot and many infantrymen were sunstruck. My men suffered from the heat, but I took much pains to keep them in the shade and none were injured.

Appendix

Report of Capt. Thomas W. Osborn, Battery D, First New York Light Artillery, of engagement at Oak Grove, or King's School House, battle of Savage Station, engagement at Malvern Cliff, and battle of Malvern Hill. [From OR, Chap. 23, Pp. 118-120.]

Camp near Harrison's Landing, July 4, 1862.

Captain: In reporting the part taken by this battery in the late engagements before Richmond, and in the march from the position of General Hooker's division at the intrenchments to the bank of James River at Harrison's Landing, I would report that on the 25th of June, General Hooker's division having been engaged during the morning, I was ordered up about 3 p.m. in front of the redoubt, taking position on the right of the road and 500 yards from the woods. I commenced shelling the opposite side of the woods to protect the passage of Generals Hooker's and Kearny's troops through them, giving my guns 4° and up to 6° elevation, and using fuse from 5" to 7", being directed both as to elevation and direction by the lookout in the tree in front of our center redoubt. We threw 60 fuse shell, 55 case-shot, and 14 percussion shell. We used the ammunition originally prepared for the 3-inch wrought iron regulation guns, and the paper fuses worked very indifferently, but the percussion well. From the position of the battery we could not see the enemy, but the lookout reported to me that our shells did good execution on the column of the enemy as they were marching down the road from the direction of Richmond toward our forces.

On the 30th [29th] of June, about 6 a.m., we were ordered to take position behind the rear line of intrenchments, as General Hooker's division was at the time falling back from the front. I placed the battery 300 yards from the road on the right. We were subject during the engagement of the morning to the shelling of the enemy's artillery, but as neither the enemy's artillery nor infantry approached us in such a manner that we could employ the battery without endangering General Sumner's corps on our right, I did not open fire. At 2.30 p.m. we were ordered to fall back. Having reached the corner of the open field in which Savage Station is, I was ordered, together with Lieutenant Nairn, Fourth New York Battery, by General Heintzelman, to report to General Smith, near the station.

At 4 p.m. General Smith moved forward, leaving the field, and we were ordered to report again to General Hooker. I then learned that General Hooker had retired from the left of the rear intrenchments to the left. I rode back again to learn whether the passage was clear, but just as we reached the intrenchments they were being occupied by the enemy's skirmishers. I immediately reported this to General Sumner on the field, and found that Lieutenant Winslow had already placed the battery in an admirable position, 200 yards in rear of a perpendicular line from Savage Station to the main road and 300 yards from the road. I do not know the regiments which supported the battery, only that they belonged to Sedgwick's division.

At 5 p.m. the enemy opened fire on the infantry of Sedgwick's division lying near this battery from a battery planted at the skirts of the woods to the right of the railroad and 1,400 yards from us. I directed the fire of the battery on it, and in a few minutes silenced it, dismounting one piece.

About this time Captain Pettit (B), First New York Artillery, took position on our left, and soon after a portion of another battery on our right. The enemy soon showed the masses of his infantry near where the battery had been in position, and was moving to the right. We opened fire and drove them under shelter of the woods. We now learned the position of the enemy in the woods by our skirmishers to be directly in front of us, and by turning the fire of the three batteries on their masses, held them at bay for an hour, their prisoners affirming that we did splendid execution among them, the range being good and the shells exploding well. A few minutes before sunset the enemy opened a battery from near the railroad bridge, in rear of the former site of General Keyes' headquarters. This was silenced in a few minutes by the fire of the three batteries.

Fifteen or twenty minutes before sunset the infantry of the two armies became engaged, and the roar of musketry was incessant and terrific till after dark, when the enemy was routed, and fled before our forces at least a half mile. Our infantry made charge after charge upon the enemy's front, and the determined shouts and huzzas rang distinctly above the roar of the musketry. I consider the whole affair a splendid and magnificent one. The enemy's troops fought bravely, but our own surpassed them in every particular, and in two and a half hours from their first appearance had fought, defeated, and driven them from the field. During the engagement I fired 90 fuse shell, 40 case shot, and 11 percussion shell.

At 10 p.m. I was ordered to move to the rear, and at 1 in the morning I crossed White Oak Swamp Bridge. In the morning (July 1) [June 30] I reported to General Hooker for duty.

July 1 [June 30], having been ordered by General Hooker to pass on before his division and report to any commanding officer at the front, I proceeded to the hill on which the battle of July 2 [1] was fought and reported to General Sykes, but he not having a position for me, I afterward reported to General Morell, and was ordered into position

"PLANNED WITHDRAWAL" OR HASTY RETREAT 81

near the large white house which the general occupied that evening as headquarters. Captain Bramhall's battery (Sixth New York Battery) occupied my right, and still another battery at Captain Bramhall's right.

About 5 p.m. a battery of the enemy opened fire on us from the woods on our left and about 1,300 yards distant. General Morell ordered me to open fire on it, and at the same time shell the woods in its vicinity. I threw 50 shell at an elevation of 3° to 4°. During the firing there was a heavy explosion in the immediate vicinity of the enemy's battery, resembling the explosion of a caisson, upon which the enemy's firing immediate ceased. We remained in this position during the night. While in this position we were supported by the Fifty-seventh Regiment Pennsylvania Volunteers.

July 2 [1], at 6.30 in the morning, I left the battery in charge of Lieutenant Winslow, to search for and report to yourself. At 7 a.m. the enemy appeared in large force on the main road on our front, coming forward rapidly, driving our pickets in, and yelling desperately. General Griffin ordered Lieutenant Winslow to open fire upon them, which he did, firing at 3° elevation 5" fuse, and having a most admirable cross-fire on the enemy with Captain Bramhall's battery. Lieutenant Winslow and Captain Bramhall fired rapidly and their ammunition worked well. There were two other batteries in position, but were not firing so rapidly. The enemy retreated under the artillery fire in a very few minutes, our infantry not becoming engaged.

Immediately after this very brief engagement the battery was ordered to report to General Couch, on General Morell's right, and before coming into position was again ordered to report to General Hooker, on General Couch's right. These orders were by General Heintzelman. From this last position we participated at several different times during the day in assisting in driving the enemy's batteries from the open field, where he persisted in placing them at short intervals during the day. They were about 1,500 years from us and shelling our troops. During the very severe engagement late in the afternoon I was in position too far to the right to bring the battery to bear upon the enemy. That day I fired 55 fuse shell, 20 case shot, and 4 percussion shell. The firing was mainly good, excepting that 4 shell in the afternoon failed to take the rifling of the piece, and revolving rapidly in their flight fell one-third of the distance short of their intended destination. At 2 a.m. I was ordered to fall back with the body of the army, and reached camp near Harrison's Landing.

It is a source of great satisfaction to me that none of my officers or men were injured in any of the engagements. I brought the battery through complete, and only suffered in the loss of several horses, brought about by excessive labor. Also the personal effects of many of the men.

I am, captain, respectfully, your obedient servant,
THOS. WARD OSBORN
Captain Battery D, First New York Artillery.

Captain De Russy
Chief of Artillery, Third Corps, Army of the Potomac.

Chapter 5

Fredericksburg

*We have been terribly whipped.
A lack of competent generalship is the only explanation I can see.*

In June 1862 following the Confederate evacuation of Corinth, Mississippi, Major General John Pope, who had been serving there under General Henry W. Halleck, was called east to take command of the newly formed Army of Virginia. Formed to consolidate under one command the scattered forces of Fremont and Banks in the Shenandoah Valley and McDowell's corps spread from Fredericksburg to Manassas Junction, it numbered approximately 50,000 men. Pope's task was not only to protect Washington but to serve as a threat against Richmond and to relieve Confederate pressure against McClellan.

After McClellan withdrew to Harrison's Landing, Lee became convinced that the Union forces on the Peninsula no longer threatened Richmond, and he detached the divisions of Jackson and Ewell to move north to meet Pope's advance. On July 29th, when Pope reached the Rapidan River, A. P. Hill's division also left Richmond to join Jackson. McClellan continued to believe that he was outnumbered. After ordering Hooker to reoccupy Malvern Hill on August 5th, causing Lee to move toward Hooker, the latter was ordered to withdraw again to Harrison's Landing. McClellan continued to request more reinforcements and argued against Washington's decision to withdraw his army from the Peninsula. He maintained that his continued presence there threatened the Confederate capital and represented the best defense of Washington.[1] Lee apparently viewed Pope's overland approach as more of a present threat.

---

1   Johnson, R. V. & Buel, C. C. (Eds.) (1956) *Battles and Leaders of the Civil War, Vol. 2*. New York. p. 187.

On August 3rd, Halleck ordered McClellan to abandon Harrison's Landing and to return to northern Virginia. The Union Army left Harrison's Landing on August 16th and reached the Fort Monroe embarkation point between August 18th and 22nd. Franklin's and Sumner's corps were delayed three days, and neither reached the Manassas field in time to support Pope. Both were within marching distance of Pope on August 28th and by forced marches could have reinforced him by August 30th. Porter's and Heintzelman's corps did arrive in time to participate in the action. Although Hooker's batteries left Yorktown on August 28th and arrived at Alexandria on the 29th, they were too late to participate at Second Bull Run (Manassas). It is debatable whether McClellan cooperated fully with Pope and if he moved as quickly as possible to assist him. Osborn's battery was assigned to the Washington fortification following Second Bull Run (Manassas) and did not participate in the Maryland Campaign.

As Pope's defeated army retreated to the Washington defenses, Lee sidestepped the forts that surrounded the capital and headed for Maryland. McClellan, after being temporarily without an army, was restored by Lincoln to his former command. McClellan followed Lee with characteristic caution. Following the drawn Battle of Antietam at Sharpsburg, Lincoln lost patience with McClellan's slow pursuit of the Confederate Army as it withdrew into northern Virginia and appointed Major General Ambrose Burnside to replace him.

Burnside's plan to cross the Rappahannock River at Fredericksburg and mount an overland offense against Richmond was frustrated by the delayed arrival of his pontoon bridges. The delay gave Lee time to prepare a strongly fortified position along a series of ridges west of the river. Determined to succeed, Burnside foolishly threw Sumner's and Hooker's "Grand Divisions" against the Confederate lines in repeated and impossible attempts to storm Marye's Heights. Franklin, with the Left Grand Division, had crossed the Rappahannock south of the city with the First and Sixth Corps and had enjoyed some early success as Meade's division broke through a portion of Jackson's line before being driven back. Franklin failed to reinforce Meade's First Corps Division as the Sixth Corps stood idly by. Burnside failed to follow up this partially successful effort against the Confederate right flank and called off further Union attacks against Jackson.

Battery D rejoined the Army of the Potomac at Fredericksburg on December 6th and served during the battle with Brigadier General William Burns's First Division of the Ninth Corps, which had been Burnside's corps prior to his appointment to command the Army of the Potomac. Brigadier General Orlando Willcox had replaced Burnside as corps commander. The Ninth Corps had returned from service in North Carolina to join Pope at Second Bull Run (Manassas) and had been an active participant at Antietam.

Although Osborn and Burns's two regular U.S. Third Regiment Batteries L and M crossed to the west side of the river below town and to the left of the main Union attack against Marye's Heights, their position prevented them from actively supporting the Union assaults.

Osborn enjoyed an excellent observation post from Stafford Heights to describe the Union bombardment of Fredericksburg and to view the Union efforts to construct a pontoon bridge in the face of Confederate rifle fire. The location also afforded Osborn a view enabling him to describe the Union slaughter.

The Editors

Battery D, 1 N.Y. Lt. Artillery
2 Division, 3 Corps
Fort Taylor, Va.
September 8, 1862

[To A. C. O.] We have moved from Arlington Heights to Fort Taylor east of Alexandria and joined the 3rd Corps from which we were separated at Yorktown.

When the troops of the Army of the Potomac were sent to General Pope, General McClellan was not relieved from the command of the Army. The troops were detached and ordered elsewhere. The artillery of General Hooker's division did not arrive in Alexandria early enough to be ordered into the fight at the front and so no order detaching it was issued. Consequently, when we arrived at Alexandria, the artillery of which Major Wainwright is chief and perhaps the detachments of cavalry attached to his headquarters for orderlies constituted the entire troops under General McClellan's command and in that way the entire Army of the Potomac. Upon our arrival Major Wainwright,[2] who had preceded the batteries, brought us orders from General McClellan to obey no orders except from him. The batteries which that day constituted the entire Army of the Potomac were Webber's, Bramhall's, Smith's, Clark's,[3] and Osborn's. Strange things happen in times of war.

---

2 Wainwright had succeeded Col. Bailey as Commander of the First New York Light Artillery Regiment in June following the latter's death at Seven Pines.
3 Capt. A. Judson Clark, Second NJ Artillery, was transferred from Osborn's command to Commanding Officer, First Division Artillery, Third Corps just before Chancellorsville.

Battery D, 1 N. Y. Lt. Artillery
2 Division, 3 Corps
Fairfax Seminary, Va.
September 13, 1862

[To S. C. O.] The battery is again with the 3rd Corps which is now camped within the lines of the fortifications around Washington. There is but very little if any probability that this command will have any fighting to do in this vicinity. If any fighting is to be done, it will be in western Maryland or Pennsylvania. The latest reports which appear reliable state that the head of the enemy's column has arrived at Hagerstown, Md. I hope a general battle will not be fought until General McClellan is fully prepared for it, but I do hope, growing out of this movement by the enemy, one will be fought, let the results be what they may. A good deal of fighting has been done by this army, but up to this time no battle has been fought in which both armies have been fully engaged. I may be overconfident, but I think such a battle would be to our advantage.

I have been commissioned as Major to command one of the battalions now being organized at Sackets Harbor, and I have telegraphed that I will accept.[4] The commission must reach here before I can be released from the command of this battery. I do not look upon the promotion as altogether desirable as the future of that command I consider uncertain. Here I have a very satisfactory command. I have telegraphed Mr. Starbuck thanking him for the kind interest he has taken in my advancement.

Battery D, 1 N. Y. Lt. Artillery
2 Division, 3 Corps
Fairfax Seminary, Va.
October 2, 1862

[To S. C. O.] The new men forwarded to this battery by Lieutenant Winslow, about 100 of them, are doing well and are contented. They are a remarkably fine body of volunteers.

---

4 Slow promotion within the artillery made this opportunity an attractive one, but one he eventually decided against because it would remove him from command of a battery in the field. Some eight months later, after Wainwright's intercession, he received both the promotion and a field command. His letters will reflect his indecision.

Many troops are being moved about and past us, but it is done so quietly that no one knows from where they come or where they are to go. It would seem from all we can see that an effort is being made to bring on another general engagement. The last, that at Antietam, was a victory for us, and that is a good deal gained after all we have gone through.

I have finally declined to accept the commission of Major in the regiment being organized at Sackets Harbor. It was understood to be for light artillery service and was so enlisted. It is now heavy artillery and has been so accepted. I believe in the end it will serve as infantry. I prefer service in the Light Artillery.

Battery D, 1 N.Y. Lt. Artillery
2 Division, 3 Corps
Fairfax Seminary, Va.
October 24, 1862

[To S. C. O.] Doctor Hubbard[5] is here and has passed considerable time with me. I do not think he will accept a commission in the Sackets Harbor regiment. It is badly officered, organized, and disciplined.

Battery D, 1 N.Y. Lt. Artillery
2 Division, 3 Corps
Centerville, Va.
November 16, 1862

[To S. C. O.] Today we have orders to move, or rather be ready to move, to the main army and report to "Major General Hooker, commanding the Center Grand Division, of the Army of the Potomac, opposite Fredericksburg." I am rather glad this change has been made. In fact, we have been doing picket duty, *i.e.*, the entire corps has on this part of the line, and I do not like it. For a few days past, the battery has been occupying an old fort of the enemy at Manassas Junction. General Hooker will do all the fighting with his Grand Division that the General commanding the Army will permit him to do. So we may rest assured that we shall see more active service.

---

5 George N. Hubbard from Carthage, NY, who had married Osborn's sister, Amelia. He later became Osborn's personal physician.

I do not think the removal of General McClellan will be in any way injurious in so far as the fighting qualities of the Army go, but I am not prepared to say I think it was altogether for the best.

I am not an ardent admirer of the General by any means, nor can I see how anyone can be who watched that Peninsula Campaign closely. His three-quarters success at the Antietam battle was better, but as I was not in it, I do not know so much about it. While, however, it does not strike me his removal was a wise act, yet the Army will fight just as well under its new commander as under him.[6]

Battery D, 1 N.Y. Artillery
2 Division, 3 Corps
Wolf Run Ford, Va.
November 23, 1862

[To S. C. O.] Last Tuesday we moved from Centerville to this place in a drenching rainstorm. We made the march 18 miles in a day and a half.

We are now stationed at a ford across the Ocquacon River and occupying the forts constructed by the enemy when they held the lower Potomac River with their blockade batteries. The position in a military sense is very strong, but of all the desolate and dreary spots I ever saw I think this the worst.

General Frank E. Patterson, who commanded one of the brigades in this division, committed suicide by shooting himself through the heart yesterday.[7] He was a son of General Patterson[8] of the Army. I was well acquainted with him. He was a noble hearted and brave man. My battery is designated to fire a salute at his burial in honor of his memory tomorrow.

---

6   Osborn's final judgment of McClellan.
7   Brig. Gen. Francis E. Patterson, commanding officer of the Third Brigade, Third Corps, committed suicide after censure for an unauthorized retreat at Catlett's Station in November, 1862.
8   Maj. Gen. Robert Patterson was relieved of command and mustered out of service July 1861, for failure to prevent Johnston's forces from participating in First Bull Run (Manassas).

Battery D, 1 N.Y. Lt. Artillery
1 Division, 9 Corps
Before Fredericksburg, Va.
December 8, 1862

[To A. C. O.] On the sixth inst. by orders of General Burnside, Headquarters of the Army, I was ordered to report to General Burns, commanding the 1st Division of the 9th Corps, for temporary duty.[9] I find the General a pleasant officer, and so far as I have seen him, I like him. I learned both Generals Hooker and Sickles were much dissatisfied with the transfer of the battery and both remonstrated with General Burnside when the order was made, but without effect. I should have preferred to remain with the old command, but any remonstrance from or by me would have been more than useless.

General Hunt, Chief of Artillery of the Army,[10] tells me I am to take my battery to the Reserve Artillery of the Army as soon as the present necessities have passed. This is a decided compliment as only the choice batteries of the Army are selected for that command.

All we see now looks as if a general movement of the Army is to be made or is now being made. All officers with whom I have talked are confident a general battle will take place before long. The pontoon train has come up; the Army is swinging around as if changing position for some specific purpose. This is something more than a change in winter quarters. Commissary, quartermaster's, and ordnance stores are being brought to the front in large quantities. One of two conclusions can be reached. First, that we are about to attack the enemy and are preparing for it. Second, that we are about to settle in winter quarters, and the attention of the enemy is being drawn to us for some ulterior purpose. Without doubt every move made and every act done is as well known at General Lee's Headquarters as at those of General Burnside. The movements of General Lee's Army from day to day show such is the case. This division lies near the river and the nearest of any portion of our Army to Fredericksburg.

The snow is three inches deep, and for a few days it has been very cold. Ice forms in the tents wherever there is no fire. The enemy's campfires are very numerous during these cold nights and are very bright. Judging by their campfires, General Lee has a very large Army in front of us.

---

9 Brig. Gen. William W. Burns commanded the First Division, Ninth Corps at Fredericksburg.
10 Brig. Gen. Henry J. Hunt.

Battery D, 1 N.Y. Lt. Artillery
1 Division, 9 Corps
Before Fredericksburg, Va.
December 9, 1862

[To S. C. O.] This battery has been transferred from the 2nd Division, 3rd Corps to General Burns' Division, 9th Corps, and from the Center Grand Division to the Right Grand Division of the Army. This separates us entirely from General Hooker. We are told it is a temporary assignment, but I imagine in the same sense that the war is a temporary affair. I dislike very much to pass out from under the command of General Hooker, and I understand he protested against the transfer and failed to influence General Burnside to permit us to remain with the old Division. I consider General Hooker the best general in this Army and would prefer to remain with him.

Appearances indicate that we are again to have a battle of considerable importance. I think before this can reach you, this Army will have crossed the Rappahannock and if so, of course, will be compelled to fight. Judging from present indications, Generals Franklin and Hooker will have the heaviest work to do. The battery is in perfect condition.

There is a report that General Franklin[11] is crossing the river this evening, but I am not able to vouch for the truth of the rumor. The enemy is heavily fortified in rear and on both the flanks of the city of Fredericksburg, but as I understand, General Franklin is to cross below the works and turn the enemy out of them and bring on a battle in the open field.

For several days we have had very cold weather and some snow. It has required a very liberal use of firewood to make the men comfortable.

Battery D, 1 N.Y. Lt. Artillery
1 Division, 9 Corps
Before Fredericksburg, Va.
December 9, 1862

[To A. C. O.] Everything points to a general engagement tomorrow or very soon. I think not later than the 11th, General Franklin or General Hooker will open the battle, but as General Franklin is now

---

11 Maj. Gen. Franklin commanded the Sixth Corps on the Peninsula. He was chosen by Burnside to command the Left Grand Division at Fredericksburg, composed of the Sixth Corps and John F. Reynolds's First Corps. Hooker commanded the Center Grand Division and Sumner the Right Grand Division.

said to be crossing the river below the enemy's works he probably will open the fight. I am writing at nine o'clock in the evening. General Hooker's pontoon train left its camp at two o'clock in the afternoon and I presume will bridge the river tonight.

Battery D, 1 N.Y. Lt. Artillery
1 Division, 9 Corps
Before Fredericksburg, Va.
December 11, 1862

[To S. C. O.] I have just been a looker-on in a new phase of military operations, that of shelling a city. The bridge train moved to the bank of the river opposite Fredericksburg last night and at daylight commenced to lay the bridges to the south side of the river. General Sumner's Grand Division was to lay three of them, one above, one in the center, and one below the city. The firing from 147 guns commenced this morning at six o'clock, the immediate occasion being the enemy opening with musketry upon our men putting down the bridges. The enemy had taken shelter in the houses or were covered by the streets or other obstructions forming temporary shelter.[12]

When the enemy fired on our men, our batteries opened on the position held by the men and on the city. The firing was very rapid and continued until considerably after noon. It has been the most severe artillery fire I have seen. Judging from the fires in the city and its general appearance together with the number of shells thrown into it, the city must be nearly or quite ruined. Late in the afternoon by the aid of the partly finished bridges and the assistance of boats, a considerable force was put over the river and now occupies the city. It is said at Division Headquarters that General Hooker's Grand Division is crossing tonight. I presume this report is correct.

It is possible a battle will be in progress tomorrow. At all events we may expect one very soon, and just now it looks as though heavy fighting was in the very near future.

---

12 Gen. William Barksdale's Mississippi brigade opposed the laying of the pontoon bridge. Osborn justified the shelling of the city because of this opposition.

Battery D, 1 N.Y. Lt. Artillery
1 Division, 9 Corps
Before Fredericksburg, Va.
December 11, 1862

[To A. C. O.] Today the city of Fredericksburg has been shelled—bombarded, I presume the newspapers will say. Our camp is directly opposite the city and I have had a good opportunity to watch the work though I took no part in it. The Engineer Corps began the work of bridging the river a little before daylight. At half past five this morning the enemy threw a few shells across the river into our camps and then withdrew their artillery. General Franklin's bridges are laid below the city, say two miles, while General Sumner's are laid to the city.

A little after daylight the enemy's sharpshooters opened fire from the houses and from other cover upon the men laying the bridges, killing and wounding about 50 men. Upon the enemy opening this fire, General Sumner withdrew the men from the bridges and opened fire on the city with 66 guns, all firing very rapidly. In the entire line of guns, those covering the city and those above and below it, there were 147 guns. The most of them were field pieces, but some siege guns were in line.

The sharpshooters were in this way quieted a little while when the men were again put to work on the bridge. He thus alternated between work on the bridge and shelling the city nearly all day. Late in the afternoon a few regiments were sent over the river in boats and captured all the men in the city, in the aggregate a considerable number.

After General Sumner commenced operations in the morning, no considerable force of the enemy showed itself this side of the low and fortified hills in the rear of the city. I cannot satisfactorily explain to myself why General Sumner laid his bridges just in front of the city where of necessity he must suffer from the fire of many sharpshooters and lose a good many men. To me it appears the same object would have been attained by putting the bridges above or below the city where the sharpshooters would have had little cover and our men would have suffered less. When the city was occupied from above or below, as many bridges as might be desirable could have been laid wherever thought best.[13] The city as such is of no importance excepting as it is the point where all the roads of the country center.

---

13 Osborn's critique seems valid.

The houses of the city are thoroughly riddled by the solid shot and shells. Several buildings took fire during the day, but there was no wind and the fires did not spread, but had the wind been high the entire city would have been burned. As a fact, the shelling made no difference in the relations between the sharpshooters and the men laying the bridges. When General Sumner had shelled the city as long as he saw fit, he put men enough across the river in boats to take possession of the sharpshooters and the city at the same time. This he could as well have done at sunrise as at sunset.

The troops in this section of the Army have been ordered to go into camp and make themselves comfortable for the night. I have been notified that my battery will be in the open field in the approaching battle with General Burns' Division. I think it is still uncertain whether we shall move in the morning.

Battery D, 1 N.Y. Lt. Artillery
1 Division, 9 Corps
Before Fredericksburg, Va.
December 16, 1862

[To A. C. O.] Only a line before the mail closes. I have seen no papers yet, but presume they report a victory. If so, it is a great error. We have been terribly whipped. A lack of competent generalship is the only explanation I can see. Our killed and wounded are not less than 15,000 men.[14] My battery lost but one man.

Battery D, 1 N.Y. Lt. Artillery
1 Division, 9 Corps
Before Fredericksburg, Va.
December 17, 1862

[To S. C. O.] We have had a desperate battle and have been defeated. We were not routed, but I am not sure it was not by the enemy's miscalculations that we were not. At all events, we are whipped so far as this last battle has influence. General McClellan was removed from command of the Army because he was slow and inefficient. General

---

14 Livermore, T. (1900) *Numbers and Losses in the Civil War in America 1861-65.* Boston & New York, counted 12,653 Union casualties.

Burnside was put in command because it was believed he possessed the opposite qualities, and the result is we are worse whipped than we were on the Peninsula.

The field between Marye's Heights and Fredericksburg was a slaughter pen. At that point which was the main point of attack, we did the enemy no damage while the field in their front was black with our dead. We did not gain an inch, and the enemy is stronger than before the battle. At this point our men were put in like grain in a hopper, and had we still been fighting them, there would still be no change, excepting we should have more dead and fewer living men.

My battery was south of the city with General Burns' division. This division did not make an assault on Marye's Heights but at one time was moved out to do so. Most of the day it laid a little to the west of the field over which the several assaults were made. I lost one man killed and one wounded.

I think General Burnside's incapacity to command so large an Army accounts for this misfortune.[15] I know it is believed here that his better judgment was against fighting this battle but that he was urged on by the authorities in Washington. Many prominent Generals, I am informed, believe this. Be this as it may, it was a very bad job.

Battery D, 1 N.Y. Lt. Artillery
1 Division, 9 Corps
Before Fredericksburg, Va.
December 17, 1862

[To A. C. O.] I dislike to write about the battle of the 13th. It is too long a story to tell if I attempt to give you any comprehensive idea of it. The newspapers will furnish you a map of the battlefield and an account of the battle as nearly accurate as the men who write these reports can pick it up. That is, they will tell it as nearly accurate as they can gather the information from the officers after the fight was over. This is the way all information is gathered from the "Cannon's Mouth." No reporter ever sees a battlefield while a fight is in progress.

In brief, the country back of the city rises into a sharp ridge which forms a crescent around the city, the points of the crescent resting on the river above and below the city. This range of hills is strongly fortified, and every yard of ground inside this crescent is commanded

---

15 Osborn's opinion seems to have been a nearly unanimous one.

FREDERICKSBURG

by the guns on the hills. Rifle pits on the crest command the slope of the hill, and a stone wall running along the base of the hill commands perfectly the plain in front.[16] This is true of General Sumner's front, but I understand General Franklin's front was not so strongly fortified—still it was very strong, and altogether it was a very unequal field to fight on.

At half past nine in the forenoon, the battle opened on General Franklin's front, that is on our extreme left and from one mile to two miles from us and down the river. A heavy fog which had lain close to the ground obscured everything until that hour when it lifted and the battle opened. We crossed the river the day before without special annoyance from the enemy. At noon General Sumner assaulted the enemy covered by the stone wall, mentioned, just in rear and about three-quarters of a mile or a mile from the city. This stone wall was a perfect fortification and was manned by two full lines of battle while the guns in the works on the crest of the hill perfectly commanded the ground over which our line of battle moved. In 15 or 20 minutes he was repulsed. An hour later he tried it again, and then again, and again. Either General Sumner or General Hooker attempted to carry this wall and crest until after dark and each time was repulsed as easily as at first. We did not once, with the best troops in the Army, reach the wall, nor even did a single man reach it. These tactics were not once changed. Each charge was an effort to carry that wall with the hope of then carrying the fortified crest beyond it. Any man with plain farmer's common sense would have seen when the first assault was made and, indeed, before the assault was made that any attempt to break the enemy's line at that point and gain the fortified crest beyond was utterly hopeless. Colonels, captains, lieutenants, and enlisted men saw it and knew every attempt would result in nothing but the slaughter of men. The enemy were completely covered and in strong force, while our line moved over an open incline where no part of a line of battle could live long enough to get to the wall. No men would be left standing on their feet long enough to get to the wall, much less to the crest.

No men could have fought better or shown more bravery than did ours in these repeated charges. Of course, such violent tactics must have been ordered directly from General Burnside. We have no Grand Division, corps, or division commander, who would voluntarily slaughter his men as was done here. As rash as General Sumner is, he would not have continued this hopeless and useless assault without specific

16 Marye's Heights.

instructions to do so. Neither would General Hooker have done it. The nature of the field and fortification was such that the enemy's artillery and infantry cooperated perfectly, and the killing of our men was so great that before night the ground over which these charges were made was literally black with the dead. In this work our artillery could not cooperate, only one battery firing at all and that only now and then at long intervals.[17] From my position we had a full and perfect view on this part of the field. The Army certainly did not lose, all told, less than 15,000 men, and I surmise many more.

I understand General Franklin was more successful, but I saw no part of his field or the fighting there and so know only what you can know. I will do my best to find out enough of that part of the battle to satisfy my own curiosity.

Today General Sickles informs me that I am to be returned to his corps. I find this a pleasant command to be with, but the 3rd Corps is much more like home if that expression can be used in Army life.

Battery D, 1 N.Y. Lt. Artillery
1 Division, 9 Corps
Before Fredericksburg, Va.
December 23, 1862

[To A. C. O.] All I see and learn tends to prove that our defeat was more emphatic and severe than we had at first supposed. There is a feeling in camp that another engagement will take place soon. I do not think so. We have been too badly whipped to undertake the job again right away.

I would like to know what the feeling of the common-sense businessmen of the country is at present as to Army matters and the future of this contest. The officers of the Army do not show any feeling of discouragement,[18] but we are certainly very inefficiently commanded. The condition of the Army in camp is at present very bad. For two weeks past the thermometer has registered below zero, wood is scarce, open shelter tents, one blanket for each man, clothing badly worn, wounded men frozen to death, half rations for the artillery, horses, etc., etc. In a word, this Army has never been so badly provided for as now. There is a decided lack of ability somewhere in the command of it.

17 Union artillery with Franklin played an active role.
18 It is difficult to believe that the majority of Union officers shared his optimism.

FREDERICKSBURG

Battery D, 1 N.Y. Lt. Artillery
1 Division, 9 Corps
Before Fredericksburg, Va.
December 24, 1862

[To A. C. O.] We have just come in from a review of the Right Grand Division which passed off well. Yesterday my battery received a high compliment from a Prussian Artillery officer who is here inspecting the Army. While I was on drill, this officer watched us for an hour and then inquired the name, age, etc. of the battery. He then told me it was the best he had seen in America. Today Colonel Wainwright said it was the best in the regiment. At the review General Hooker said that in discipline, drill, and soldierly bearing I had surpassed K, 4th U.S. Artillery.[19] This was the highest possible compliment as that battery stands at the head of the batteries in the regular Army and has served 17 years as a light battery under the choicest officers of the regular Army.

I am very proud of this battery, and I believe I have good reason to be. There are reasons, however, for its appearance and efficiency which are not known to the officers who inspect it and speak so highly of it. I have spared no labor in keeping its discipline and drill up to the highest standard. I have exerted myself to maintain perfect harmony among my officers, and I have had K, 4th U.S. Artillery, in the same division, as an example to follow—that being recognized as the most perfect regular battery in the service and that I have been determined to surpass. I have taken advantage of every available circumstance which was offered. After the battle of Williamsburg superior officers refused us nothing we made requisition for, and as in subsequent battles we have been able to maintain the reputation we gained then, this liberal feeling toward us has continued.

The number of men and the equipment of a battery are prescribed by General Orders. By these orders we are allowed 156 men; I have 170. We are allowed 110 horses, and I have 150. We are allowed no tents, and I have 40. We are allowed three baggage wagons, and I have six. The men are allowed one blanket each, and my men have three. My men have the full amount of uniform allowed by orders and, in addition, one complete outfit extra to be used only on reviews and kept in perfect order. Thus, at any hour I can bring out my battery as clean and fresh as if I were in permanent garrison. The discipline and drill the men have had enables me to maneuver and move on review equal

---

19 Lt. Francis Seeley's Battery K, Fourth U.S. Artillery.

to any regular battery. The cleanliness and neatness of the men, of the battery, the horses, and equipment puts us ahead of any battery at any review and far ahead of the average batteries in the Army. But in fact in nearly all particulars, K, 4th U.S. Artillery, and this battery are about equal.

My senior First Lieutenant Geo. B. Winslow was a hardware merchant in Gouverneur. J. L. [A.] Matthewson, Junior First Lieutenant, was editor and associate owner of the Mohawk Valley Register. A. N. Ames, Senior Second Lieutenant, was partner in a woolen factory in Oswego. J. L. Richardson was a bookkeeper in Geneva.[20] All are of New York. None married, except Winslow.

I am told there is much feeling still existing by reason of our transfer from the 3rd to the 9th Corps. Generals Hooker and Sickles still demand our return to the 3rd Corps while General Sumner demands the battery shall be retained in its present assignment. As we are with the corps formerly commanded by General Burnside and his decision is final, I presume we shall remain where we are. Of course, I am not consulted and have nothing to say about it. With the 3rd Corps, I should be more at liberty to take care of the battery as I choose. In case of a battle I should be much more recklessly exposed and used, in all probability, there than I would be in this corps.

In this letter I have lauded myself and battery very freely. I think, however, no more than the facts will bear me out.

Battery D, 1 N.Y. Lt. Artillery
1 Division, 9 Corps
Before Fredericksburg, Va.
December 26, 1862

[To A. C. O.] Another Christmas has gone, and so far as one can see we are no nearer the close of this war than we were one year ago.

The Engineer Corps has gone to Belle Plain[21] to build a wharf. The sick are being sent out of the Army and the field hospitals are being

---

20 Lt. J. L. Richardson and Lt. Angell Matthewson both later served as Commander of Battery D following Winslow's retirement due to ill health resulting from a wound at the Battle of the Wilderness. Lt. Richardson succeeded Winslow. Following Spotsylvania, Matthewson briefly commanded the battery relieving an exhausted Richardson. Richardson resumed command following Matthewson's serious leg wound at the North Anna which ended his military career.

21 Belle Plain, VA, on the Rappahannock River served as a Union supply base and evacuation center for the wounded.

FREDERICKSBURG

sent away. These movements would appear to indicate some change, but I do not see what advance movement can be made now with any prospect of success.

General Willcox,[22] commanding this corps, said today, "This is the best volunteer battery I have seen and I am sure eclipses any regular battery in this Grand Division."

Battery D, 1 N.Y. Lt. Artillery
1 Division, 9 Corps
Before Fredericksburg, Va.
January 1, 1863

[To A. C. O.] You speak in your last about the discipline in the Army. As a whole in this Army it is good, but of course in a good many regiments and batteries, it is loose; still, as a rule it is good. Judging from all we see and experience, I should say the enemy has better discipline than we. The results[23] of the campaigns thus far indicate this.

The discipline, the bravery, the endurance, the willingness, the all of an Army is in the capacity and industry of its officers. An Army officered as it should be, disciplined as it should be, and led as it should be will fight if occasion demands until four out of every five of the men are shot down. It does not require a long series of years to bring an Army serving in the field into this condition. Months will accomplish it, say from six to ten months. But competent commanding and subordinate generals are required as well as competent field and line officers. I think now everything should give way to making this Army perfect in all particulars. If we lose in this war, the country is lost and if we win it is saved. There is no middle ground.

Battery D, 1 N.Y. Lt. Artillery
1 Division, 9 Corps
Before Fredericksburg, Va.
January 5, 1863

[To S. C. O.] We are having beautiful weather but it is natural to expect a change before long, and whenever a change does come, we

---

22 Brig. Gen. Orlando B. Willcox, Ninth Corps Commander at Fredericksburg.
23 Osborn's opinion is debatable.

will surely be tied up till spring. After the rains begin, it will be impossible to move the Army any distance on these roads. There are as many people in this Army as in a large city and to move all at once with the necessary trains on two or three country roads with the mud knee-deep approaches very nearly the impossible.

This division is a half mile from the riverbank and looks down upon the city. We are in easy range of the enemy's guns and they of ours. Since the battle the picket lines have been very quiet. An almost good will exists between the enlisted men of the two armies, and no firing is done on either side.[24] The commanding generals do not apparently wish to annoy each other or to be annoyed by picket firing.

Battery D, 1 N.Y. Lt. Artillery
1 Division, 9 Corps
Before Fredericksburg, Va.
January 7, 1863

[To A. C. O.] The news we get from the west today is encouraging and is some amend for our great loss here. It was reported here yesterday that General Rosecrans had surrendered his Army, and this report was believed and it seems was also believed in Washington. The news we have today looks well and I trust may be confirmed. If General Rosecrans has compelled General Bragg to abandon Murfreesboro and has relieved Nashville, a great point has been gained.[25] If now Vicksburg can be taken and the Confederacy cut in two, a still greater advantage will be secured. I have no doubt but in the popular mind the taking of Richmond would be considered of greater advantage, but I believe the opening and possession of the Mississippi River would be of far greater military importance.[26]

From present indications I do not think anything will be done here for some weeks and perhaps months.

---

24 Peaceful period during which Union and Confederate pickets bartered coffee and tobacco across the Rappahannock in small toy sailboats.
25 Union Maj. Gen. William S. Rosecrans defeated Confederate forces under Maj. Gen. Braxton Bragg on January 3, 1863, at Murfreesboro or Stone's River, TN. This Union victory helped dispel some of the gloom caused by Fredericksburg.
26 One of Osborn's valid judgments.

Battery D, 1 N.Y. Lt. Artillery
1 Division, 9 Corps
Before Fredericksburg, Va.
January 11, 1863

[To A. C. O.] If you can gain access to General Rosecrans' Army and spend three or four weeks there, I should be glad to have you do so. In that time there would probably be more or less fighting and by improving your opportunities you would acquire a great deal of knowledge you can obtain in no other way and such as will benefit you in after life. If at any time you should give yourself to literary work, you will find such an experience and information obtained of especial advantage. I have never yet seen a description of a battle, battlefield, or a campaign which conveyed to the reader any comprehensive idea of either.

Battery D, 1 N.Y. Lt. Artillery
1 Division, 9 Corps
Before Fredericksburg, Va.
January 16, 1863

[To A. C. O.] We are rapidly approaching another engagement or at least everything points that way now. We have been ordered to be ready to move at daybreak tomorrow and are told by our immediate superiors a battle will be fought tomorrow or next day at fartherest.
    The Richmond papers say General Foster[27] has been badly whipped in North Carolina.

---

27 Maj. Gen. John G. Foster, Union Commander of the Department of North Carolina.

Chapter 6

After Fredericksburg

I think the President's Emancipation Proclamation precludes the possibility of any settlement except by absolute subjugation, and even that carried to the last extremity.

During the Civil War civilian morale seemed to fluctuate in accordance with military success and failure. The ultimate outcome of the war seemed to hinge on civilian morale and the civilian will to continue the struggle. Until the last few months of the conflict, both armies seemed to maintain relatively high morale even under seemingly impossible circumstances.

Perhaps a belated salute is owed the Army of the Potomac, whose men in the ranks in the face of continued defeats maintained their belief in their ability to win. This Army lacked the victories and brilliant leadership that fed the morale and inspired the men in Lee's barefoot brigades. From McDowell through Hooker, the Army of the Potomac suffered through successive failures of command, their spirits apparently sustained by the hope that things would improve. It was a determination born in defeat that seemed to reflect the courage, patience, and endurance of Lincoln, their President and Commander-in-Chief.

The morale of the Army of the Potomac probably reached its lowest level following the disaster at Fredericksburg with its 12,653 Union casualties. After Burnside had sent his men against Marye's Heights in repeated, hopeless, and bloody frontal assaults, every Union soldier knew that they had suffered a humiliating defeat because of Burnside's inept leadership. The problem of low morale was compounded by Burnside's January 22, 1863, effort to cross the Rappahannock above Fredericksburg in what became known as the "Mud March." Heavy rains made the roads impassable, and the Union Army marched back to Falmouth amid the jeers of Confederate pickets.

AFTER FREDERICKSBURG

Burnside, who never wanted to command the Army of the Potomac, accepted blame for the crushing defeat. Lincoln accepted his resignation and on January 25th appointed Hooker to replace him. Hooker's appointment was well received by the men who apparently believed that he could do no worse than Burnside. The new commander reorganized the Army doing away with Burnside's "Grand Divisions." He looked to the neglected physical needs of his men, their rations, and clothing and provided for a system of furloughs. He created a cavalry corps and held several reviews as Lincoln visited the Army. Each of the corps adopted a distinctive patch to be worn on the men's caps as a proud badge to boost pride and corps morale. As the spring sun began to dry the Virginia roads, the Army's *esprit de corps* seemed to rise, and the Army, described by Hooker as "the finest on this planet," prepared for its second spring campaign.   *The Editors*

Battery D, 1 N. Y. Lt. Artillery
1 Division, 9 Corps
Before Fredericksburg, Va.
January 20, 1863

[To A. C. O.] Since the 16th, we have been hanging on by the eyelids under orders everyday to move. Still, we do not move. I have received printed General Order No. 7 of January 7th which says, "The commanding general announces to the Army of the Potomac that they are about to meet the enemy once more," then gives as a reason, "The late brilliant actions in North Carolina, Tennessee, and Arkansas have so divided and weakened the enemy on the Rappahannock, etc.," also a written order to "be ready to move at an early hour tomorrow morning." All this looks as if the commanding general meant to do something. But why the Army is not moved to whatever point it is to go is more than I can tell.

The above is all I know of any success in North Carolina. We have the report of the capture of Arkansas Post,[1] but we can get no definite idea of what General Grant is doing. He must have a large Army; otherwise, the enemy would crush him.

---

1 On January 11, 1863, Union forces under Maj. Gen. John A. McClernand, with the assistance of Porter's gunboats, captured Arkansas Post (Fort Hindman) on the Arkansas River.

If we are to fight here now, I wish we might be better commanded than we were at Fredericksburg. I have more confidence in each one of the Grand Division Commanders[2] than I have in the Commander of the Army.

It is now three o'clock in the afternoon and we have no orders to move yet, and I do not think we will break camp this evening.

Battery D, 1 N. Y. Lt. Artillery
1 Division, 9 Corps
Before Fredericksburg, Va.
January 21, 1863

[To A. C. O.] Since I wrote you last evening, a heavy rainstorm has been in progress. Rain fell all night and has fallen all day at a fearful rate.

At nine o'clock last evening, I was ordered to be ready to move at four o'clock this morning—another order at eleven o'clock last evening not to turn out unless the storm abated. At ten this morning, that unavoidable causes had delayed the pontoon train and that we would probably move sometime this afternoon and to be ready at a half hour's notice. It is now half past four in the afternoon, and we have no further orders.

The Left and Center Grand Divisions moved at nine o'clock yesterday morning and have since been out in this storm. The ground is softened by the rain, and the roads are next to, or quite, impassable. The river is rising rapidly.

In this movement the Army has changed flanks—General Sumner had the right, General Hooker the center, and General Franklin the left; but the disposition made for this movement gives General Franklin the right, General Hooker the center, and General Sumner the left. The Army has swung around on General Sumner as a pivot with the view of crossing the Rappahannock above Fredericksburg. General Sigel's[3] command is not mentioned in these orders, and I assume he is to be left on this side of the river to protect our communications and supply depots.

As General Burnside is still determined to fight the enemy again, it is probably unfortunate this storm has stopped us now. I have no

---

2 Sumner, Franklin, and Hooker.
3 Maj. Gen. Franz Sigel commanded the Eleventh Corps. He was succeeded by Howard before Chancellorsville, a move resented by the German-American regiments.

information that the plan of fighting a battle has been abandoned, but I do not see how the Army can be moved now. It will be several days before the roads can be used and meanwhile the enemy will have provided against a flank attack.

Battery D, 1 N. Y. Lt. Artillery
1 Division, 9 Corps
Before Fredericksburg, Va.
January 22, 1863

[To A. C. O.] Today the Army is all returning to its old camp. The proposed battle has been prevented by the mud. I presume now that by way of vanity we shall soon learn that General Burnside has been removed on account of the mud. He failed at Fredericksburg on the 13th of December and on the 21st of January got stuck in the mud;[4] consequently, he will be removed, not that he was responsible for the mud, but the lack of success will be sufficient and I think he will now go. But surely the mud is horrible and no train can now be moved. The rain has continued to fall today but not so rapidly as yesterday.

I think the President's Emancipation Proclamation precludes the possibility of any settlement except by absolute subjugation, and even that carried to the last extremity.[5]

Battery D, 1 N. Y. Lt. Artillery
1 Division, 9 Corps
Before Fredericksburg, Va.
January 23, 1863

[To S. C. O.] I understand the wagon train which went out with the Army three days ago is fast in the mud, and 12,000 men have been left with it to guard it.

---

4 Osborn describes Burnside's celebrated "Mud March."
5 Osborn's judgment of Burnside's future and the Emancipation Proclamation's impact both proved to be correct.

Battery D, 1 N. Y. Lt. Artillery
1 Division, 9 Corps
Before Fredericksburg, Va.
January 26, 1863

[To S. C. O.] Just now the principal item of interest is that General Hooker takes command of the Army today.[6] I hope now the country will hear better things from this Army.

The letters you speak of in the Mohawk Valley Register are written by Lieutenant Matthewson[7] of this battery. He is a bright and energetic young man and a good officer.

While I am writing, one of the enemy's bands is serenading us from the opposite side of the river. It plays very well.

Battery D, 1 N. Y. Lt. Artillery
1 Division, 9 Corps
Before Fredericksburg, Va.
January 26, 1863

[To A. C. O.] Long before this reaches you, you will know that General Hooker has been placed in command of the Army of the Potomac. No change could have been made more agreeable to me and I believe to the mass of the Army.

General McClellan has still many admirers in the Army, but I do not think he can recover from the effects of the cashiering of General Porter.[8]

Office, Chief of Artillery
2 Division, 3 Corps
Falmouth, Va.
February 22, 1863

[To A. C. O.] I have been home ten days on leave of absence.

---

6 Hooker replaced Burnside on January 26, 1863.
7 Lt. Matthewson joined the battery in December of 1862 after serving with Battery K. He also had served as Col. Wainwright's Adjutant. His service was ended by a serious leg wound received at North Anna on May 23, 1864.
8 Porter faced a court martial for his performance at Second Bull Run (Manassas). He was a close friend of McClellan.

On the 6th of February, my battery was ordered back to its old place in the 3rd Corps. On my return I was ordered to duty as Chief of Artillery of the 2nd Division, 3rd Corps, on the staff of General Berry commanding the Division, with the office at the headquarters of the division. This is a position I have for some time hoped for, and now I am notified that I have been commissioned as Major in the 10th New York Heavy Artillery. I have once before received a commission as Major of these same troops but they were at that time organized only into battalions and allowed a Major as commanding officer. I have hardly determined yet whether to remain here in this superior position by assignment or to accept the superior grade and go to the regiment. I am inclined to stay here.[9]

The winter is severe and the snow now eight inches deep. General Hooker gains favor with the Army, and all about us looks better. The enemy is very busy strengthening the works on the south side of the river.

Office, Chief of Artillery
2 Division, 3 Corps
Falmouth, Va.
March 6, 1863

[To A. C. O.] My command now consists of five batteries of six guns each and is for an officer of my grade and rank a very satisfactory one.

You are I think wrong in saying the Army of the Potomac is now on the defensive. It is a necessity now that we wait for spring. An army cannot move in this country in the winter. I am told the effective strength of this Army is 130,000 men, that is, men available for their proper use in an engagement. In every way this Army is better cared for now than it has ever before been. I have large hopes for the future. So I had a year ago, but it appears to me now that I have a better foundation for these hopes.

If each army that is strong enough to make a forward movement in the spring will do it at the same time, it will be better. If we should then lose at one point, we would win successes at the others. This would prevent the enemy from moving troops from one point to

---

9 Maj. Gen. Hiram G. Berry had assumed command of Hooker's former division of the Third Corps after Hooker's promotion. Following Osborn's promotion to command of Berry's artillery in Sickles's corps, he chose to wait for his commission as Major.

another on interior lines and thus in each battle have the greater part of their entire effective force engaged against one of our armies.[10]

As to the cause of the removal of Generals Sumner and Franklin from their commands I, of course, cannot give reasons. The change was made at Washington, probably at the request of General Hooker. I have my personal ideas about it. I think General Hooker never forgave General Sumner for his refusal to help him at Williamsburg. There, he let General Hooker's division be cut to pieces while he was in easy helping distance with about 30,000 men. I am told by officers here that General Sumner was unnecessarily slow in going to General Hooker's assistance at the Battle of Antietam. General Franklin is currently reported in this part of the Army to have more retarded the fighting at Fredericksburg than to have aided it as he might. I know by current conversation at different headquarters that much fault was found with him during the late movement when the Army was driven back to its camp by the storm and mud. It is also believed by those officers who talk about such matters that these two Generals would have been unreliable in service under General Hooker.[11]

You say I am inconsistent in my statement regarding the removal of General Burnside. If I recollect rightly, I said that after his great failure at Fredericksburg for which he should have been removed, he was not; but for an accident, the storm, for which he was in no way responsible, he was removed. This is the fact anyway.

Office, Chief of Artillery
2 Division, 3 Corps
Falmouth, Va.
March 10, 1863

[To A. C. O.] This afternoon I received notice that my commission as Major of the 10th New York Artillery had been forwarded to me. General Hooker asked that I be mustered under this commission and then detailed to duty in this Army. General Barry, Chief of Artillery at Washington,[12] hearing this, said that if he thought General Hooker's application would be granted, he would stop the commission

---

10 Osborn anticipates General Ulysses S. Grant's 1864 strategy.
11 Franklin's performance at Fredericksburg was not outstanding. After forcing Crampton's Gap on South Mountain in the Antietam Campaign, he had failed to follow up his advantage and made only a weak effort to relieve Harpers Ferry.
12 Brig. Gen. William F. Barry

at the War Department and have it returned to Albany. That the 10th New York Artillery was the most demoralized body of men he had yet seen. That he wanted me with the regiment, and if General Hooker wanted me with the Army he must keep me with my present grade. I don't know how it will all turn out. I got this information from General Hunt's Adjutant General.[13]

Have you noticed the compliments the battery received in General Orders No. 18 and published in the New York papers about the 6th or 7th inst.? The *Herald* and some other papers published it.[14]

Office, Chief of Artillery
2 Division, 3 Corps
Falmouth, Va.
March 15, 1863

[To S. C. O.] A commission as Major in the 10th New York Artillery has been sent me and I have accepted it.[15] I shall probably go to Washington Tuesday or Wednesday next. I do not know where I will be assigned to duty; part of the regiment is in Washington and part in New York City. General Berry has just told me he shall again apply to the War Department for me to be assigned to duty with the new rank as his Chief of Artillery. If he is successful, it will be gratifying to me. I prefer to be with the active Army rather than be disciplining new troops. At present my future movements are a little uncertain.

Office, Chief of Artillery
2 Division, 3 Corps
Falmouth, Va.
March 20, 1863

[To A. C. O.] You again speak of the lack of discipline in the Army. I conclude from what you say, the discipline is not as good in the western armies as in this and yet in the main I agree with you. The discipline here, as I see it, is very good, but I am where I can see only

---

13 More influential intercession on Osborn's behalf.
14 Battery D on March 3, 1863, was one of 11 volunteer batteries cited for meeting Hooker's "acceptable standards" for artillery.
15 A temporary decision.

the best of it. What is to be seen about the edges and in the rear, I know little about. That is what you see the most of. I do not, however, put the enemy's discipline so far in advance of ours as you do, or as I did.[16] We have so far failed in generalship and not in the rank and file of the Army. When we get the right men at the heads of the several military departments, if we ever do, we shall succeed and not till then. I know from personal experience that in a square stand up fight our men are superior to the enemy. In commanders we have been deficient. I have confidence in Generals Hooker, Rosecrans, and Grant—not so much in several of the others and in some, none at all.

Office, Chief of Artillery
2 Division, 3 Corps
Falmouth, Va.
March 31, 1863

[To A. C. O.] Colonel Wainwright, having learned that I was about to accept a commission in the 10th New York Artillery, telegraphed me that he had sent my name forward for a commission in my own regiment as Major and requesting me to wait for it. This I have concluded to do.[17] The grade of Major in the 1st New York Artillery is much to be preferred to that in the 10th New York Artillery. The first being Light, the second Heavy Artillery.

Office, Chief of Artillery
2 Division, 3 Corps
Falmouth, Va.
April 14, 1863

[To A. C. O.] Preliminary orders have been issued for a movement of the Army, and very extensive preparations are being made for it. At six o'clock this afternoon we were ready to move but did not receive final orders to do so. The preparations which have been made for the approaching campaign have been such as to indicate we shall move very rapidly. The Army is cut down in its baggage to the last possibility; no surplus men are allowed, no tents even for General officers, no baggage wagons, and only pack mules for the transportation of ammunition. The Army was never in so fine condition as now and it

---

16 Osborn retracts an earlier judgment.
17 Wainwright intercedes for Osborn and expresses his confidence in him.

AFTER FREDERICKSBURG

appears to have the necessary confidence in itself. We are expecting to be ordered out of camp tomorrow though long experience has shown that in such matters we may be and very likely will be disappointed. We may go and we may not.

Two days ago General Stoneman moved out with the cavalry corps, said to be about 12,000 strong.[18] Today we have heard a little firing up the river, and we surmise the cavalry went that way. More active service must be close on us now, and the indications are that General Hooker intends to fight hard and rapidly. I have gotten the artillery under my command in excellent condition. I think no artillery in the Army surpasses it. General Hunt, Chief of Artillery of the Army, says this is true.

It is my impression from what I have seen that this time the Army will go down the river and cross and I feel confident, too, that wherever we fight we shall be successful this time.[19] But even if such should be the case, we cannot avoid fighting again very soon. If the enemy are beaten now, they will fight again as soon as they have had time to take breath. I have always believed this Army would defeat General Lee's Army and take Richmond and I still believe so, but just now I am more hopeful of reaching this end soon than I have been for some time. I think I appreciate the difficulties but believe they will be ultimately overcome.

The camp reports are to the effect that we have here 125,000 men, all of whom may be called veterans. We are also told that General Heintzelman will move from Washington with a large force to be employed in the general movement of this Army in such manner as may be best on occasion called for. It is also understood that General Hooker is anxious to fight in the open field, and to do so to force the enemy away from their works.

The President and Mrs. Lincoln arrived here a week ago Sunday and remained until Friday evening. Monday, the President reviewed the cavalry; Tuesday, he rode through the several camps; Wednesday, he reviewed the 2nd, 3rd, 5th, and 6th Corps. Friday, he reviewed the 11th and 12th Corps. He expressed himself as much pleased with all he saw. On Tuesday, I was introduced to him.[20]

By the way, in your last you ask me what my sources of information are and say I frequently use the expressions "It is said" and "It is

---

18 Hooker intended for Maj. Gen. George Stoneman's force to cut Lee's supply line, forcing his retreat.
19 Osborn was proved wrong on both counts; Hooker moved up the river and Chancellorsville was a Confederate victory.
20 Osborn's failure to comment further is surprising.

reported" without giving sources of information.[21] In a word, I am on most excellent official terms at this corps headquarters and the same of each of the divisions and nearly all the brigades of the corps. I have become well acquainted with nearly all the officers about the Army Headquarters and especially with those who comprised Hooker's staff when he commanded this division, etc., etc., besides a considerable acquaintance with many field and line officers. Here, all conversation nearly is of military matters, and a person with ordinary shrewdness can after talking with many people, each one of whom knows a little or has made a good guess, put the results of his several conversations together and reach a generally correct conclusion. You, of course, understand we can get nothing direct from the commanding general, and even if I did so I should not write it.

If our movement to the front at all corresponds with our expectations, our communications will for a time be cut off.

Office, Chief of Artillery
2 Division, 3 Corps
Falmouth, Va.
April 17, 1863

[To S. C. O.] For three or four days we have been continually expecting to move and are now ready to do so at an hour's notice. We are not informed why there is a delay, but doubtless there are good reasons and we shall soon leave our camps and wherever we go we shall have a desperate battle. The enemy will meet us wherever we offer to fight. It is believed here that General Heintzelman will occupy this camp with a large force when we move out of it.[22]

Office, Chief of Artillery
2 Division, 3 Corps
Falmouth, Va.
April 18, 1863

[To A. C. O.] The cavalry force of General Stoneman, I mentioned in my last, has been hindered in its operations by the violent rains which have fallen since they left. It appears the cavalry was to have

---

21 Osborn unwittingly uses a newspaper reporter's expression.
22 An unfounded rumor. Heintzelman had been returned to Washington following Second Bull Run (Manassas).

crossed the river yesterday at Rappahannock Station, but the river rose so rapidly they could not do it. I understand these rains increased the depth of the water seven feet, and that is more than they can get over or through. They are now waiting for the water to fall. The movement of the Army depends much upon the movements of the cavalry. Today the weather is fine, and the roads are again passably good.

You will remember I am now attached to the division commanded by General Berry, a volunteer officer from Maine. He has a most excellent reputation as an officer. Previous to this assignment he commanded a brigade in General Kearny's division and the brigade which led the advance and helped General Hooker in the afternoon at Williamsburg. I should know him better after the fight.

Office, Chief of Artillery
2 Division, 3 Corps
Falmouth, Va.
April 21, 1863

[To A. C. O.] We are still prepared to move at an hour's notice, but the orders to do so have not yet reached us. When we were ready, the enemy by some means knew of it and concentrated all their force near the river and opposite to us. Previous to this they were laying along the railroad between Fredericksburg and Richmond where they could be more easily supplied.

Yesterday we had another heavy rain and the streams are again swollen and the roads bad.

Office, Chief of Artillery
2 Division, 3 Corps
Falmouth, Va.
April 24, 1863

[To S. C. O.] Still, the Army remains in its camp and as I understand is waiting for the weather to become sufficiently settled and the roads fit for a campaign. Apparently this has occurred two or three times, but just as the conditions were satisfactory another storm has set in.

The peach trees are in bloom.

Office, Chief of Artillery
2 Division, 3 Corps
Falmouth, Va.
April 26, 1863

[To A. C. O.] The weather is beautiful and the roads are pretty well settled. I do not think we shall remain here many days longer. Governor Parker of New Jersey[23] has been here for several days and today reviewed this division which never appeared better. The Governor was much pleased and gave the division the highest praise. In speaking to me of it, he said it was a greater and better display than he had ever before seen or had expected to see. He expressed himself as much gratified that he had made the visit.

The Governor of Maine arrived here this morning.[24]

Office, Chief of Artillery
2 Division, 3 Corps
Falmouth, Va.
April 27, 1863

[To S. C. O.] We have orders this evening which look as if we will move tomorrow. They are preliminary only, but I think we shall go tomorrow.

Today this corps was reviewed by Secretary Seward,[25] and by the Prussian and Swedish Ministers. The review passed off well.

Office, Chief of Artillery
2 Division, 3 Corps
Falmouth, Va.
April 27, 1863

[To A. C. O.] We have orders to move in the morning, but the hour is not given. The 5th, 11th, and 12th Corps are moving today and are headed up the river.

---

23 Gov. Joel Parker. There were five New Jersey regiments in Berry's division.
24 Gov. Abner Coburn. Gen. Berry was a native of Rockland, ME.
25 William A. Seward, Lincoln's Secretary of State.

Today this corps was reviewed by Secretary Seward, the Prussian and Swedish Ministers, the Governor of Maine, and others. The review passed off very creditably.

I think this review was had to attract the attention of the enemy in order to cover the movement of the other corps. It took place in plain view of the enemy.

Chapter 7

Chancellorsville

The only possible termination of this war is to destroy the armies of the Confederacy. The South will not stop fighting and the North cannot.

Chancellorsville is frequently considered to have been Lee's greatest victory and his most brilliant command performance. Outnumbered two to one, he boldly chose to divide his army, and to outmaneuver and outwit his Union adversary. Chancellorsville is the story of two flanking movements. Hooker's initial flanking movement that forced Lee's withdrawal from his fortified Fredericksburg position is sometimes forgotten in the wake of Jackson's more spectacular and much publicized movement against the unsupported Union right flank. Both movements were successful in achieving their objectives. Lee followed up his initial success. Hooker did not.

On April 27, 1863, Hooker sent three of his corps, the Fifth, Eleventh, and Twelfth, up the left bank of the Rappahannock to cross at Kelly's Ford. On April 29th, they crossed the Rapidan at Ely's and Germanna Fords and arrived at Chancellorsville on April 30th, well in the rear of Lee's army. At the same time, the Sixth Corps, supported by the First, Second, and Third Corps, crossed the Rappahannock at Franklin's old crossing below Fredericksburg. Lee learned of Hooker's move to Chancellorsville on April 30th. On the same date, two divisions of Couch's Second Corps, followed on May 1st by the Third Corps, crossed the Rappahannock to Chancellorsville by way of United States Ford. Reynolds's First Corps joined them on May 2nd.

Earlier, in a move he later regretted, Hooker had sent all but one brigade of his cavalry toward Richmond in an effort to cut Lee's supply line hoping to force him to retreat. Stoneman's cavalry raid failed to achieve either objective and left Hooker with a cavalry force too small to protect his exposed right flank. Lee perceived Hooker's intent, left Early's division to face Sedgwick at Fredericksburg, and on May 1st ordered Jackson to move toward Chancellorsville to engage Hooker's main body. Jackson moved swiftly toward Chancellorsville on the Old Turnpike and Orange Plank Roads to seize the commanding ridge near the Tabernacle and Zoan Churches.

After entrenching his position around Chancellorsville, Hooker, on May 1st, moved the four Union corps there toward Jackson who had moved to seize the strategic ridges west of Fredericksburg. When Sykes's division of the Fifth Corps encountered the advancing Confederates, a sharp fight followed between Sykes and Brigadier General Paul J. Semmes's Confederate brigade. Hooker ordered his advancing units to withdraw back to their defensive positions at Chancellorsville, an order that angered his corps commanders. Hooker's strategy to force Lee out into the open to fight had been accomplished but after Lee accepted the challenge, Hooker backed away.

It was not the Confederate leader's nature to "ingloriously fly" or to refuse "to give battle on our own ground." The quotes had been contained in Hooker's congratulatory message to his troops on the previous day. The May 1st confrontation proved to be the high water mark of Hooker's offense, and his quickly adopted defensive attitude may have reflected his loss of self-confidence.

Rather than attack Hooker's entrenchments, Lee chose the risky alternative of sending Jackson's 24,000 man corps on a 12 mile march in a flanking movement around Hooker's vulnerable right flank that rested on the Old Turnpike west of its junction with the Orange Plank Road. Lee remained at Chancellorsville with the 16,000 men of Major General Lafayette McLaws's and Major General Richard H. Anderson's divisions to face Hooker's six corps.

It was around 6 p.m. on May 2nd when Jackson's men emerged from the Wilderness to strike the rear of the Eleventh Corps positions, most of which faced south and not toward the Confederates advancing from the west. The scattered brigade-size Eleventh Corps units, many not entrenched, were ill-prepared to resist Jackson's sudden, surprise attack.

Jackson's flanking march had not gone unnoticed. Birney's division of Sickles's corps, from its vantage point at Hazel Grove, sighted Jackson's column moving by its front near Catherine Furnace headed in a southwesterly direction. Birney attacked the column and captured most of the Twenty-third Georgia Regiment. The attack delayed the two rear Confederate brigades for an hour. Sickles reported the movement to Hooker as either a Confederate flanking movement or retreat. Both Generals chose to interpret it as a retreat.

Having been forced to move at a slow pace over narrow roads and forest trails, Jackson's 10 mile long column took longer than planned to reach its destination, and four of A. P. Hill's brigades arrived too late to join in the initial attack. Five of Jackson's brigades were not deployed for other reasons, leaving only six brigades to participate in the attack against the Union Eleventh Corps. Confederate Colonel E. P. Alexander noted that the ensuing conflict was a case of one Union brigade at a time facing six Confederate brigades and called the Union resistance, "a gallant effort," adding that "no troops could have acted differently."[1] Fortunately for Hooker, because of unanticipated delays, the attack was not launched until 6:00 p.m. and the Confederates ran out of daylight. Eleventh Corps resistance also slowed the Confederate advance.

In their pursuit of the retreating Eleventh Corps, Jackson's brigades had become disorganized and exhausted. A. P. Hill's fresh division was pushed to the front to lead a renewed attack. Near the junction of the Bullock Road with the Plank Road, Lane's North Carolina brigade formed its line across the Plank Road with its center guiding on the road as Jackson impatiently urged Hill to move forward. Uncertain of the location of the Union defense line, Jackson and Hill each separately sought to reconnoiter the Union positions. Both Confederate Generals were wounded, Jackson mortally by his own men, and Hill by Union artillery fire coming from Dimmick's advance section located in the Plank Road in line with the entrenched Union infantry on either side of the road. North of the road were two brigades of Berry's division of Sickles's Third Corps who had remained near Chancellorsville on May 1st when Sickles's other two divisions had moved to Hazel Grove. Initially, Berry's men and an organized remnant of Colonel Adolphus Buschbeck's Eleventh Corps brigade were the only infantry present to oppose Jackson.

Berry's Third Brigade (Mott) and Hays's brigade of Major General William H. French's Second Corps division arrived to reinforce the Union line on the north side of the Plank Road. Brigidier General Alpheus S. Williams's Twelfth Corps division and Best's Twelfth Corps guns joined the Union defense on the south side of the road. These units had occupied different positions, but had been quickly turned to face Jackson's advance. Sickles's two Third Corps divisions at Hazel Grove, Birney and Major General Amiel W. Whipple, protected the Union left flank. Winslow, McClean, and four of Dimmick's guns were on the crest of the ridge on and to the immediate left of the Plank Road.

Osborn's batteries followed Berry's division down the Plank Road. In his letter to A. C. O. and his official report, he vividly describes the flight of those disorganized Eleventh Corps men who had become separated from their units. It was with difficulty that his three

---

1   E. P. Alexander (1977) *Military Memoirs of a Confederate*. Dayton, OH. p. 337.

batteries were able to force their way through the human mass blocking their way. (See Chapter Appendices B and C.) Both Osborn and Lieutenant George Winslow confirm in their reports that one section of Lieutenant Dimmick's battery was placed in the road near the infantry line of battle at the foot of the hill, well in advance of the batteries located at the edge of the Chancellorsville plateau.

Brigadier General Robert Rodes, who commanded Jackson's initial attack, after reconnoitering the road toward Chancellorsville, informed Colonel Crutchfield, Jackson's Artillery Chief, that there were no Union troops in front of them, whereupon Crutchfield's batteries opened fire. The Confederate artillery fire caused Winslow's Battery D to respond, in Rodes's words, "by a most terrific fire, which silenced our guns . . . a fire mainly directed down the Plank Road."[2] During the exchange Crutchfield was wounded and removed from the field in the same ambulance with the wounded Jackson.

In his May 8th letter to A. C. O., Osborn narrates the events of the next 15 hours, events in which he and his batteries played a key role. Osborn viewed these events, which occurred along a narrow one mile front, from his vantage point on the Plank Road. His batteries served as a roadblock across the road which was the most accessible approach to the Union position.

When Jackson and Hill became casualties, the Confederates were forced to cancel Jackson's plan for a night attack.[3] Osborn and Dimmick's advance section claimed credit for Hill's wounding. Generals Henry Heth and James Lane, Brigade Commanders of A. P. Hill's division, indicated in their battle reports that the fire from Union guns at Fairview interfered with their efforts[4] to organize their men in the woods on both sides of the Plank Road. Union artillery fire also interfered with removal of the wounded Jackson.[5]

Early on the morning of May 3rd, the Confederates now commanded by General "Jeb" Stuart resumed their attacks. Confederate artillery had been denied clear fields of fire until Hooker ordered Sickles to withdraw from Hazel Grove. Colonel E. P. Alexander, who had replaced the wounded Crutchfield, quickly took advantage of this excellent artillery position that overlooked Fairview and placed 40-50 guns at the abandoned site, a move that contributed to the Confederate victory.

---

2 *OR.* Vol. 25, Part 1, Pp. 941-942.
3 *Ibid.*
4 *Ibid.,* Pp. 890, 920.
5 Johnson, R. V. & Buel, C. C. (Eds.) (1956) *Battles and Leaders of the Civil War.* New York. Vol. 3, p. 212.

After three hours of intensive fighting and a countless series of charges and countercharges by both sides along and in the woods adjacent to the road, Jackson's men overran the Union position and joined forces with Lee's two divisions at Chancellorsville. After a brief stand near the Chancellor House, Hooker withdrew to a strong defensive position that had been prepared the previous evening, one that protected the United States Ford crossing. Sedgwick, after defeating Early at Fredericksburg, attempted to join Hooker's force at Chancellorsville but on May 4th was turned back by Lee at Salem Church. Sedgwick recrossed the Rappahannock at Bank's Ford and on May 5th Hooker's army withdrew by way of the United States Ford.

Many of Hooker's men may have felt that it was he and not they who had lost the battle. Osborn seems to agree, noting that it was along the May 3rd line that the battle should have been won. Failure to replenish Union artillery ammunitions and to reinforce the Third and Twelfth Corps infantry from the nearby idle First, Second, and Fifth Corps defies explanation. Hooker's action or inaction on May 3rd seems to reflect the behavior of a commander resigned to defeat. Perhaps, partially mesmerized by his belief in Lee's almost superhuman abilities and still stunned by Jackson's sudden attack, his ability to command seemed paralyzed on May 3rd. The blow to the head suffered late in the battle, inflicted by the falling debris of the Chancellor House, had little impact on the final outcome. Jackson had delivered the fatal blow on the evening of May 2nd.

From their positions on and near the Plank Road along the brow of the Chancellorsville plateau, Osborn's batteries enjoyed a relatively open field of fire. Along with Best's Twelfth Corps guns, they had halted the initial rush of Jackson's men down the Plank Road and had interfered successfully with Confederate efforts to launch a night attack. Their defense on May 2nd prevented a Union defeat from becoming a disaster.

Standing in the road with Lieutenant Dimmick's advance section, Osborn had been a forward observer (See chapter Appendix A.) and had suffered three slight wounds. He had been a close witness to the mortal wounding of General Berry and Lieutenant Dimmick.

One hundred and thirty years later, the Union location of the Fairview artillery line remains quite visible, still marked by the lunettes constructed on the night of May 2-3, 1863, by Captain Charles W. Squier, Chief Engineer of General Berry's staff (Second Division, Third Corps). When the original Orange Plank Road was replaced by the present Route 3, a divided four lane highway, some of the lunettes adjacent to the old road were destroyed by the widening of the cut through the ridge west of Chancellorsville. The remaining lunettes are

CHANCELLORSVILLE

no longer level with the present highway but are several feet above its present grade.

This formidable collection of Union guns has come to be known as "Best's Artillery" line, named for Captain Clermont L. Best, Fourth U.S. Artillery, Chief of Twelfth Corps Artillery. Upon Jackson's advance down the Plank Road, Best gathered 14 of his Twelfth Corps guns which had faced McLaws's and Anderson's divisions and moved them to the Fairview site to face the new Confederate threat. Best counted 34 Union guns present at Fairview on the evening of May 2nd. Bigelow, the respected Chancellorsville historian, sets the number at 37.[6] Not counting Dimmick's advance section, there were 14 Twelfth Corps guns, 7 Eleventh Corps pieces and the balance, 16 guns, of Osborn's command. According to Bigelow, the numbers varied during the course of the engagement as batteries were removed and as others arrived.

Bigelow incorrectly credits Best for giving the order for the opening response of the Union guns to Colonel Crutchfield's Confederate fire down the Plank Road.[7] Lieutenant George Winslow, Commander of Battery D, takes credit for firing the Union response from Fairview and lays claim to being the first battery on line at Fairview. (See chapter Appendix B.)[8] Captain Best would not have given orders to Third Corps batteries with Osborn and divisional commander General Berry both present.

In his report, Osborn noted, "Two batteries of the 12th Corps were on the left of Winslow's battery, commanded by Captain Best as chief, but their position was inferior to our own, yet doubtless they did good service." Osborn apparently felt that his batteries closer to the road enjoyed a more open field of fire.[9]

Osborn's letter and his battle report (See chapter Appendix C.) contradict another historian's account that the Fourth New York Independent Battery was left at the crossroads because of past controversies over its alleged unreliability. It was placed on the brow of the Chancellorsville plateau along with Winslow and Dimmick and gave a good account of itself until 3:00 p.m. on May 3rd when ordered to the rear by an aide of General Hooker, a move deplored by Osborn.

For the Confederates, Chancellorsville was a costly victory. Jackson's three divisions, in a series of frontal assaults, had suffered 7,158

---

6 Bigelow, J. (1910) *The Campaign of Chancellorsville: A Strategic and Tactical Study.* New Haven: Pp. 318-319.
7 *Ibid.*, p. 312.
8 *OR. op. cit.*, p. 487.
9 *Ibid.*, p.484.

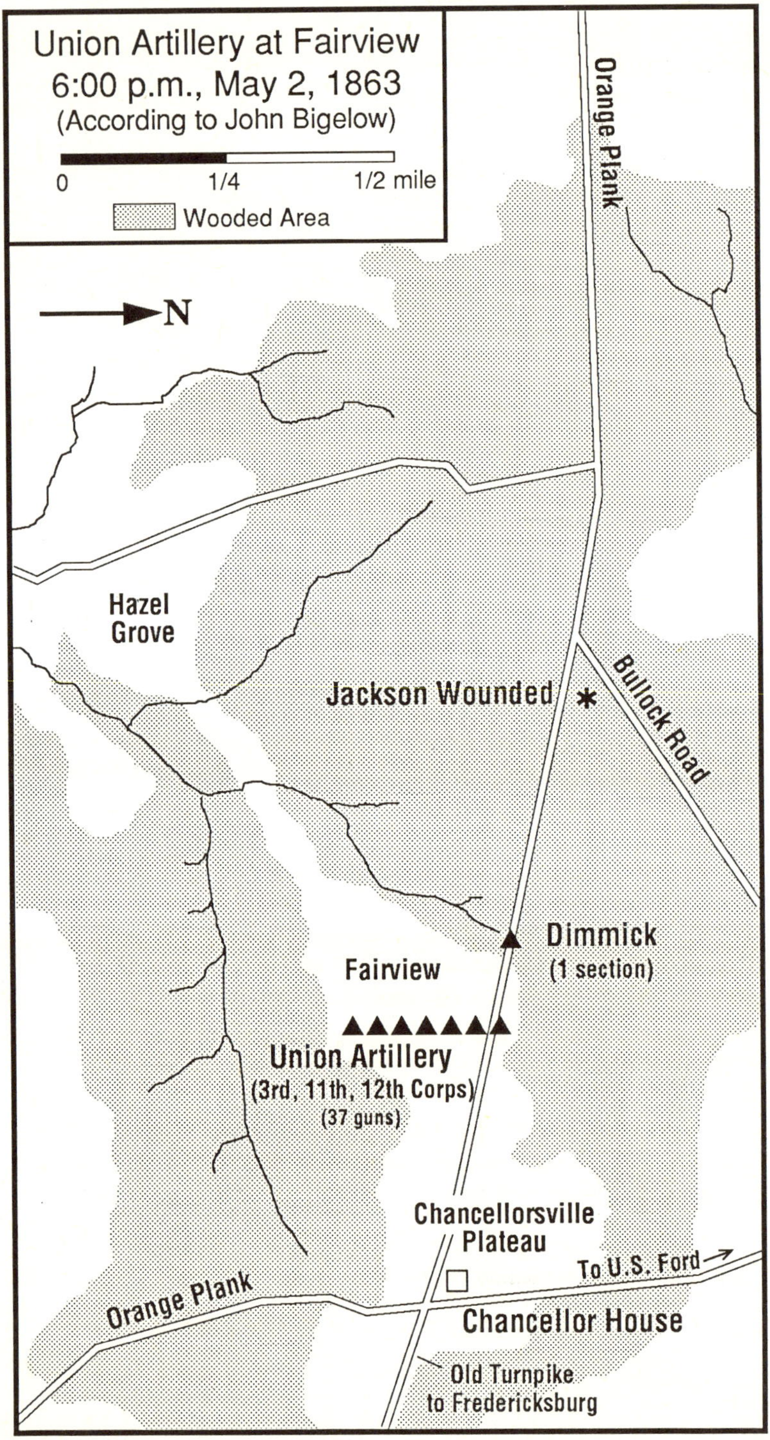
Union Artillery at Fairview
6:00 p.m., May 2, 1863
(According to John Bigelow)
0
1/4
1/2 mile
Wooded Area
N
Orange Plank
Hazel Grove
Jackson Wounded
Bullock Road
Dimmick
(1 section)
Fairview
Union Artillery
(3rd, 11th, 12th Corps)
(37 guns)
Chancellorsville Plateau
To U.S. Ford
Orange Plank
Chancellor House
Old Turnpike
to Fredericksburg

casualties, nearly 30 percent of their numbers. Fighting from behind entrenchments, the Union Third and Twelfth Corps had lost 4,703 men. The loss of Jackson may have been the greatest Confederate loss. Forced to reorganize his army into three corps, Lee promoted A. P. Hill and Richard Ewell to corps command, a position that neither man was prepared to handle. The failure of the Confederate command structure at Gettysburg proved to be an added and unforeseen cost of the Chancellorsville victory.
—*The Editors*

Office, Chief of Artillery
2 Division, 3 Corps
Falmouth, Va.
May 7, 1863

[To S. C. O.] On that part of the field in the late battle of Chancellorsville where I was, the fighting was more severe than any part of the Army of the Potomac has before seen or done. In the entire battle perhaps the losses were not quite so heavy as the same we have before had. But in our front, for stubborn and persistent fighting it has at no time been equalled.

I took a somewhat conspicuous part and have everywhere been congratulated upon the service my command performed as well as upon the fact that I am still living. I commanded in the fight four batteries, three of which were at the front and engaged. All did excellent work. My loss in brief was one battery commander killed, one officer wounded, and 86 men killed and wounded. I lost no guns and not a single man attempted to avoid duty. General Berry who commanded the division was killed. I was standing by his side when he was shot. I received three slight wounds, no one of which is serious and I shall not go off duty.[10]

The fighting on our front by the infantry was wonderful for its determination and desperation. I cannot even guess what will be the general results of this battle; certainly, we were not successful. Since the battle I have been so closely confined to my command I know but little outside of it.

10 Osborn with Lt. Justin E. Dimmick's section was located well in advance of the other Union batteries. Lt. Dimmick was killed and Osborn received three slight wounds, his only wounds during the war.

Battery D, First New York Light Artillery on the shore of the Rappahannock River before the Battle of Chancellorsville. (*Courtesy of the Library of Congress.*)

Office, Chief of Artillery
2 Division, 3 Corps
Falmouth, Va.
May 8, 1863

[To A. C. O.] In the operations between the 29th of April and the 5th of May, I had under my command the following batteries: K, 4th U.S. Artillery, Light 12-pounders, First Lieutenant F. W. Seeley; H, 1st U.S. Artillery, Light 12-pounders, First Lieutenant J. E. Dimmick; D, 1st N. Y. Artillery, Light 12-pounders, First Lieutenant G. B. Winslow; B, 1st N. J. Artillery, 10-pounder Parrott guns, Captain A. J. Clark.

On the 29th of April at two o'clock in the afternoon, I received orders from General Berry to move the batteries with the infantry to near the bank of the Rappahannock and about midway between the crossings of Generals Sedgwick's and Reynolds's Corps. At eleven in the evening we went into camp for the night. At sunrise on the 30th, I reported by order to General Newton[11] on the bank of the river and placed the batteries in position to sweep the plain on the south side of it. At three in the afternoon I was directed to move with the 3rd Corps to the United States Ford. At midnight we camped a mile south of the Hartwood Church and on the morning of the 31st crossed the river.

At noon on the 29th Captain Clark's battery was transferred to the 1st division, and the 4th New York Independent Battery reported to me.[12] I had done all I could to make Captain Clark's battery perfect, and I very much regretted this change. It was in most excellent order.

On May 1st at three in the afternoon, we moved with the division about three miles to the front, excepting Lieutenant Seeley's battery which remained with General Mott's[13] brigade at the Ford. Brisk skirmishing was going on at the front in the evening. At night we camped near a plantation residence designated the White House.

Heavy skirmishing commenced early in the morning of the 2nd. This continued until afternoon with now and then heavy firing indi-

---

11 Brig. Gen. John Newton, Commander of the Third Division, Sixth Corps.
12 The Fourth New York Independent Battery, previously commanded by Capt. James E. Smith who again commanded it at Gettysburg, was under the command of Lt. George F. Barstow at Chancellorsville but was led into battle there by Lt. William T. McClean. The battery had previously suffered from internal dissension and some sources claim that it was held back near the Chancellor House when the other Third Corps batteries advanced down the Plank Road. Osborn disputes this assertion, praises its performance on May 2nd, and protested the battery's removal to the rear during the night of May 2nd-3rd.
13 Brig. Gen. Gershom Mott commanded the Third Brigade of Berry's division.

cating sharp collisions. At four in the afternoon the firing became very heavy and when the firing was at the heaviest, the sound indicated that our men were giving way.

While this firing was in progress, this division was near the road a little in rear, say 200 yards, of the Chancellorsville House. The sound of musketry had fallen off a little when we were ordered in to the support or more properly to the protection of the 11th Corps which had been routed. The infantry of our division moved in advance followed by the artillery in the order of Dimmick, Winslow, and McClean of the 4th N. Y. Independent Battery. General Hooker had made his headquarters at the Chancellorsville House. We had just passed him when we encountered the head of the column of the 11th Corps coming to the rear in complete disorder.[14] The men and officers were moving in a solid mass, filling the road its entire breadth. Our infantry had forced its way through them by might of numbers and organization, and they, having passed the men, filled the gap and the mass was again solid. I could not move the guns without injuring the men as they would not give way. I hesitated a minute or two in hopes they would make an open way but they would not do so, and seeing no alternative I ordered the batteries forward and by the force of the weight of the teams and guns, I passed through. I presume a few men may have been hurt but if they were I could not help it. This mass of men extended about a half mile before we passed through it.

About three-quarters of a mile and on the right of the road after we passed the Chancellorsville House, the timber comes to the road and a quarter of a mile further it crosses the road covering the entire front.

Major General Hiram G. Berry
(From *Battles and Leaders of the Civil War*.)

---

14 Osborn's official report contains a more graphic description.

Present-day View of Hazel Grove
as seen from Best's 12th Corps Artillery Position.

The field on the left of the road and next to the woods is about a half mile wide. It was here the battle was mainly fought. About 400 yards before we reached the farthest timber, that is the timber on the left of the road, the ground slopes off gradually towards the timber making a low hill or ridge 25 or 30 feet in height. On this ridge I put the batteries in position—Dimmick on the right resting on the road, Winslow on his left, and McClean on his left. One section of Dimmick's battery I took forward to where the timber crossed the road and where the infantry were forming the line and put it in position on the road. This was done at General Berry's request. The position these two guns occupied was in the line of battle. I was with this section and placed it in position to command the road in front of our line.

At sunset, a battery of the enemy opened fire on us and succeeded in dropping their shells among the batteries on the ridge.[15] This battery was about 1,000 yards distant. Winslow and Mason of Dimmick's battery opened fire on it and in a few minutes silenced it. After this little flurry with the battery, our front became quiet. I remained with the section at the front in the line of battle. Our line had its right

---

15 Under the command of Col. Stapleton Crutchfield, Jackson's Artillery Chief.

resting in the woods on the right of the road and extending on the left of the road along the edge of the timber. From my place with the section I could distinctly hear the enemy in our front. It was then after dark or rather just at dark. They moved down the road, and when within 200 or 300 yards of our line filed off of the road to the right and left and formed line of battle that distance in front of us and parallel to our line. We could distinctly hear the commands of the officers and the steps of the troops. Everything indicated that the force in front was large as we afterwards found it to be.

While these movements were going on in our front, a good many of the enemy's scouts who were sent forward to determine our position were taken and sent to the rear. Several of the enemy's officers scouting ahead of their line were also taken in. An artillery team of four horses and four or five men were sent for this section which they had seen through the twilight and supposed to have been abandoned by the 11th Corps. They were all captured and sent to the rear. It was plain the enemy had not yet located our line and were forming their line in the woods in order themselves to be under cover of the timber, and it is possible they may have suspected they were in our immediate neighborhood.

The orders I gave to the batteries on the crest were to govern their fire by the fire of the section at the front, to open fire when I opened and to cease firing when I ceased, and that I would remain at the front. General Berry had told me about dusk that my position on the road enabled me to watch the movements of the enemy more closely than he or any other officer could do. That he desired me to exercise my own judgment and if I saw any necessity to open fire, or if I thought it advisable to do so, to open. That he would give instructions to the infantry to open fire if I opened and cease if I ceased. General Berry's headquarters in the line was about 100 yards to the right of the two guns and from where I stood.[16]

At half past nine in the evening, the night was very light. The road through the tall timbers in our front was wide and straight for a considerable distance. At that time the field was very still. We saw as plainly as could be seen in the clear evening light the head of a column of mounted men coming down the road towards us. They were moving slowly and with evident caution. When within 150 yards of us, they halted and were inspecting their front and apparently this section of artillery. I concluded this was some prominent general and his staff. I think they stood still at least two or three minutes, evidently

---

16 In the wooded area north of the Plank Road, close enough to provide overall direction for Osborn.

consulting, after which the leading horseman turned to the left and countermarched on his column, those in rear following this movement. All this convinced me this was a prominent general, and no one but a prominent one would have been so separated from his command. Acting on this conclusion, I directed Lieutenant Dimmick to open fire on this column, which he did. Of course, the horsemen dashed into the woods on either side of the road and I saw no more of them, but the effects of the fire from these two guns were surprising to say the least. I had ordered the batteries on the crest to govern their fire by the fire of this section, and they opened instantly. The infantry in compliance with General Berry's orders opened at once, and the entire line of battle of the enemy also opened. They were close to us and were ready. The firing of one gun was the order for the entire line to open, and the enemy replied instantly.

Now, about these horsemen who drew our fire. When the fire opened from both lines, they were midway between the lines. From the first gun it was less than half a minute before both lines had opened a full volley fire. Undoubtedly, this was Stonewall Jackson and his staff.[17] There are two reports regarding him, one that he was killed and another that he was badly wounded and will die, though I think it is now conceded that he is dead. All that I have seen and heard is to the effect that he fell between the lines at the hour this firing occurred. So far, this answers to the conditions given. But the Richmond papers say that he was shot by his own picket or from the picket line by the men mistaking him for one of our men. This certainly is an error. No man can know who shot him. He was between the lines when both were firing a full volley, and it is not to be assumed that a man in that position could live a minute. If he was hit by a bullet striking him in the front, he was probably hit by his own men. If in the back of the shoulder, by our men as he was doubtless facing his own line when struck. He had already turned his face towards his own line when I fired, and the natural impulse would have been to get back to his own line. This fire lasted about fifteen minutes when it slackened away.

General Jackson was thought by many to be the greatest General the enemy had and I think with very good reason. I, however, consider General Lee the greatest man they have developed. You will see more or less in the papers concerning General Jackson's death if he is really dead, and I have been particular in giving you these facts as I understand them.

---

17 Osborn is mistaken as he later admits. Gen. A. P. Hill was the victim of fire from Osborn's advance section.

Looking East down the Plank Road toward Chancellorsville. Jackson Monuments are in the Left Foreground. Osborn's Batteries were Located on the Rise seen in the Distance. Dimmick's Section was in the Preceding Hollow. (From *N.Y. Monument Commission Book*, p. xxx)

At half past ten in the evening, a movement in our front caused us to open on the enemy again but principally with artillery. Our fire was directed to the road in the rear of the enemy's line in order to annoy the columns moving to their front to strengthen and extend their line. The batteries on the crest were increased to five by the addition of two batteries from the 12th Corps.[18] They each fired very carefully and very deliberately. The elevation of the guns being as slight as possible passed the shells over our line, and the fuses were so cut that the shells exploded immediately after passing our line of infantry. The flight of the shells could be followed by the burning fuze until they had exploded or had passed into the woods. It was a display of beautiful fireworks, not so brilliant as that at Malvern Hill but still very fine. The enemy's artillery replied, but to that we paid no attention and confined our fire to their infantry. While this artillery fire was in progress, the infantry skirmishers or pickets several times became sharply engaged; this firing lasted about half an hour. After midnight there was another conflict of the same nature but not so long continued.

At two o'clock in the morning, Lieutenant Seeley reported with his battery and went into position extending the line of the batteries to the left. At three o'clock in the morning, an aide of General Hooker's ordered the 4th N. Y. Independent Battery to some other point. I have been unable to learn the occasion for this order but presume it was an arbitrary act by some staff officer whose stupidity was much more fully developed than was his good sense. That battery went somewhere to the rear and took no further part in the battle.

After midnight Captain Squire, Engineer for the division, threw up slight earthworks in front of the batteries on the crest, which proved the next morning to be of value.

Between two and three o'clock, General Sickles moved General Birney's division, which was on our left, forward against the enemy's line for the purpose of recovering some guns said to have been left by the 11th Corps as it fell back. This brought on a very sharp collision, but as General Sickles reports, the enemy's line was thrown back some distance and I think the guns recovered—but of that, I am not certain. The line of General Birney[19] then fell back to its position.

On the morning of the 3rd at five o'clock, the enemy made the principal attack of the battle on this division. The troops making the attack were massed and moved against us with great force and weight. We had but a single line of battle. From the moment the attack was

---

18 Bigelow J. (1910) *op. cit.,* credits Best with having 14 guns at Fairview.
19 Brig. Gen. David Birney commanded Sickles's First Division.

Staying Jackson's Advance, Saturday Evening, May 2, with Artillery Placed Across the Plank Road. (From *Battles and Leaders of the Civil War*, Vol. 3, p. 166.)

made, they held persistently to their work, gaining an inch at a time and holding every inch they gained until, inch by inch, they crowded our line back from its position. Our men did all they could, but the line was neither strong enough nor extended enough to hold the enemy back. The attack was upon this division alone with its single line. On our left was General Birney's division and on our right General Hays' brigade.[20] These, in fact, were practically all the troops that fought the battle and of these, this division did four-fifths of it.

The enemy's force was concentrated to break our general line at the point occupied by this division. If successful in this, they would occupy the crest upon which the artillery was and the open plain in rear of it to the Chancellorsville House.

It would be useless for me to attempt to describe the fighting at this point. It was desperate beyond the power of description. No division of the Army can surpass this in its power to fight and to hold to its work. It was placed at a great disadvantage by having but a single line in fighting a force continually reinforced to any extent required to accomplish the object to be attained. After our line was thrown out of its position, it continued to fight between the woods and the ridge on which our guns were, as long as it was possible for them to remain. The two lines of battle came together and intermingled actually crossing each other and swinging clear around so that the fronts were changed. The bayonet was several times used by both lines. This method of fighting continued until our force was becoming too seriously reduced and the ammunition was exhausted, when our line fell back in good order, fighting as it retreated. Reinforcements were several times asked for, but none were sent and in my opinion here was the error of the day.

The place and time to have fought this battle out was right then and there. The battlefield to have won or lost the fight on was that where the fighting was done and the open plain right back of it, that is between the woods and the Chancellorsville House. A heavy reinforcement put in on our right would have localized the fighting, and then by reinforcing the line in our front we could have fought out the battle and won it in the open field.

This is no afterthought of my own. After the battle had fairly opened, I listened every minute for the battle to open on our right by an attack on the enemy's left and also looked each moment for the arrival of reinforcements to strengthen our line. But neither occurred, and when we could no longer stand up, our line withdrew. The tactics

---

20 Brig. Gen. William Hays commanded the Second Brigade of the Second Corps.

General Sumner adopted at Savage Station would have won this fight. Larger forces would have to be sent in to relieve the lines in front as they became wholly or partially exhausted, but otherwise the same, and before more than half of our unoccupied and available forces had been brought up and put in, the enemy would have been whipped. This was my opinion on the field and I have not changed it.

The artillery did all and more than I could reasonably expect of it. Dimmick fought with the section at the front until the enemy had passed his flanks, and he was wounded twice, the last time fatally. The batteries on the crest fought until our infantry was driven back of them, and they had for some time protected their front with cannister. Nothing was in the power of the batteries to do they did not do to aid the infantry. Seeley had taken position on the left and front of the 12th Corps batteries, and thus he had the advantage of not only protecting his own front but sweeping that of the others. He did much to prevent the capture of any of our guns.

The enemy's forces were moved against us in two and three lines while we had but a single line.[21] The fighting was so stubborn that the lines came together and wound in and out with each other and in many places actually coming together and using the bayonet. Winslow, in his report of the part his battery took, says of the time when our line was being forced back, "Our left having fallen back our troops in front were exposed to a heavy fire, both in front and flank and finally fell back a short distance, but in good order, the batteries keeping the enemy in check while our infantry rallied and advanced regaining their former position. Four or five times our infantry reluctantly retired a short distance and again advanced, driving the enemy who seemed to outnumber them two to one. At each successive attack the enemy's numbers increased, the reinforcement coming down the hill in almost solid masses. Our artillery did much to check them with shot and shell causing perceptible destruction to their ranks.

"Just before the last charge of the Jersey brigade,[22] in front of my battery, the enemy came down the slope in solid masses covering, as it were, the whole ground in front of our line, and with at least a dozen stand of colors flying in their midst. I ordered the guns loaded with solid shot and as our line fell back and wheeled to the left, unmasking

---

21 Prior to the May 3rd Confederate assault, E. P. Alexander, *op. cit.*, counted two Union defense lines. After the conflict moved back and forth, it is likely that the two lines became joined and took on the appearance of one no longer occupying its original entrenchments.
22 Mott's Third Brigade.

the battery, I fired at one and a half degrees elevation. The effects were remarkable. A few rounds threw them into great confusion and drove them up the hill whereupon our infantry again charged and took several stand of colors.

"The enemy then crossed the road and came down the road on the right. The section of Dimmick's battery at the front and the remainder of his battery on my right had been compelled to withdraw. The enemy continued slowly to advance and our troops to withdraw. In a few moments, the enemy planted their colors in the road 100 yards to my right and on my flank and with their sharpshooters were busy in picking off my men and horses.

"When about 20 had gathered about the colors, I turned my guns with cannister upon them and drove them back. This was several times repeated. They were however rapidly closing around us in the woods upon the right and not more than 25 or 30 yards from my right gun when I received your order to limber up and retire. I had expended all my ammunition. I limbered from the left successively, continuing to fire until the last piece was limbered and then moved off."

I noticed this battery move off the field under this heavy fire as an exhibition of coolness and discipline I have not seen surpassed. Many of the horses were killed and some of the men but when they left the face of the enemy, they moved off at a walk—every officer and every man at his post and with the precision and exactness each would have shown on drill or at a review.

I will also give an extract from the report of Lieutenant Seeley upon the part taken by his battery in the battle of the 3rd inst. He says, "Early in the morning on which the enemy vigorously attacked our lines I was ordered by an aide-de-camp of General Hooker to a position on a rising ground in an angle made by the position of our infantry, which was on two sides of a square facing outward. I saw after bringing my pieces into position one of the enemy's batteries placed behind the crest of a hill some 500 yards in front and which opened a destructive fire on my battery. I replied from the left half of my battery, commanded by Lieutenant Arnold, vigorously for 15 minutes, when finding that my shells and case shot exploded well on the crest of the hill behind which the enemy's battery was yet failed to do any damage owing to the fact that the enemy's guns were perfectly screened by the crest, I desisted and made no further effort to dislodge them. I then turned my attention to the enemy's infantry, a brigade of which had gained a temporary advantage on our right and had forced a portion of our first and second lines to retire on their supports. A few well directed shots from the right section caused them to hastily retire after which I ceased firing. The battery in my front keeping up meantime a well directed fire, killing and wounding several of my men and horses. I held my position about half an hour longer when the battery on my right left the field and the infantry retiring behind my flanks I received your orders to retire.

"I again took up position near the Chancellorsville House encountering a very destructive fire from the enemy's line, then 450 yards distant. In order to check the advance of the enemy, who was pressing on in front and on both flanks, I loaded with cannister and reserved my fire until the enemy were within 350 yards of me and then opened on them with effect causing their troops to break and seek cover on my left and front where I followed them with solid shot until my ammunition was exhausted. I then withdrew from the field with the remnant of my men and horses and the debris of my battery."

While the fighting was at the severest, I found the batteries were slacking fire on account of the ammunition giving out. No reserve ammunition was within reach. I therefore applied to Captain Randolph,[23] Chief of Artillery of the Corps, for either ammunition or other batteries to relieve those whose ammunition was exhausted. The Captain said there was no ammunition available and the only battery available was that of Captain von Puttkammer,[24] 11th N. Y. Indt. Battery. The Captain of that battery refused to go to the front and emphatically showed the white feather. Not being able to procure either ammunition or other batteries, I was compelled to withdraw the batteries at the front as their ammunition gave out.

If I had been able to have supplied them, I would have formed line again between this, their position, and the Chancellorsville House. As it was, I could not do it. As each battery was withdrawn, it was sent to the ordnance train and in three hours would have gone to the front again had the changes in the battle required their services.

Nothing further of special interest transpired with the batteries. On the 5th, General Hunt,[25] Chief of Artillery of the Army, ordered us to recross the river and to reoccupy our old camps.

In refitting the batteries for whatever service they might be called upon to perform, I was compelled to unhorse and partially unman the 4th N. Y. Indt. Battery . When I did this, I placed that battery on the north side of the river, on the bluff and commanding the ford and the plain south of it. That battery was as speedily as possible made serviceable and its men restored and a full quota of horses provided.

I believe I am justly entitled to feel proud of these batteries, their commanding and subordinate officers and the men. They did in this

---

23 Capt. George E. Randolph, Third Corps Artillery Chief.
24 Capt. Albert A. von Puttkammer, Eleventh New York Independent Battery, was found absent from his command and later dismissed from the service.
25 Brig. Gen. Henry J. Hunt.

battle all that could be done. No batteries could have done better. The infantry fought to the full extent of its ability and endurance, and the artillery rendered it every assistance in its power.

The ammunition expended by the artillery of the division was 2,400 rounds. The loss in materiel: 94 horses, two empty caissons abandoned for lack of horses to bring them off, one gun carriage knocked to pieces—gun saved. In officers, Lieutenant J. E. Dimmick killed and Lieutenant J. Arnold wounded. In men, K, 4th U.S. Artillery, killed 7, wounded 30; H, 1st U.S. Artillery, killed 2, wounded 18; D, 1st N. Y Artillery killed 2, wounded 12.

The reports from Captain Clark's battery detached and sent to the 1st. Division are all good.

The death of General Berry, our division commander, was not only a severe loss in itself but the occasion of special sadness to those who knew him well. His reputation was that of an exceptionally brave and reckless officer. He was exceedingly ambitious and was gaining prominence rapidly. He was fully aware of the desperate position in which his division had been placed and was determined to carry it through its work successfully. When the enemy attacked in the morning, he ordered his officers and men to cover themselves as much as possible by the earthworks the men made during the night. These were about 18 inches high and gave good protection to the troops lying on the ground. He, however, refused to make any effort to screen himself, but walked to and fro along the line encouraging all to hold the line and keep themselves well covered. In this way he was exposed to the fire of the sharpshooters and four-fifths of his person to the general fire of the enemy. He had escaped a considerable time and was confident he would not be struck. While standing close to me and near the section on the road, he was hit by a musket ball in the breast and in a few minutes after died. His body was at once carried to the rear, and a few hours later Lieutenant George W. Freeman of my staff was detailed to proceed at once to Washington with the body.

I have thus given you an outline of that part of the battle which I saw and of the part I took in it. I have made no effort to describe anything which occurred in other parts of the Army or the fighting done by other troops than those immediately about me.

N.B.[26] The exhaustive investigation of Colonel Hamlin[27] into the operations at Chancellorsville show that but a moderate percentage

---

26 Osborn apparently added this note to his letters at a later date when he was preparing the letters for publication.

27 Col. Augustus C. Hamlin, Eleventh Corps historian and author of *Eleventh Corps:*

of the mass of troops coming to the rear as we went to the front belonged to the 11th Corps, the greater part of them being members of other corps. Also, that the General and body of officers and men I opened upon in the evening was General A. P. Hill,[28] staff and escort, that Stonewall Jackson fell farther to the rear and was shot by a North Carolina regiment. Hill was wounded by my fire upon him.

Office, Chief of Artillery
2 Division, 3 Corps
Falmouth, Va.
May 14, 1863

[To A. C. O.] I do not need now to comment further on the late expedition. The failure is apparent to everyone, yet I do not think it as bad as represented at the north. The defeat at Chancellorsville was bad enough but not so bad as Fredericksburg.

I do not think the Army can move again soon. The terms of service of the two years and the nine months men are expiring, and many are going out of service. Just now the Army is decreasing in numbers.[29] I still have confidence in General Hooker and hope the President will retain him, at all events sufficiently long to give him another opportunity to show his skill and ability as a commander.

Office, Chief of Artillery
2 Division, 3 Corps
Falmouth, Va.
May 17, 1863

[To S. C. O.] I have written A. C. quite at length of the part I took in the battle of Chancellorsville, and if you think it worthwhile you can send to him for that letter. I have not the time to write it again.

On General Sickles' front both armies fought to the full extent of their ability. The almost hand-to-hand contest lasted from daylight till about nine o'clock. The ground upon which most of the fighting took place had less than a half mile front. The enemy made the attack and then by rapidly reinforcing their line with fresh troops bore back

---

The Battle of Chancellorsville, an authority on Chancellorsville and a leading source for John Bigelow.

28 Osborn admits his mistake.
29 Most of the two year enlistments had expired.

our line which was not reinforced at all. By this method of fighting, they lost more men than we but at the same time they won the battle. Excepting General Sedgwick's force in and near Fredericksburg, only one and a half of our corps did any fighting worth speaking of.[30] In forcing us back, the enemy became much exhausted, and why General Hooker did not take advantage of this fact is more than I can tell. It is a mystery and I presume will remain so. I have great confidence in him, but he certainly failed in this great battle to take advantage of all the opportunities which were open to him.

While the battle was progressing, the General was severely hurt by a solid shot striking a pillar of the Chancellorsville House against which he was leaning. He was unconscious from the effects of the blow for a half hour, and it is not unlikely he was seriously affected by it all day. I am inclined to think the battle was lost by reason of this accident. I have the utmost confidence in his ability, and aside from the great misfortune to the country I regret the loss of the battle on his own account.[31]

My old battery did splendidly and has by its service richly repaid the country for all it has cost. Winslow is a splendid officer and in this battle did remarkably well.

The Army is now precisely where it was before the battle and with a present prospect of remaining some time. The nine month men and two years' regiments are now going home, and I regret that far too many of them are going for the good of the Army. We shall continue to be strong enough to resist any attack but I think not strong enough for a good while to move against the enemy.

I very much regret the death of General Berry. He was a good soldier, a good man, and a good friend. The division could but illy spare him.

The 35th New York Infantry goes home this week.[32] It is a two years' regiment and their term of service has expired. Any of the officers or men will be glad to tell you about us.

---

30 The First, Second, and Fifth Corps were not heavily engaged.
31 Osborn is charitable and slow to criticize his earlier longtime division commander.
32 The Thirty-fifth New York Regiment of Maj. Gen. Abner Doubleday's First Corps Division were from Jefferson County, NY. Their two year enlistments had expired.

Office, Chief of Artillery
2 Division, 3 Corps
Falmouth, Va.
May 18, 1863

[To A. C. O.] In reply to your questions. Considering the number of troops actually engaged, which was but a small section of the Army, the battle of Chancellorsville was the most persistently fought and most destructive open field fight which has yet occurred between these two armies or sections of them. The front over which the severe fighting actually took place was not more than a half mile. Of course, the troops covered more ground, but I speak of that portion of the field where the desperate fighting of the morning of the 3rd occurred and on which the battle to us was lost and by the enemy won.

The battle lasted from daylight until about nine in the morning. Nearly all of this time the lines were within a few yards of each other and at times actually came together and intermingled. From the position I occupied, nearly all of the time the lines of battle were in plain view and the bullets about me were lively.

We have every prospect of being here for some time. We are now occupying precisely the same ground and camps we occupied before we went to Chancellorsville, and indeed before the battle of Fredericksburg.

Office, Chief of Artillery
2 Division, 3 Corps
Falmouth, Va.
May 27, 1863

[To S. C. O.] I have been commissioned as Major[33] of my own regiment and mustered in that grade. Winslow has been commissioned and mustered as Captain and is in every way worthy of the place. This separates me permanently from the battery with which I have done so much service.

We are still quiet and so far as I can see shall continue to be for some time.

I am assigned to the command of a brigade of artillery in the Artillery Reserve of the Army.[34] I shall go to that command as soon as I can turn over the command here.

---

33 Thanks to Col. Wainwright, Osborn finally received his promotion to Major.
34 This assignment was of short duration.

Headquarters, 2 Brigade
Volunteer Division, Artillery Reserve
Near Falmouth, Va.
May 30, 1863

[To A. C. O.] I have been mustered as Major of the 1st New York Light Artillery and have been assigned to the command of the 2nd Brigade of the Volunteer Division of the Artillery Reserve, Army of the Potomac. I have now seven batteries, 5th, 15th, 29th, 30th, 32nd New York Independent, and B and M First Connecticut Artillery. The two Connecticut batteries have 32-pounder guns. The 5th, 15th, 30th, 32nd New York Independent have 20-pounder Parrott guns, and the 29th New York Independent has 3-inch regulation rifle guns. This gives me all the siege guns of the Army of the Potomac. I am not over-pleased with this command. Several of the batteries are German and indifferent. I would prefer light batteries and it is not unlikely the command will be considerably changed this evening, that is, a part of the batteries I have will be taken from this brigade and others assigned to it. The name and designation of the brigade will not be changed.

There is a wonderful lack of grade and rank in the artillery service of the Army and more especially so with the Light Artillery.[35] With the grade of Major I now command a brigade of artillery. I am entitled to a full brigade staff and will soon have it. A corresponding command of infantry, with no more men and not a fourth of the responsibility or a hundredth part of the value of materiel to look after, is commanded by a Brigadier General. Still this is held to be the aristocratic arm of the service, quite as much or even more so than the cavalry.

I am only fairly getting into my work here. In a few days I shall know myself and my command better.

The exact figures, as given to us from Headquarters, of the losses at Chancellorsvllle are killed and wounded, 8,200 men and missing, 4,700, total 12,900.[36]

There was an incident connected with the battle which I do not think has been made public to any great extent in the country but for what reason I do not know. While the fighting was going on and early in the morning of the 3rd, General Hooker stood leaning against one of the pillars in the front of the Chancellorsville House, at which he had

---

35 Gen. Hunt frequently voiced this complaint.
36 The casualty count according to Livermore, T. (1900) *Numbers and Losses in the Civil War in America 1861-65*. Boston & New York. Union: 1,575 killed; 9,594 wounded; 5,676 missing. Confederate: 1,665 killed; 9,081 wounded; 2,018 missing.

made his headquarters. A solid shot struck the pillar and a splinter from it hit General Hooker knocking him down and senseless. This the officers who were with him report. One of my officers saw him a few minutes after he was hit lying upon a stretcher. An hour later I saw him and spoke to him. And at that time he did not appear to have fully recovered.

As to the report which has been published that he was intoxicated, I do not believe it or that there was any approach to such a condition. Certainly when I talked with him, there was nothing of the kind noticeable, and all officers who were with him or saw him during the day say that he was perfectly sober and free from the influence of liquor.[37]

Headquarters, 2 Brigade
Volunteer Division, Artillery Reserve
Near Falmouth, Va.
June 3, 1863

[To A. C. O.] I have said before I thought we would remain here this summer, and I see nothing yet to change this opinion. The enemy are known to be active, and I hear it frequently said we shall have them to fight on this side of the river soon. I do not think so as while we are weaker than we were at the time of Chancellorsville we are yet too strong for such a movement to be made by General Lee.

The Artillery Reserve of the Army is being reorganized as a corps under the command of General O. H. [R. O.] Tyler.[38] It is still in a state of most glorious confusion. The batteries as such are well enough but are poorly commanded by field officers or in its field organization. I will put my brigade in perfect condition if my superiors will permit me to carry out my own views. My adjutant general's department is now better organized than that of any one of the brigades, divisions, or the corps.

---

37 Osborn as an eyewitness would seem to be a reliable reporter.
38 Brig. Gen. Robert O. Tyler.

CHANCELLORSVILLE 143

*Headquarters
Artillery Brigade, 11 Corps
Stafford Court House, Va.
June 11, 1863*

[To S. C. O.] A few days ago I sent you a copy of a special order by which I was assigned to the command of the artillery brigade of the 11th Corps. I have been on duty with it since last Thursday[39]

You will recollect it was this corps which first broke at Chancellorsville. I am told I have been highly complimented in being assigned to this corps to reorganize its artillery, but to me it is an unpleasant job. I found the batteries in a most deplorable condition and in a state of complete demoralization. So far, I have been in the saddle the most of everyday and taxing my ingenuity to determine how best to make the batteries serviceable again. So far, I am succeeding well, but there is much to do yet. I left the best artillery in the Army when I left the 3rd Corps, and when I came here I took the worst. If we lie still two or three months, I can put it in good shape. If we move soon, I do not see how it can be done. The officers are willing but have never been subject to any discipline or military supervision whatever. All their military habits are excessively loose. I will do my best to bring these batteries up to a good standard of efficiency.

*Headquarters
Artillery Brigade, 11 Corps
Stafford Court House, Va.
June 11, 1863*

[To A. C. O.] My last letter to you was written from the Artillery Reserve of the Army. Thursday morning of last week I was ordered to report to General Howard,[40] commanding the 11th Corps, as his Chief of Artillery. I soon found I had been assigned to perform a difficult task. The artillery of this corps has been known throughout the Army as the worst in the Army. I am told that my assignment here was a compliment. General Tyler remonstrated against the order transferring me from the Artillery Reserve, but General Hunt said he considered me equal to the work required and I must go. He said the batteries were worthless, and a disciplinarian and industrious officer was required. So I am here.

39 Osborn assumed his new command on June 3, 1863.
40 Maj. Gen. Oliver O. Howard.

I have nowhere seen anything to be compared to these batteries with the exception perhaps of Captain Dilger's battery.[41] They have scarcely a resemblance to light batteries. Generals Hooker, Hunt, and Howard have each assured me that I should have everything I wished to re-equip and get them into serviceable order. I have confidence in my ability to bring them out so, providing the Army lies still a considerable time, as it will require quiet to accomplish much with and for them. These batteries have evidently never had a commander, that is, an officer who exercised any control over them.

The first thing I did was to ride through the camps and look over the debris of what should be and once was light batteries—the next, to quietly but firmly let the captains know I commanded the artillery of this corps. A part of them were willing to accept the situation and a part of them were not. I very soon stopped all foolishness by informing those who developed a disposition to be fractious that a disobedience of military orders would not be overlooked. One battery I have broken up and sent the men to Washington. The others I have inspected and had nearly every part of their materiel condemned even going so far as to condemn the clothing the men had on. I have directed the officers of each battery to make requisition for a new outfit in place of materiel condemned. I have ordered them to change their camps to get them out of the reach of the refuse of the old camps. In every step I have taken, I have directed the officers to comply strictly with the requirements of the artillery tactics. I have ordered them to drill certain hours of the day, and most assuredly they needed it. I have established my brigade headquarters in the immediate vicinity of the batteries and have organized a brigade staff. Indeed, I have undertaken a complete and thorough reorganization of these batteries. I think by close attention and constant watching I can soon get them into fair condition and fit for the field. They are not so now.

Our cavalry crossed the Rappahannock River last Friday and are reported to have had a severe engagement,[42] but I know little about it. The cavalry movement is said to have called General Lee's Army back this way after it had gone towards Western Virginia.

---

41 Capt. Hubert Dilger proved to be a premier artillery officer, one of the Union's finest.
42 Brandy Station, June 9, 1863.

CHANCELLORSVILLE   145

*Headquarters
Artillery Brigade, 11 Corps
Centerville, Va.
June 16, 1863*

[To A. C. O.] We left our camp at Stafford Court House between three and four o'clock on the 12th inst. and marched 13 miles. The next day we made Catlett's Station 20 miles, next day Centerville 20 miles, and tomorrow move again. I think now we are going towards Harpers Ferry. The Army now is all here. You know as much of the enemy as I do.

*Headquarters
Artillery Brigade, 11 Corps
Middletown, Md.
June 27, 1863*

[To A. C. O.] We reached here last evening, and as we are in the advance we may be here all day for the Army to close up. On the 25th this corps marched 27 miles. The enemy is reported to have left Boonsboro 12 miles from here yesterday going north. The citizens estimate the force all the way from 20,000 to 60,000 men.

General Hooker's headquarters will reach here today. I have no idea how long we are to remain here but probably only a day or two.

You ask me about the brigading of the artillery. After the battle of Chancellorsville, General Hooker ordered a reorganization of the artillery.[43] Each Army corps was allowed a brigade of five batteries with a brigade staff and organization. Any surplus batteries beyond this allowance to the corps were sent to the Artillery Reserve of the Army, there to be organized into brigades of seven batteries each and then into divisions of two brigades each—Brigadier General Tyler to command the Artillery Reserve; the volunteer division, to which I belonged, to be commanded by Major Tompkins of the Rhode Island Artillery,[44] who ranks me by more than a year.

I have learned since I came here that after I had taken command of the brigade in the Artillery Reserve that General Howard applied to General Hooker for an artillery officer who could fit his batteries for

---

43 After being denied an active role at Chancellorsville, Hunt was finally given the reorganization plan he had urged upon Hooker since late January.

44 Maj. John A. Tompkins.

the field. They were by his own representations very bad. After some hesitation General Hooker transferred me. I knew nothing of all this until I received the order assigning me as Chief of Artillery of the 11th Corps.

We are now in sight of the battlefield of South Mountain.[45] I never saw a more beautiful country. It is finely cultivated.

*Headquarters
Artillery Brigade, 11 Corps
Gettysburg, Pa.
July 3, 1863*

[To S. C. O.] We have been fighting three days. This has been the severest[46] battle of the war.

N.B.[47] This letter was on a slip of brown wrapping paper one inch by two and was the only letter I wrote about the battle in which I took the most prominent part of any during the war.

*Headquarters
Artillery Brigade, 11 Corps
Middletown, Md.
July 8, 1863*

[To A. C. O.] All looks favorable. I think we shall be engaged again this afternoon and probably tomorrow.[48] My command fights well.

---

45 The scene of the fighting at South Mountain that preceded Antietam on September 17, 1862.
46 Osborn's two sentence report of Gettysburg. Some 20 years later, he penned a fuller account, titled, "Experiences at Gettysburg." His account was published in 1991 as, *The Eleventh Corps Artillery at Gettysburg: The Papers of Major Thomas Ward Osborn*, edited by Herb S. Crumb.
47 Osborn apparently added this note to his letters at a later date when he was preparing the letters for publication.
48 Maj. Gen. George B. Meade is in cautious pursuit of Gen. Lee's army, his retreat stalled at Williamsport by the rising waters of the Potomac.

CHANCELLORSVILLE

*Headquarters
Artillery Brigade, 11 Corps
New Baltimore, Va.
July 24, 1863*

[To S. C. O.] Our rapid movements for the last six weeks have made many and singular changes for us. Indeed, it has been a lifetime done up in a few days. We are now nearly halfway from the field of Gettysburg to Richmond, but whether we are to stop in this neighborhood or push on further south I do not know. I shall not be surprised in either event. The Army is very much worn, and the drafted men will soon begin to arrive. When they do, we shall need quiet to make soldiers of them; perhaps, however, the enemy will not be willing we should take a rest for this purpose, but nothing is to be feared if the enemy will attack us. Some of our Generals think it will be the plan of General Meade to move forward and attack General Lee before he has time to recuperate his Army. This Army, although it is tired and worn, never was in better condition for fighting than it is now.

For the last two months the tide has set heavily against the enemy and they cannot forever hold out. In my opinion, the last month has been the beginning of the end. Of late, the larger successes have all been on our side, Gettysburg, Vicksburg, and Port Hudson.[49]

Since the 13th of June, this Army has marched more than 300 miles, fought three days at Gettysburg and many smaller battles dependent on the main one at Gettysburg.

This valley is a very fine country and formerly was well cultivated. No able-bodied men are to be found here at present. The crops sown in the spring will not be harvested, and the meadows which are very fine have not been mowed and now will not be. The Negroes are all gone, either sent south or escaped to the north.

The only possible termination of this war is to destroy the armies of the Confederacy. The south will not stop fighting and the north cannot.[50] Whenever their armies shall be destroyed, the war will close and not till then. The able-bodied men of the south have already all been absorbed, and from this time forward a man lost to them is lost permanently. His place cannot be filled.

---

49 Port Hudson surrendered on July 9th following the fall of Vicksburg on July 4th.
50 Another accurate forecast by Osborn.

*Headquarters
Artillery Brigade, 11 Corps
New Baltimore, Va.
July 24, 1863*

[To A. C. O.] We crossed the Potomac at Berlin on our way to Warrentown, and we are now six miles south of that place. The Army is all about here. Whether we are to remain here for some days or to go on in the morning, we are not informed. Since crossing the Potomac, Mosby's men[51] have been following us in considerable numbers but only in squads of two or three together. If one of our men falls out or behind, he is picked up; if a team stops or gets out of the column, it is picked up; but if five or six mounted men go out and remain together, they are not disturbed. If a straggler gets off a few hundred yards from the column, he is taken charge of by Mosby's people. Major Howard,[52] brother and aide to the General, was captured yesterday while carrying dispatches to the headquarters of the Army.

I am told the Army has been reinforced up to its numbers before the battle. I think we have now made the first serious impressions on the enemy's Army. I do not believe that hereafter they can recruit men as fast as they will lose them.

This is a beautiful country but it is temporarily ruined. It has been denuded of everything except a few women.

*Headquarters
Artillery Brigade, 11 Corps
Manassas Junction, Va.
July 28, 1863*

[To A. C. O.] Everyday we are led more and more to believe that in the late campaign General Lee lost from 30 to 40 percent of his Army.[53] The troops engaged on both sides were veterans. The fighting was severe on both sides and the losses very heavy.

---

51 John Singleton Mosby, leader of the Confederate Partisan Rangers in Northern Virginia.
52 Maj., later Col., C. H. Howard.
53 Livermore, *op. cit.*, sets Confederate Gettysburg casualties at 28,063 out of an effective force of 75,054.

CHANCELLORSVILLE 149

The papers today tell us that the city of Jackson, Mississippi, has been taken and that General Morgan[54] has been captured. These are certainly bright spots after we have been so long and so persistently beaten.

The enemy's method of fighting has in a great measure been their ruin. They have fought for success on the field and have gained most of their successes through a great sacrifice of men. I do not think I have been in a single engagement, except at Savage Station and Fredericksburg, where the enemy's losses in men have not been greater than ours. At Savage Station the method of fighting was reversed, and we lost the majority of men and at the same time gained the battle. The battle at Fredericksburg was on our part an act of concentrated folly by the commander. It was a killing time of our own men. In some of the battles I have been in, the enemy's force at the point of attack could not have been less than two to our one and in others three to our one. Their plan of massing men at the point of attack results in a fearful loss of men even while it results in success on the field. By thus exposing their men, they have won many victories, but the loss has been greater than they could bear and from this time forward will tell heavily on them by continually reducing the fighting strength of their Army.

---

54 Brig. Gen. John Hunt Morgan was captured at Salineville, Ohio, on July 26, 1863.

Appendix A

Forward Observer

The Civil War battery Commander, unlike his Twentieth Century counterpart, had no bombproof shelter. His command post was with his battery, more often than not in an open field and exposed to enemy rifle and artillery fire. He and his section chiefs served as the battery's forward observers without benefit of range finder, radar, or other modern remote fire control devices. He often sighted the guns making azimuth and elevation adjustments to correct the direction and range of battery fire. Because of the limited range of Civil War artillery, targets were usually visible and direct fire the rule. Chancellorsville and Gettysburg were notable exceptions when Union gunners fired over their own troops at invisible targets. The Commander and his lieutenants usually selected the targets. The battery's mobility and survival depended upon its horses, and the Commander had to be ever vigilant to protect them from enemy rifle fire. Because of the short range of the guns, a battery could not hold its position long without the close-up support and protection of its infantry. The position of Battery Commander required a leader who remained cool and clear-headed under fire, who could make split-second decisions, and who possessed the personal courage to lead by example in order to maintain control of his battery under the most adverse conditions.

Thomas Ward Osborn's career as Union Battery Commander in the field with the Army of the Potomac from March 1862 through May 1863 involved all of these duties. In every sense he seemed to embody those characteristics demanded of a Battery Commander as forward observer.

Appendix B

[Excerpt from the] *Report of Lieut. George B. Winslow, Battery D, First New York Light Artillery.* [From the *OR.*, Series 1, Vol. 25, Part 1, Chapter 37, p. 487.]

Hdqs. Battery D, First New York Artillery,
May 8, 1863.

About the middle of the afternoon of the 2d instant, there was heavy firing in front of General Hooker's headquarters, and we moved by orders rapidly forward. Soon after arriving at the front, the firing ceased, and we again returned to our position in the rear. The horses were then unharnessed, and were being watered, when very heavy firing of artillery and infantry opened upon our right and front. The battery was immediately harnessed, and again moved with the utmost rapidity to the front. As we neared General Hooker's headquarters at Chancellorsville, the shot and shell from the enemy's guns fell thick and fast around us, causing no little haste and confusion among the supply teams then moving to the rear. The road was soon cleared, however, by General Patrick, and the battery moved on, turning at Chancellorsville to the right down the Fredericksburg and Gordonsville Plank road. Here an indescribable scene of confusion and disorder presented itself. Our way was literally blocked with the artillery and infantry of the Eleventh Army Corps, who were flying to the rear apparently in the utmost terror, begging in many instances by word and gesture that nothing might impede their cowardly and disgraceful flight. To turn them out of the way, much less back, was impossible, and some time elapsed before we could advance, and then only by turning into the field to the left of the road. A section of Battery H, First U.S. Artillery, then in front of me, advanced to the foot of the hill near our line of battle. I passed the remaining four guns, and placed my battery in the first eligible position I could find, which was upon the brow of the hill some 500 or 600 yards in rear of our advance line, my right resting upon the Plank road. The position, as the battle developed, proved an admirable one.

The enemy opened upon us from a battery in the road on the hill less than 1,000 yards in front. I immediately brought my guns to bear upon the enemy's, using solid shot, and after a few rounds succeeded in silencing them for a time. One man was killed and 1 severely wounded at my right gun just as they were in the act of firing the first round. Soon after, four guns of the First U.S. Artillery (Battery H) came into position in the road on my right, and Best's and other batteries on my left. By this time, night had come upon us, but a cloudless sky and a bright moon enabled us to sight our guns with a considerable degree of accuracy.

I am, Captain, very respectfully, your obedient servant,

GEO. B. WINSLOW
First Lieut. First New York Artillery, COMDG. Battery D.

Capt. Thomas W. Osborn
Chief of Artillery, Second Div., Third Army Corps.

Appendix C

Report of Capt. Thomas W. Osborn, First New York Light Artillery, Chief of Artillery.[From the *OR*, Series I, Vol. 25, Part 1, Chapter 37, Pp. 482-486.]

Office of Chief of Artillery,
May 8, 1863.

Major: I have the honor to report the movements of the light batteries of the division—Company K, Fourth U.S. Artillery, light 12-pounder guns, commanded by First Lieut. F. W. Seeley; Company H, First U.S. Artillery, light 12-pounder guns, commanded by First Lieut. J. E. Dimick [Dimmick]; Company D, First New York Artillery, light 12-pounder guns, commanded by First Lieut. George B. Winslow, and Company B., First New Jersey Artillery, 10-pounder Parrott guns, commanded by Capt. A. Judson Clark—between April 29 and May 5.

On the 29th ultimo, at 2 p.m., I received orders from Major General Berry to move the batteries, with the infantry, to near the bank of the Rappahannock, and about midway between the crossings of Sedgwick's and Reynolds' corps.

We rested for the night at 11 o'clock, and at sunrise of the 30th reported, by orders, to General Newton on the bank of the river. I posted the batteries to sweep the plain on the south bank, but at 3 p.m. I was ordered to move with the corps to the United States Ford. At midnight, we halted a mile south of Hartwood Church, and in the morning crossed the river.

At 12 m. of the 29th, Captain Clark's battery was transferred to the First Division of this corps, and the Fourth New York Independent Battery to this. I regret this change very much; it was a rifled battery, and splendid in its officers, men, and all its equipments. It has been my especial delight to assist it and to make it perfect for the field, and the effort has not been in vain.

At 3 p.m. the division was ordered to the front about 3 miles, with the exception of General Mott's brigade and Seeley's battery, which were left at the ford. Brisk skirmishing was going on at the front; at night we rested near the white house.

The morning of May 2 brought a day filled with the variable incidents nearly always attendant on the immediate proximity of contending armies on the eve of battle—the small but vigorous attacks of each on the other's lines, to learn the points of strength and weakness. At 4 p.m. we realized a heavy attack was being made on the left, and the varying direction of the sound showed us too plainly our forces were giving way. The division was soon ordered to the front, the batteries following the order of Dimick [Dimmick], Winslow, and the Fourth New York Independent Battery. As we passed General Hooker's headquarters, a scene burst upon us which, God grant, may never again be seen in the Federal Army of the United States. The Eleventh Corps had been routed, and were fleeing to the river like scared sheep. The men and artillery filled the roads, its sides, and the skirts of the field, and it appeared that no two of one company could be found together. Aghast and terror-stricken, heads bare and panting for breath, they pleaded like infants at the mother's breast that we would let them pass to the rear unhindered. The troops in the old division, unwavering, and the artillery, reckless of life or limb, passed through this disorganized mass of men. Reaching the crest of the hill, I left the batteries of Dimick [Dimmick] and Winslow on the brow, taking position perpendicular to the road, Dimick [Dimmick] taking the right, excepting one section of Dimick's [Dimmick's] battery, which I took about 400 yards to the front, on a line with the front of the woods, and only a few yards in the rear of our line of battle.

At this time (a little after sunset), a rebel battery opened fire on the batteries on the brow of the hill, and less than 1,000 yards from them. Winslow and Mason, in command of two sections of Dimick's [Dimmick's] battery, accepted the challenge, and almost immediately silenced them.

All was now quiet, excepting that we could constantly hear the enemy, from 300 to 1,000 yards in our front, massing their troops and moving their artillery. It was now evident that their force was large, as the swearing of officers and giving orders sounded like the chattering of a multitude. This continued until 9.30 o'clock, during which time several commissioned officers rode within our lines of pickets and were captured. At this time, I distinctly saw the head of a column moving down the road, it being a beautiful moonlight night. The column seemed to cover the entire breadth of the road, and moved very cautiously until within 150 yards of us, when it began to deploy in line of battle. At this moment, I directed Lieutenant Dimick [Dimmick] to open with canister, clearing the road almost instantly. The batteries on the crest opened, at the signal, upon the road beyond, and, taking the reports of prisoners as reliable, the havoc in their ranks was fearful.

This same movement of the enemy occurred again at 10.30 and at 12 midnight, excepting he did not move his forces upon the open road, but in the woods, and the challenge to open fire was given by the enemy's infantry against our own, but the results were each time the same, the enemy being at each assault repulsed. He used his artillery considerably, but to no great effect, only wounding a few artillerymen and killing a few horses. The practice of the artillery this evening was the most splendid I ever saw. The lines of battle at several times became closely engaged, but the batteries on the crest varied their elevation most admirably, keeping precisely the time of fuse required and the exact elevation necessary to strike the rebel line of battle, and I have yet to learn that one Federal soldier was struck by one of our shots or a premature explosion of a shell; yet we repeatedly tore the rebel lines to fragments, and assisted our gallant infantry to drive them, shattered, to the rear. The artillery fire of the evening, although perhaps not quite so heavy as at the world-renowned battle of Malvern Hill, I consider far more perfect in time and accuracy. During the firing of this evening, the rifled guns of the Fourth New York Independent Battery, although stationed at some little distance to the rear of the 12-pounder batteries, did excellent service, and assisted in driving the enemy back. Two batteries of the Twelfth Corps were on the left of Winslow's battery, commanded by Captain Best, as chief, but their position was inferior to our own, yet doubtless they did good service. These batteries remained in this position during the next day's engagement.

At 2 a.m. Seeley's battery reached the field, with General Mott's brigade, from the ford.

At 3 a.m. the Fourth New York was ordered to the rear by an aide-de-camp of General Hooker, and I regret to say that, though we needed it much through the day, the order carried it beyond my reach and beyond the battle-field.

During the night, Captain [Charles W.] Squier, chief engineer of General Berry's staff, threw up small works in front of the guns, which were of great benefit during the engagement of the following day.

At 5 o'clock in the morning, the enemy attacked us in force, and, after a very severe fight by our men, the Federal line began to fall back. From the first moment I learned the position of the enemy, I played upon him with the artillery, the section in the road using a very short fuse and canister as the enemy moved to and fro. In the movement of this section, securing and defending the front of our line from the persistent attacks of the enemy, notwithstanding its own exposed condition, and under a most galling fire from the rebel sharpshooters and line of battle, Lieutenant Dimick [Dimmick] showed the skill and judgment of an accomplished artillery officer and the intrepid bravery of the truest soldier. After holding this position for upward of an hour, his men fighting bravely, but falling rapidly around him (his horse being shot under him), and our infantry crowding back until his flanks were exposed, I gave him the order to limber and fall back. In doing this his horses became entangled in the harness, and in freeing them he received a shot in the foot. This wound he hid from his men, but in a moment received one in the spine, and from the effects of it died in two days after. I would, if possible, here pay a slight tribute to his memory, but I cannot. He was an educated and accomplished officer, just budding into the full vigor of manhood. As a line officer he has shown fine abilities, and on the battle-field was unsurpassed for gallantry. Lieutenant Sanderson, before and after the fall of Lieutenant Dimick [Dimmick], conducted himself with great courage, judgment, and decision.

The division artillery was now confined entirely to the brow of the hill, but Seeley was to the left and in front of the Twelfth Corps batteries. Seeley took this position by order of General Hooker, and it being so far removed from the other batteries (about 600 yards), I could pay no personal attention to it; besides, I had unbounded confidence in his judgment and in his battery. The best report I can give will be the body of his report, which will be found below. The battle was now beginning with almost unparalleled fury, the enemy throwing his troops upon us in double and triple lines, and then in solid masses. The infantry of the division fought with stubborn desperation, and the contending forces surged backward and forward like two huge waves, mingling and unmingling as the one or the other gained a momentary advantage.

It was at this time that the artillery carried the most fearful havoc among the enemy's forces. The batteries of Winslow and Dimick [Dimmick] here bore the same part, and I can do no better in giving you a clear understanding of the part each bore in the engagements than to quote from Winslow's report. He says:[55]

To the part Lieutenant Seeley bore, I quote from his report. He says:[56]

During the heat of the battle, I perceived the firing of my guns began to slacken, and learning the ammunition was giving out, I applied immediately for another battery of Captain Randolph, chief of corps artillery, and though he gave me orders for Captain von Puttkammer's Eleventh New York Independent Battery, I could not get him to the front, and I was compelled to withdraw my guns, and thus caused the gallant old division to fall back before the rebel masses. I withdrew the batteries to the ammunition train, and in three hours they were ready for service again.

On the 4th, nothing of special interest transpired to the batteries.

On the 5th, we were ordered by General Hunt to recross the river, and to proceed to our present camp.

---

55 The tenth, eleventh and twelfth paragraphs of Winslow's report (No. 157, p. 486) here quoted.
56 The third and fourth paragraphs of Seeley's report (No. 158, p. 489) here quoted.

In refitting the batteries for whatever service they might be called to perform, I was compelled to resort to the unpleasant alternative of temporarily unhorsing the Fourth New York Independent Battery, Lieut. William T. McClean commanding, and putting it in position on the bluffs on the north side of the United States Ford. It has since been again placed on its original footing.

I am frank to say that I feel the utmost gratification at the management of the artillery by its immediate commanders, and the favorable results it produced on the battle. I can scarcely conceive it possible that more destruction could have been carried into our enemy's forces by three light batteries than was apparently by our own; how the firing could have been more accurate; the coolness and judgment which directed each battery; how the men could have been more heroic, noble, and true than all were; how commanders and subalterns could surpass these noble men.

The ammunition used by the division artillery was about 2,450 rounds. The loss of material was 94 horses, 2 empty caissons (by horses being killed), and 1 gun-carriage broken, but gun secured.

In officers and men we lost First Lieut. J. E. Dimick [Dimmick], Battery H, First U.S. Artillery, killed; Second Lieut. Isaac Arnold, Battery K, Fourth U.S. Artillery, wounded. Battery K, Fourth U.S. Artillery, 7 men killed and 37 wounded; Battery H, First U.S. Artillery, 2 men killed and 18 wounded, and Battery D, First New York Artillery, 2 men killed and 12 wounded.

Before closing, I wish to call the attention of the general commanding to the following officers as especially worthy of promotion, by brevet or otherwise, for their very gallant and meritorious conduct at the battle of Chancellorsville on the 2d and 3d instant: First Lieut. F. W. Seeley, Battery K, Fourth U.S. Artillery; First Lieut. George B. Winslow, Battery D, First New York Artillery, and Second Lieut. J. A. Sanderson, Battery H, First U.S. Artillery.

I am, major, very respectfully, your obedient servant,
THOS. WARD OSBORN,
Capt. and Chief of Artillery, 2d Div., 3d Army Corps.
Maj. Charles Hamlin
Asst. Adjt. Gen., Second Division, Third Army Corps.

Chapter 8

Chattanooga

... few battles ever fought have offered finer exhibitions of the charge of one army against another than did this.

Until his promotion to Major and his assignment to command of the Eleventh Corps Artillery on June 3, 1863, Osborn's letters record the history of Battery D. Even after Osborn's promotion to artillery chief of Berry's division, when George Winslow, now a captain, assumed command of the battery, Battery D had remained part of Osborn's greater command. Now they were to be permanently separated as Osborn assumed command of the Eleventh Corps Artillery. Both men served at Gettysburg in different corps, Winslow in the Wheatfield and Osborn on Cemetery Hill, almost a battlefield apart. Thereafter, Battery D became known as "Winslow's battery." Following his promotion Osborn had written S. C. O. on May 27th, "This separates me permanently from the battery with which I have done so much service." It was with mixed emotions and some regret that he left the men that he had known and had worked with for nearly 22 months.

Osborn's frequent letters to his brothers in the latter part of June record the movement of the Eleventh Corps to Gettysburg. He had written of his struggle to improve his new command and to turn them into first-class batteries within the brief period between Chancellorsville and Gettysburg, about a month—less time than he had thought necessary to accomplish the task.

Osborn wrote no lengthy accounts of his three days at Gettysburg. There were only two short notes between June 27th and July 24th. One of them, written on July 8th, simply states, "My command fights well." It would be some 20 years before he would leave a written record of those three days. He had written a short manuscript later found among his papers in the Colgate University Special Collections enti-

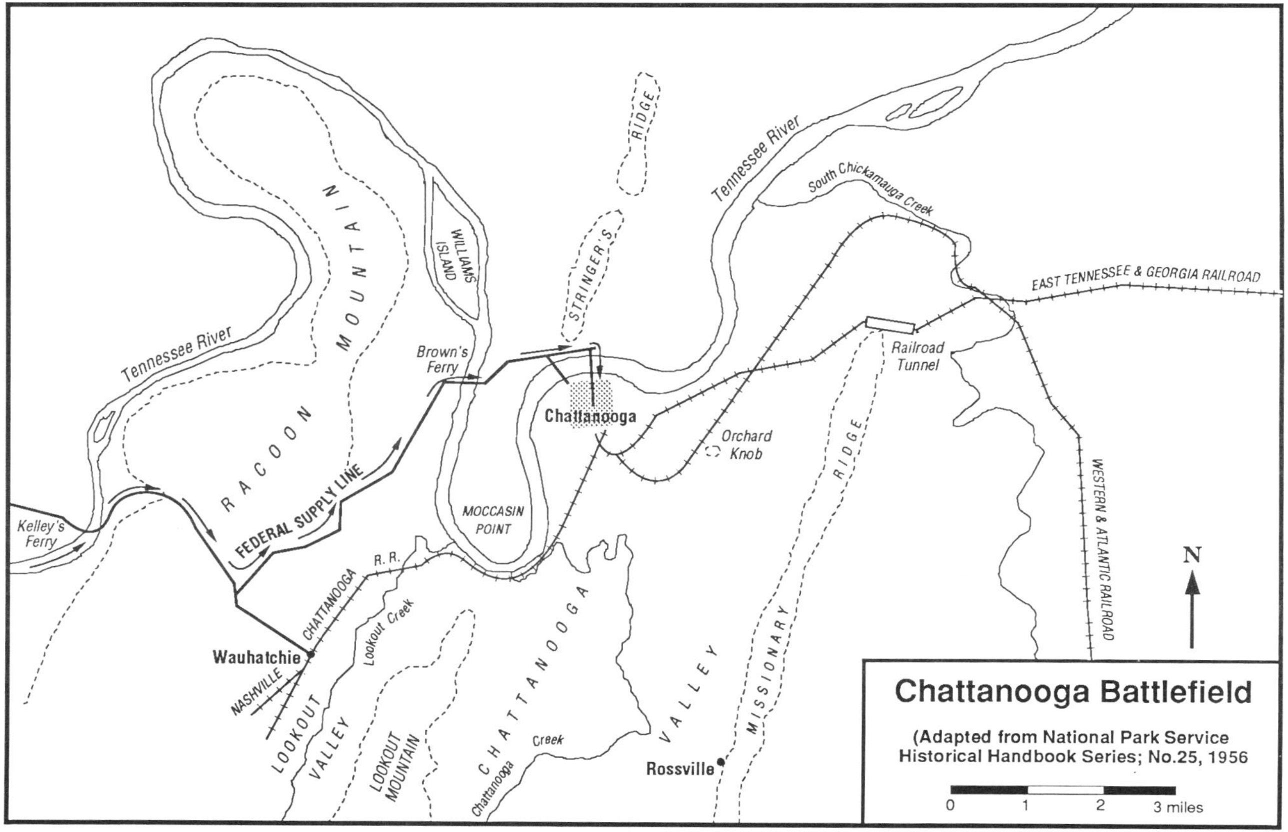

Chattanooga Battlefield
(Adapted from National Park Service
Historical Handbook Series; No.25, 1956
0
1
2
3 miles
N
Tennessee River
Kelley's Ferry
RACOON MOUNTAIN
FEDERAL SUPPLY LINE
WILLIAMS ISLAND
Brown's Ferry
STRINGER'S RIDGE
Chattanooga
MOCCASIN POINT
Wauhatchie
NASHVILLE
CHATTANOOGA
R. R.
Lookout Creek
LOOKOUT VALLEY
LOOKOUT MOUNTAIN
CHATTANOOGA VALLEY
Chattanooga Creek
Rossville
MISSIONARY RIDGE
Orchard Knob
Railroad Tunnel
South Chickamauga Creek
EAST TENNESSEE & GEORGIA RAILROAD
WESTERN & ATLANTIC RAILROAD

tled "Experiences at Gettysburg," which was published in 1991 as *The Eleventh Corps Artillery at Gettysburg.*

After Gettysburg, the Army of the Potomac followed Lee into Virginia and for two months the two armies quietly eyed each other during a peaceful interlude marred only by an occasional cavalry skirmish.

On September 25th, the Union Eleventh and Twelfth Corps departed by rail for the western theater in an effort to relieve General Rosecrans's Army of the Cumberland which, since its defeat at Chickamauga on September 21st and retreat to Chattanooga, had been bottled up there by Bragg's victorious Army. With its main supply routes by river and by rail having been cut, the Union Army was threatened with starvation and surrender. The Eleventh and Twelfth Corps arrived at Bridgeport, Alabama, on the Tennessee River in early October.

Hooker's command advanced east along the Tennessee River to Lookout Valley near Chattanooga in an effort to break the Confederate siege. On the night of October 28th-29th, the two corps turned back a Confederate attack at Wauhatchie. There would be no further Confederate interruption of the Union supply route into Chattanooga.

Osborn's Eleventh Corps batteries participated in the engagement at Wauhatchie and in the battle of Chattanooga as Grant's assault broke the Confederate siege of that city. Two of Osborn's batteries supported Hooker's attack on Lookout Mountain and one battery served with Howard as the Eleventh Corps supported Sherman's attack against the Confederate right flank. Osborn and two of his batteries were attached to Sheridan's division that formed the right wing of Thomas's Army of the Cumberland as it stormed up Missionary Ridge. As a member of Sheridan's staff, Osborn viewed the spectacular Union assault and accompanied Sheridan to the crest of the ridge. *The Editors*

Headquarters
Artillery Brigade, 11 Corps
Catlett's Station, Va.
August 9, 1863

[To S. C. O.] So far as we can see there is no prospect of the Army moving soon. The heat is so great that we are not anxious to be put on the march now. Still, the command is kept in readiness to move at any hour.

You speak of the hard things said about General Hooker. I think a large majority of the Army would have preferred to have had him remain in command. So far as the fighting qualities of the Army go, they would be the same under one commander as another. The troops are veterans and will fight when called upon to do so. But there is a vast difference when in battle, whether the commander is fully competent or not. I do not think the government gave General Hooker a fair trial. General Meade gained the Battle of Gettysburg by following the plan of the campaign perfected by General Hooker, but in addition the troops on the battlefield were well-handled.[1] Of course, General Meade gets the credit of this and as he was responsible he should have it.

But in regard to the profane expressions said to have been spoken by General Hooker, I have no idea he used them. To assert that he did so is, I think, both wrong and foolish. I wonder that people are so credulous as to believe every falsehood told about prominent public men[2] and especially the prominent generals. The General is not a religious man nor is he a fool. The latter would need to be assumed if it is believed he used the language accredited to him. In addition, he is not a drunkard nor can he rightly be called a dissipated man.

Among the wounded of my old battery at Gettysburg was Oren Munger. If he is home, say to your friends that he is an excellent soldier and a fine man and I will be gratified if he receives the attention due him as a good soldier and a brave one.

*Headquarters
Artillery Brigade, 11 Corps
Catlett's Station, Va.
August 20, 1863*

[To A. C. O.] There has been no change in the position of the Army but changes are going on in regard to some of the troops. Different brigades and divisions have been sent to Washington and then shipped on transports down the river. I do not know where they are to go but surmise somewhere on the Southern coast.[3]

---

1 Osborn is right. The superior performance of Meade's unit commanders, Maj. Gen. Winfield S. Hancock, *et al.*, on all three days contributed to the Union victory.
2 Osborn wonders about a constant characteristic of human nature.
3 On August 7th, Brig. Gen. Alexander Schimmelfennig's First Division of the Eleventh Corps departed for Charleston, SC. On August 16th, 10,000 Union troops, some from the Twelfth Corps, departed for New York City to deter possible rioting following resumption of conscription. The troops returned on September 12th.

To keep you up a little in the organization of the Army, I will go over it in brief. We have the 1st, 2nd, 3rd, 5th, 6th, 11th, 12th Corps and one corps of cavalry. Each corps has a brigade of Artillery. In addition, we have the Reserve Artillery which is not attached to any corps.

If General Lee has made no changes in the strength of his Army corresponding to those made in this, he could do us mischief now. If he should attack us, I think the Army would fall back to the defenses of Washington. I am inclined to think anyway it would be good military sense to do so even now, but from a political point of view it is probably best that the Army should stay here.

Headquarters
Artillery Brigade, 11 Corps
Catlett's Station, Va.
September 5, 1863

[To S. C. O.] Everything goes on here quietly as usual and so far as we can learn or see, there is no prospect of a movement. We were never more comfortably located. My own headquarters are a mile from the railroad station in the edge of a forest and very pleasant. I see the authorities of Madison University[4] have put my name at the head of the "Roll of Honor" of the college men who have gone into the service. I am a little surprised at this as I have not kept up close relations with the college, nor am I aware through what channels they have followed my course in the Army. However, it is very gratifying to be thus remembered and recognized.

Yesterday the Artillery of this corps was reviewed by several general officers and by General Hunt, Chief of Artillery of the Army, who pronounced it to be in better condition than it has been at any time since it entered the service. Certainly it has undergone a wonderful change for the better.

---

4 Osborn was a 1860 graduate of Madison University (now Colgate University) at Hamilton, NY.

CHATTANOOGA 163

*Headquarters
Artillery Brigade, 11 Corps
Catlett's Station, Va.
September 22, 1863*

[To A. C. O.] The main body of General Lee's Army has moved back to the bank of the Rapidan River. This corps is guarding the railroad from Bull Run to the Rappahannock River. We have entrenched here to some extent as a rallying point in case of a necessity suddenly arising.

*Headquarters
Artillery Brigade, 11 Corps
Catlett's Station, Va.
September 24, 1863*

[To S. C. O.] We are breaking camp and move in an hour to Alexandria. I understand the 11th and 12th Corps, under the command of General Hooker, are to go to the Army of the Cumberland. We are directly or indirectly to assist General Rosecrans. I do not regret making the change although for many reasons I dislike to leave this Army where all my service so far has been performed.

*Headquarters
Artillery Brigade, 11 Corps
Catlett's Station, Va.
September 24, 1863*

[To A. C. O.] In less than an hour we will leave for the Army of the Cumberland at Chattanooga.

*Nashville, Tenn.
October 8, 1863*

[To A. C. O.] I arrived here from Washington after a tedious journey of 12 days.[5] We reached here at midnight of Tuesday and find commu-

---

5 It is surprising that Osborn did not make further comment regarding the transfer

nication cut between here and Chattanooga. My batteries are at Bridgeport, Alabama, while my horses are all here. The infantry of the 11th and 12th Corps, under General Hooker, is at Bridgeport. I learn from the officers of the Quartermaster's and Commissary Departments that General Rosecrans' army is very short of rations and without forage. As soon as the railroad can be opened, it will be used solely for carrying supplies for the Army.

Nashville is under martial law and is a dirty and illy cared for city. So much of the Army as I have seen here is not in good condition and the discipline appears to be loose. Perhaps if a firmer hand were over the city and a stronger man in command, the first impressions would be better.

Nashville, Tenn.
October 10, 1863

[To A. C. O.] I have not yet been able to procure transportation for that portion of my command I have with me, but I hope to get it on the road tomorrow. I will go by rail while my command, some quartermasters, and animals with supplies will march down. The column will consist of 270 wagons, 69 ambulances, 1,500 extra horses, and one battery under the charge of my Adjutant General, Lieut. George W. Freeman and one of my Captains. The whole will have a guard of 1,800 infantry under the command of a Colonel. I had expected to go with them, but General Howard telegraphed me not to do so as the chances of capture by the enemy were excellent. Still, as a fact there is not much choice as it is but little less precarious in going on the railroad as it is broken at some point every day or two.

I am told at the headquarters of the Quartermaster's Department today that General Rosecrans' Army has already been a week without forage and the men on minimum rations. General Rosecrans has ordered that the railroad be permitted to carry nothing but infantry and supplies for the troops at the front.

---

by rail of the Eleventh and Twelfth Corps to Tennessee, which began with their departure on September 25th from Virginia, with the vanguard arriving five days later on September 30th at Bridgeport, AL, a trip of 1,157 miles. The significance of the event may have escaped Osborn since it took 12 days for the artillery to reach Nashville, a trip he described as "tedious."

*Headquarters
Artillery Brigade, 11 Corps
Bridgeport, Ala.
October 17, 1863*

[To A. C. O.] This is the southern terminus of the railroad now open and the nearest rail communication with General Thomas' army at Chattanooga. The 12th Corps is guarding the railroad from Murfreesboro to Stevenson and the 11th from Stevenson to this point, with one brigade six miles up the river.[6] There is no town here, but the railroad crosses the river at this place. The bridge has been destroyed but preparations are now being made to build a new one, which will be put up in a few days.

By wagon road Chattanooga is about 30 miles from here. On account of the mountainous character of the country, a very strong guard is necessary to keep the railroad north of us open. This duty has been placed upon General Hooker, and all the men who were doing this duty before our arrival have been relieved. Our Quartermaster of the 11th Corps, Colonel Le Duc, has built a sawmill and is now building a steamboat and several barges to supply the Army at Chattanooga when the river route shall be opened and made available.[7] But to accomplish this, the enemy will need to be driven from the bank of the river. Between Bridgeport and Chattanooga the mountains come to the river banks on both sides, and it will be no easy task to dislodge the enemy. Come what may, I do not think there is any intention of giving up Chattanooga.

---

6 Confederate cavalry attacks against the railroad continued to disrupt the Union supply line and made necessary the detachment of Maj. Gen. Alpheus Starkey Williams's division, Twelfth Corps, for guard duty.

7 Col. William G. Le Duc, Eleventh Corps Quartermaster supervised the construction and launching of a steamboat by mounting an engine, boiler, and sternwheel on a flat-bottomed scow for carrying and towing supplies to Kelley's Ferry, 45 miles upriver, the first link in what was dubbed the "Crackerline" to supply Union forces in Chattanooga. From Kelley's Ferry, supplies were transported by land across Raccoon Mountain to Brown's Ferry, crossing into Chattanooga. After 4,000 troops from Maj. Gen. George H. Thomas's corps, under the supervision of Grant's Chief Engineer, Maj. Gen. W. F. Smith, secured the crossing from a Confederate picket force, part of the force floated on pontoon boats downstream landing on the south bank where they overcame the Confederate pickets. The other Union force marched down the north bank with bridge-building materials. Following construction of the bridge, the 28 mile "Crackerline" from Bridgeport to Chattanooga functioned without interruption.

166 NO MIDDLE GROUND

I am informed from very high authority that the cause of the removal of Generals Rosecrans, McCook, and Crittenden was that they retired to Chattanooga before the close of the battle,[8] and that the enemy was completely defeated and unable to make another attack when General Thomas ceased fighting at Chickamauga.

The wagon train with which are a part of my men and horses is just now arriving from Nashville. It is now near evening. A part will get in tonight and the remainder in the morning.

Headquarters
Artillery Brigade, 11 Corps
Bridgeport, Ala.
October 20, 1863

[To S. C. O.] We have finally come to a halt at this place. It will be four weeks next Thursday since we left camp in Virginia. All this time we have been on the road or laying by in the most disagreeable places. I have seen all I could see in traveling through the country in the manner we have traveled. The conveniences were not first-class and the trip was slow and tedious. The country from Louisville here is a waste the same as in Virginia where the Armies have operated. The large towns are filled by a floating and most unsavory population which is kept under restraint by military patrols.

This is only a place in name but at present of considerable military importance. There was once a house and a sawmill here, but the house has been burned and the mill torn down. It is on the bank of the Tennessee River, which the Nashville and Chattanooga Railroad crosses at this point. The country is mountainous, and this is in fact a mountain pass. The enemy left strong fortifications here when they fell back to Chattanooga. A large Army could not be whipped here, but we are weak and if attacked, will have to fight for ourselves. Such a contingency would not be altogether unexpected.

The main body of our Army is at Chattanooga about 30 miles distant and we learn is suffering greatly for food. It is to be our work to open

---

8 Rosecrans's Union forces were defeated on September 19th-20th at Chickamauga. Rosecrans withdrew to Rossville, leaving Thomas and Maj. Gen. Gordon Granger to stem the Confederate advance at Snodgrass Hill. Rosecrans relieved Maj. Gen. Alexander McCook and Maj. Gen. Thomas Crittenden from command. Both were later exonerated following a court of inquiry. Rosecrans was removed from command on October 19th and transferred to the Department of Missouri.

the railroad and river to supply it. It is not the intention to abandon this country.

Much rain has fallen since we arrived here. The days are too hot and the nights too cold. Along the river the fogs are very dense and do not rise until nine o'clock in the morning.

I brought my command through in good shape. The horses are worn and several have died, but taken altogether, the men, horses, and materiel came through better than might have been expected. In two weeks I will have all in good shape again.

I see by the papers that the Army of the Potomac has fallen back to the neighborhood of Washington. I do not consider this of any serious importance. It is as well near Washington as where it was when we left it and it can be more easily supplied.

These two Corps, the 11th and 12th, are now incorporated in and are a part of the Army of the Cumberland.

Headquarters
Artillery Brigade, 11 Corps
Brown's Ferry, Tenn.
November 1, 1863

[To A. C. O.] We were two days in coming from Bridgeport and did some skirmishing on the way at midnight on the 28th ult. While we were camped at Wauhatchie in Lookout Valley, the enemy attacked us in our camps and we had a severe battle. The most of the 11th Corps and one division of the 12th Corps men were engaged. Our loss was 500 men. The fighting lasted nearly two hours. Among the killed was Captain Geary, son of General Geary,[9] commanding the [2nd] Division of the 12th Corps.

The main part of the attack was on that division. The enemy was repulsed and we held the ground and the camps we occupied when the attack was made. The prisoners we took report that they belong to General Lee's Army and General Longstreet's[10] command.

We have opened communication with General Thomas' Army at Chattanooga.[11] Supplies will be brought to the Army here at once.

---

9 Maj. Gen. John White Geary, Mexican War hero, first mayor of San Francisco, and Governor of the Kansas Territory, was later Governor of Pennsylvania.
10 Lieut. Gen. James Longstreet.
11 Maj. Gen. George H. Thomas replaced Rosecrans in command of the Army of the Cumberland.

Just now General Hooker's command is on quarter rations. The Army of the Cumberland at Chattanooga has been living on corn alone for several days, no other food. It will be fully supplied now.

Headquarters
Artillery Brigade, 11 Corps
Lookout Valley, Tenn.
November 5, 1863

[To S. C. O.] Since the little battle of the 29th, we have been quiet and have had no opportunity of gaining military glory by being shot.

When we left Bridgeport, we brought as little with us as would support us for three days. Unfortunately, we could get no supplies for seven or eight days and have been living on as small an allowance as mortal man could well stand up under. The train is now up, and we have sufficient for our needs. I hope we shall not be so caught again. It was expected we should have a good deal of fighting to do and it was not desirable to be bothered with large trains. We got the fight and starved too.

On the night of the 29th, the enemy attacked us in our camps here in the Valley, and a sharp battle ensued lasting two hours. The moon was shining brightly. We drove the enemy back and so won the day, or rather, won the night. Our loss all told in killed and wounded was about 500 men.[12] General Hooker gained considerable credit by this affair.

By this little campaign of 28 miles from Bridgeport here, we have opened the river and railroad for the supply of General Thomas' Army. Little steamers built by this corps at Bridgeport are now carrying rations and forage to Chattanooga. I assure you the men there needed them. That Army has been living several days on corn alone, and the horses have nearly all died for want of forage. The immediate wants of the Army are now supplied.

We are four miles from Chattanooga and directly under the face of Lookout Mountain. The guns on the summit are within easy range of our camps. The reputation this mountain has as a military stronghold or position is greater than its value to the enemy will warrant. It would be much better if it was but one-fifth as high as it is.

---

12 The principal loss was sustained by Gen. Geary's Second (White Star) Division at Wauhatchie.

This country is very mountainous and the valleys are little else than large ravines. The flat lands or rather agricultural lands, for the ground is very rolling even in the valleys, are not more than a half mile wide. Lookout Mountain on one side of us is 1,400 feet high and Raccoon Mountain on the other is 800 feet. It is a picturesque country and if we were pleasure seekers I should say it is beautiful.

We have taken several prisoners here and many deserters have come in from the enemy. All unite in saying the enemy is suffering badly for supplies and that the crops in the country have been good but are being rapidly exhausted in the support of the armies.

Headquarters
Artillery Brigade, 11 Corps
Lookout Valley, Tenn.
November 6, 1863

[To A. C. O.] General Sherman[13] with his Army is now on the Memphis and Charleston Railroad somewhere west of here. General Hooker was to open the railroad and river between Bridgeport and Chattanooga, which he has done. General Grant told General Howard that he has troops enough to whip General Bragg,[14] and as soon as he is ready he will concentrate and do so.[15] There should be no question now as to the result.

A few words about our movement from Bridgeport here. We moved from there on the 27th ult. with 9,000 or 10,000 men. I think I wrote you a less number was available, but I did not know then the 12th Corps was to furnish one division. The 11th Corps and General Geary's division of the 12th Corps moved together on the main road near the bank of the river and made this point in two days.[16] No effort was made to molest or turn Lookout Mountain. On the evening of the 28th we captured a cavalry outpost; on the evening of the 29th we drove a brigade of infantry from Lookout Valley and had a brisk skirmish in doing so. I employed two batteries. At night we camped in the valley and within the range of the guns on the crest of Lookout Mountain, 26 miles from Bridgeport and 4 from Chattanooga.

13 Maj. Gen. William T. Sherman.
14 Gen. Braxton Bragg.
15 Grant, on his way to Chattanooga, met with Gen. Howard.
16 Hooker's force moved to Wauhatchie by the road on the south bank of the Tennessee River.

Precisely at midnight, it being very light from the moon, the enemy attacked us, managing to thrust the head of their column between General Geary's division and the 11th Corps[17]—then at the same time attacked both ways. Some of our officers blame General Geary for permitting this movement, but whether justly so or not I do not know. I think not. Our troops fought well on both fronts of the enemy. The fight lasted a little more than two hours and was a clear success for us, the enemy being driven from the field and our camps held and but little damaged. Our killed and wounded amounted in round numbers to 500. A remarkable circumstance of this battle is the fact that our entire command is accounted for, not one man missing. The men are all here—well, wounded, or killed—so the enemy did not get one prisoner. We took 100 prisoners, all of whom report they are from the Army of Northern Virginia and belong to General Longstreet's corps.[18]

Lookout Mountain remains in the possession of the enemy. The firing from the summit is continuous day and night, but the elevation is so great the damage done is very slight. This battery on the mountain is 1,000 feet above us and the guns used are 20-pounder Parrotts. The shells, in falling, come down so nearly perpendicular that no rebounding is possible, and for this reason the damage from them is much lessened. They plunge into the ground and even if they explode, no damage from them is possible more than a few yards from where they fall.

Since our arrival here and the line of transportation opened, the condition of General Thomas' Army has been much improved. Still, I understand only half rations are issued. That Army suffered much from hunger before we arrived. When we left Bridgeport and on the march, our men were instructed to save their rations as it would be difficult to get more. This they did until at Brown's Ferry a part of them came in contact with some of General Thomas' men and heard their story, when everyone who had an opportunity gave away the last ounce of food he had and took the chances of getting more. The result was a good many of them were for several days very hungry.

General Grant said yesterday that General Sherman will be here within three or four days.

---

17 Brig. Gen. Micah Jenkin's division of Longstreet's corps attacked Hooker's men. Maj. Gen. John Bell Hood had commanded the division until his wounding at Chickamauga.

18 Longstreet's corps had been detached from Lee's army of Northern Virginia on September 9th. Three brigades arrived in time for the first day's fighting at Chickamauga on September 19th, and five brigades arrived on September 20th for the second day.

Last night my favorite saddle horse died. There was no apparent cause for it. He was in good flesh and well yesterday and this morning was dead. He was remarkable for his beauty and training. He was known and recognized everywhere in the Army where he had been used and was always spoken of by his name "Fred." He was the most thoroughly broken saddle horse and one of the most beautiful I have ever seen.

*Headquarters
Artillery Brigade, 11 Corps
Lookout Valley, Tenn.
November 19, 1863*

[To A. C. O.] This month the weather has been very fine and the roads are good.

From all I can gather the strength of the Army here is about this: General Sherman's force, now between here and Bridgeport, is about 30,000;[19] General Thomas in Chattanooga about 40,000; General Hooker in Lookout Valley about 10,000; a total force of about 80,000 men available for an engagement.[20]

The above was written this morning. This evening I am notified to be ready to move tomorrow. I get otherwise the following information. The battle will take place tomorrow or next day. General Hooker is to open the battle by an attack on the slope of Lookout Mountain between the river and the summit, engage the enemy, and if possible draw them this way. General Sherman's troops are moving past us now on their way to some point beyond Chattanooga precisely with the intention of getting on General Bragg's extreme right. It looks as though the principal attack would be there. General Thomas is still in Chattanooga, and in front of General Bragg's center against which he is to operate.

General Bragg's army lays in a semicircle around the city of Chattanooga, two to four miles from it. His left is on Lookout Mountain and the river, his right on Missionary Ridge and the river, and the main body of his army lies on the western slope of Missionary Ridge facing

---

19 Grant had ordered Sherman on September 22nd to come to Chattanooga from Mississippi. Sherman's force was less than Osborn's estimate, nearer 20,000.
20 In Grant, U. S. (1885) *Personal Memoirs of U. S. Grant.* New York, Vol. 2, p. 95, Grant estimated his force at 60,000.

the city. The line from the river above and around the city to the river below is unbroken and well fortified.[21]

General Grant called his principal generals together last night and had a talk with them, but what occurred I have not learned.

The slope of the mountain upon which we understand General Hooker is to make his attack is such that artillery can be made of little use.

There is a rumor here that General Burnside has attacked General Longstreet[22] but we have nothing positive in regard to it—nor have I learned from what source the rumor comes.

*Headquarters
Artillery Brigade, 11 Corps
Lookout Valley, Tenn.
November 21, 1863*

[To A. C. O.] We are having a severe storm and this afternoon I am confined to my tent on account of it.

Yesterday General Bragg sent in a flag of truce to General Grant to say "prudence would dictate the removal of all non-combatants from Chattanooga." General Grant replied, "no more flags of truce will be received until after Thursday of next week."[23]

The attack on Bragg's army was to have been made at daylight this morning, but night before last a light rain fell and made the roads slippery. General Sherman's command could not all be got up yesterday. It was to have been brought here by a forced march and the movement undertaken against the enemy at once. Last night I was notified the attack would be postponed until tomorrow morning. At dusk a heavy rain set in and continued all night and today until now. The ground is saturated and the roads are spoiled. It would hardly be possible to move a body of troops with their artillery at present.

I have a good deal of confidence in General Grant, and as long as this job has to be done, I am sorry there has been a delay. It might as well be done and over with as to wait longer. General Bragg may have

---

21 A strong position, but thinly held since Longstreet's departure on November 4th for Knoxville. Grant estimated the total Confederate force at 30,000, and Longstreet's corps numbered 15,000 men, *Ibid.*

22 An engagement between Longstreet and Burnside occurred at Campbell's Station near Knoxville on November 16th.

23 Grant interpreted Bragg's request as an effort to delay the Union attack until Longstreet's return from Knoxville after defeating Burnside.

been serious in sending in his flag of truce, and we may be seriously disturbed tomorrow morning by an advance from him. Undoubtedly, General Grant intends to precipitate matters here on General Burnside's account or before General Longstreet can be recalled to the assistance of the enemy here.

22nd, Sunday.

This letter laid over last night. We have orders now to move at half past one this afternoon to Chattanooga. An occasional gun is heard at General Bragg's extreme right, the point to which Sherman was moving. I do not think we shall be engaged before tomorrow morning. The weather is beautiful but the roads very muddy.

General Grant directs that I leave two batteries here with General Hooker, send one to General Sherman above Chattanooga, and take two to Chattanooga with General Howard.[24] The last I hear of General Hooker's work is that he will remain here with one division only to make a demonstration on this face of Lookout Mountain.

Headquarters
Artillery Brigade, 11 Corps
Lookout Valley, Tenn.
December 3, 1863

[To A. C. O.] The infantry and two batteries[25] of this corps have gone to Knoxville to the relief of General Burnside and to force General Longstreet to move north and out of East Tennessee. At Red Clay the corps received orders to return to its camp in this valley. When General Howard received this order, he directed me to gather the three batteries which had been detached from the corps and get them into our old camp to join the corps when it reached here. I left the corps to execute this order, after which the corps received orders to proceed on the campaign to Knoxville under General Sherman. In this way much to my regret, I failed to go to Knoxville.

---

24 Wiedrich and Sahm were to be with Hooker, Wheeler with Sherman, Dilger and Merkle with Maj. Gen. Philip H. Sheridan. Osborn's Eleventh Corps batteries: Battery I, First Ohio, Capt. Hubert Dilger; Battery G, Fourth U.S., Lieut. C. P. Merkle; Battery I, First New York, Capt. Michael Wiedrich; Thirteenth Independent New York, Capt. William C. Wheeler; Battery K, First Ohio, Lieut. Nicholas Sahm.
25 Dilger's and Wheeler's batteries went to Knoxville.

Headquarters
Artillery Brigade, 11 Corps
Lookout Valley, Tenn.
December 5, 1863

[To A. C. O.] I will write you a sketch of the battle of the 23rd, 24th, and 25th at Chattanooga as I saw it, and I hope I will be able to give you a clearer idea of it than you can get from the newspapers—more especially so, of that portion of the battle which I saw. I have seen no account of the battle, yet I can give you what I saw or learned on the field.[26]

On Sunday the 22nd, General Grant made the distribution of troops. General Howard reported to General Thomas at Chattanooga with the 11th Corps. General Osterhaus[27] with his division of General Sherman's Army reported to General Hooker in Lookout Valley as also did two brigades of the 4th Corps. General Jeff C. Davis with his division reported to General Sherman. The Army was thus distributed: General Hooker in Lookout Valley with Geary's division of the 12th Corps, Osterhaus' division, and two brigades of 4th Corps besides two batteries of the 11th Corps. General Thomas in and about Chattanooga had the 4th, 14th, and 11th Corps, less one division of the 4th Corps with General Sherman and two brigades with General Hooker. General Sherman, above Chattanooga and nearly opposite the mouth of Chickamauga Creek, had three divisions of his own and one division from the 14th Corps.[28]

General Bragg held the line from the mouth of Lookout Creek on the river in Lookout Valley to the mouth of Chickamauga Creek at the foot of Missionary Ridge or the river. This line made a semicircle around Chattanooga from two to five miles from it, varying in distance to accommodate the topography of the country. This line was thoroughly fortified. Commencing at Lookout Creek, it ran over Lookout Mountain, thence crossed Mission Valley, which is a mile and a half wide, to the crest of Missionary Ridge, thence following the crest of the Ridge, which is about 400 feet above the level of the plain, to within

---

26 Osborn enjoyed an excellent observation post on Orchard Knob from which to describe the Union assault on Missionary Ridge. He played an observer's role at Chattanooga not unlike his Fredericksburg experience in contrast to his more active participation at Williamsburg, Savage Station, Chancellorsville, and Gettysburg. His description of the battle is an excellent one.

27 Brig. Gen. Peter Joseph Osterhaus.

28 The units of the three Union armies were mingled. Grant, *op. cit.*, p. 84, said the heavy rains and rising river prevented some units from serving with their respective commands.

CHATTANOOGA 175

a mile or so of the river where it turned back and was thrown over or near the railroad tunnel so as to face the river, at the extreme right following the crest of a lower range of hills to or across the Chickamauga Creek. It was a position which the enemy with their best military engineers had ample time to select and which after being thoroughly fortified they had published to the world was impregnable, in that their line could not be broken. To look at this position from any point in its front one would naturally conclude the enemy's claim was well-founded.

From his headquarters, which were on the crest of Missionary Ridge directly in front of the city, General Bragg could see every movement made by our Army in the valley as plainly as if he was looking on a checkerboard. This was an important circumstance in favor of the enemy all through the battle. At the time the battle opened, General Sherman's force was the only one which was not in plain view of General Bragg or his officers on Lookout Mountain. At that time General Sherman had not shown his force in the narrow valleys through which they had marched to their position.[29]

At dark on the 22nd General Grant sent out a circular saying there would be no movement the next day and that the troops should rest quietly. On the morning of the 23rd, all remained quiet in both armies and no one in General Thomas' Army, where I then was, expected a movement that day—I think not even the corps commanders. So matters remained until two o'clock in the afternoon when each corps commander received orders to turn out his command to support a reconnaissance if necessary. No one appeared to suspect what General Grant's real intention was until General Thomas' entire Army was on its feet as if falling in for a grand review. Officers and men then began to believe that a serious movement had begun.

I refer only to General Thomas' army, the other armies at that time having received no orders. Since the battle, prisoners have said that General Bragg spoke of this movement of the troops as the Army getting ready for a grand review and gave no orders looking to a defensive movement. Indeed, this Army of 40,000 or 50,000 men did fall in, as if for a review. When they were sufficiently in hand, they were rapidly deployed into two lines of battle covering the plain in front of Missionary Ridge.

The line of battle was then moved directly towards the face of the mountain, driving in the enemy's strong picket line and occupying their advanced line of works. The movement was a complete surprise

---

29 The move of Sherman's army into position had been hidden behind Stringer's Ridge.

but the enemy made enough resistance to be classed as a sharp preliminary fight although some of the line made no resistance worthy of mention. Very little firing was done considering the magnitude of the movement. General Thomas moved his line forward about a mile and a quarter and halted as suddenly and unexpectedly as he had moved forward. He at once entrenched his line thoroughly and not more than half or three-quarters of a mile from the foot of the Ridge. At dark all appeared quiet again. General Bragg had now only to wait developments. Evidently, so far as this first movement extended he was beaten!

During the following night General Sherman arrived at the river nearly opposite the mouth of Chickamauga Creek. At daylight after some opposition from the pickets, he laid his pontoon bridge over the river, crossed, and moving up along the foothills, he forced the enemy back and occupied the first range of low hills parallel to the river. This was in the morning of the 24th.

General Bragg, from his subsequent movements, appears to have concluded he had now discovered General Grant's plan of battle. He was firm in the belief that no danger was to be apprehended from General Hooker against the mountain. That could take care of itself. Missionary Ridge was too steep to be taken by assault; consequently, there was but one thing left for General Grant to do, that of driving in his right flank which he had reached by crossing the river.

The road used by the enemy to move troops upon from one flank to the other followed the crest of the Ridge. From the plain near Chattanooga, we could see a heavy column moving from General Bragg's left to his right from sunrise till noon.[30] These men were being concentrated against General Sherman, and the fighting on his front grew very heavy. After General Sherman had pushed the enemy back as far as he could easily do, he entrenched his line thoroughly after which the enemy were not able to dislodge him.

When a large proportion of General Bragg's Army had been moved to his extreme right to hold General Sherman in check or to dislodge him or else to insure his front against any movement by General Thomas, General Grant was ready for General Hooker to move and his troops were put in motion. This movement from the camps commenced in the early morning.

The General advanced a small force directly against that detachment of the enemy guarding the main bridge on the highway across Lookout Creek and making as strong a demonstration there as he

---

30 Bragg, convinced that Sherman presented the greater threat, moved Lieut. Gen. William J. Hardee's corps from his left flank to his right flank.

could with the force in hand. He succeeded in drawing the force on that face of the mountain to the threatened point. General Geary, meanwhile, went three miles up Lookout Creek; taking a trail which ran well up on the side of the mountain and near the palisades, he moved by the flank towards the river and in rear of the enemy's position at the Lookout Creek Bridge and captured much of the entire force or about 2,000 men. General Hooker then crossed the remainder of his troops by the captured bridge and moved up the side of the mountain as nearly in line of battle as the nature of the ground would permit, making a junction with the men having crossed the bridge with General Geary's division. This movement was resisted by all the men the enemy had left upon the mountain.

I have inspected the slope of the mountain over which this advance was made and fighting done and I am unable to conceive how our men could climb this very steep side of the mountain. I do not believe it could have been done unless it was for the intense excitement men labor under when under fire. However, they did climb the slope, got over the immense boulders with which the side of the mountain is covered for many hundreds of feet, and drove the enemy before them. The steepness of the hill was the chief protection of our men from the fire of the enemy which mainly passed over their heads.

About five o'clock in the afternoon the most of the face of the mountain, looking from the city, was taken. The enemy succeeded in covering and holding the road from the crest of the mountain to Mission Valley, and on that line the fighting continued till ten o'clock at night. The road by which they could retire was held from the top plateau of the top of the mountain to the valley and across the valley to Missionary Ridge.

Between five o'clock and dark a dense white cloud floated up against the side of the mountain enveloping both Gen. Hooker's force and that of the enemy. I stood near Fort Wood on the plain.[31] From the time the lines of battle reached the open field on the face of the mountain we could distinctly see the two lines of battle as they passed over the open field and around this face of the mountain called the White House Plantation;[32] after they were covered by the cloud, we saw no more of them but could distinctly hear the musketry from the two lines. The cloud did not rise again till night.

When General Hooker had become actively engaged so as to absorb the attention of General Bragg, General Sherman slackened away

---

31 Fort Wood was an elevated position well fortified with 22 artillery pieces in Thomas's defensive line during the siege.
32 Osborn most likely refers to the Robert Craven house and farm.

with his fire and rested in his trenches as quietly as the enemy would permit. He had however, during the fighting of the day, advanced and entrenched his line in a better position than he had held in the morning.

The fighting on the 24th had been much more severe and stubborn than that on the 23rd. That on Lookout Mountain was successful and had done much towards destroying the hold on this, which had been considered an impregnable position of the enemy. Lookout Mountain had been long considered the strongest position in the mountains and had been proved to be the weakest and at dark was practically in our hands. General Thomas had thrown his left forward but had failed to connect with General Sherman's right. General Howard occupied the left of General Thomas' Army.

I had been assigned by General Grant to duty with the two batteries with General Sheridan[33] for this battle and was with him near the right of General Thomas' Army. I did not again report to General Howard until the battle closed.

On the morning of the 25th, our lines had again been changed. In the night the enemy abandoned Lookout Mountain and crossed to the opposite side of Chattanooga Creek. There remained a gap between General Thomas' left and General Sherman's right, which it was necessary to close. This was partially accomplished by suddenly throwing General Howard's left forward and then closing the gap with General Baird's division.[34] This was done at about ten o'clock in the forenoon. The 11th Corps suffered severely in this advance.

General Hooker was ordered forward to connect with General Thomas' right. This connection was not fully made and the General failed to accomplish what General Grant expected of him. Still so far as practical results went, the line from General Sherman's left to General Hooker's right was complete and we had a connected line embracing the entire Army. Part of this line had two lines of battle and part but one. I have not heard of any portion of it having more than two. This much being accomplished, the Army took a breathing spell and the field was quiet about three hours.

General Bragg still held Missionary Ridge, but General Sherman was entrenched on the end of it next the river—General Thomas in the plain facing the ridge and General Hooker swinging into the pass

---

33 The two batteries belonged to Merkle and Dilger. In his battle report, Sheridan made "special mention" "for valuable services" rendered by the officers of Battery G, Fourth U.S. Artillery, Merkle's battery. *OR*. Series 1, Vol. 31, Chap. 43, p. 193.

34 Brig. Gen. Absalom Baird's Third Division of the Fourteenth Corps.

towards Rossville upon the left and the other end of the ridge from Sherman.

At two o'clock in the afternoon we received orders that at the firing of a signal gun from Fort Wood in the rear of the city, the entire line would advance and carry the enemy's position by assault. The signal being given, the entire line moved forward. The enemy was the strongest in front of General Sherman and met him with the most desperate resistance. Elsewhere, they met our line with whatever resistance they could. I was a little to the right of the center of General Thomas' Army and had a perfect view of the charge up the ridge of the entire line of General Thomas' Army. General Sherman's line I could only see or determine the position of by the smoke. I was not able to see any part of General Hooker's line.

Whatever it was possible to do with the two batteries, I did to aid in the assault. I presume few battles ever fought have offered finer exhibitions of the charge of one army against another than did this. The charge of the enemy at Gettysburg was of a more desperate character, but the force making the charge was comparatively but a small portion of General Lee's Army. Here the entire Army moved to the assault. In this charge there could not have been less than five or six miles of the line moving at once. I had a perfect view of more than two miles of it. On General Thomas' front the line moved over the plain to the foot of the mountain in good order. At the foot the enemy had a strong line of works with probably one-fourth of a full line of battle but being protected by the works were able to make a strong resistance. This line was taken and many prisoners captured.

Our line made a short halt at this line of works to reform before climbing the hill and having done this, it advanced up the face of the mountain. In our front the hill was very steep, as steep as a man could easily climb if he were laboring under no excitement. The men advanced but a few yards before the steepness and unevenness of the ground caused the line to break apart in many places and it was but a few moments before all resemblance to a line of battle was lost. Instead of a line of battle we had a great number of men climbing up the face of the mountain apparently without organization and without order. Where the ground was favorable, they moved with comparative ease, but wherever the enemy's fire could reach them they sought cover and protection in every possible manner, taking advantage of the undulations of the ground, small ravines, and any and every other thing to protect themselves from the fire of the enemy. Still, every man was going up as rapidly as he could climb the steep face of the mountain; none came back or even hesitated. Here and there a mounted officer was seen among the men taking all the chances of being hit on account of his conspicuous position on horseback.

The enemy's line on the crest had been much reduced,[35] and yet there were men enough to do a good deal of fighting and an abundance of artillery for a full line of battle. Both infantry and artillery of the enemy fought well. The steepness of the hill was a great protection to our men. The enemy's musket fire was too high, and for considerable of the distance the artillery could not be sufficiently depressed so that even cannister did mostly go over the heads of the men climbing the hill.[36] In the matter of time it did not require many minutes for our men to climb the mountain 400 feet high and which was bare of timber except here and there a tree.

General Sheridan's division reached the crest first and upon breaking the enemy's line and occupying their trenches commenced a flank fire both ways. This caused the enemy to slacken their fire on the advancing men, and in a few minutes the crest for a considerable distance, a mile or so, was occupied by our troops.

It is not to be assumed that the point where the enemy's line was first broken was the only place at which it could be broken. In a very few minutes after General Sheridan's men occupied the enemy's works, the men of other commands also occupied it. Indeed, for a little while it was in doubt whether General Sheridan's men or General Wood's[37] men were first in the enemy's works. At each point where our men reached the works, they at once opened fire and moved to the right and left on the enemy's flanks and drove them in.

As nearly as one could judge time under the circumstances, it was not more than 15 or 20 minutes after the first men gained the crest before the enemy in all General Bragg's Army were in complete rout. While this assault was being made, General Sherman was making his fight against a full line of infantry and artillery thoroughly entrenched. He was gradually throwing his left forward and gaining the enemy's rear when the line on the crest of Missionary Ridge gave way. The breaking of the enemy in General Thomas' front forced those in General Sherman's front to fall back, and the retreat of the entire force was at once precipitated.

In this final charge of the Army General Hooker's movements were to a great extent independent of the remainder of the Army. He was separated from the line and had encountered a detached body of the

---

35 The Confederate line had been reduced in numbers by the move of Longstreet's corps to Knoxville.

36 The Confederate defensive line had been constructed on the topographical crest rather than the military crest of Missionary Ridge so that Union troops advanced under the Confederate fire.

37 Brig. Gen. Thomas J. Wood, commander, Third Division, Fourth Corps.

enemy near or at Rossville, which so maneuvered as to detain him and prevented his moving towards the rear of the enemy's position as General Grant had intended and expected of him. It appears General Grant expected he would pass around to the rear of the enemy so as to intercept and take many of the enemy prisoners when they should leave his own front. In this he failed.[38]

Nearly all of General Bragg's artillery was captured, many thousands of small arms and vast quantities of military stores. There were 52 field guns captured near General Bragg's Headquarters. I rode to the crest with General Sheridan. He hastily looked over the captured artillery and then directed me to take charge of it. This I did and later turned it over to an Ordnance Officer.

General Sheridan followed a small body of the enemy, a brigade or two, beyond the ridge and forced them farther away from our line, but night came on in a few moments and gave the enemy the opportunity to escape further punishment and also gave our men a chance to sleep. The Army had gained a splendid victory, and this much talked of, much fortified, and really very strong pass in the mountains, held and defended by a force which General Bragg considered all sufficient to hold it against any army, was captured.[39]

The pursuit was commenced the next morning. On the evening of the 25th, I had reported back to General Howard with the two batteries I had with me. I served during the entire battle on the staff of General Sheridan.

On the morning of the 26th, the 11th Corps moved to Red Clay on the Dalton and Cleveland Railroad. We did not meet the enemy but found and destroyed some military stores and destroyed a section of the railroad, after which we returned to the neighborhood of Chattanooga. The weather was cold and the roads bad. General Hooker found the enemy near Ringgold and attacked them, losing heavily in doing so and gained no material advantage.[40] The enemy were in a mountain pass where they had much the advantage in position. At all other places where the enemy were found, they were easily driven.

---

38 Hooker's failure here may have contributed to his not being promoted to replace Brig. Gen. James B. McPherson upon the latter's death at Atlanta. Sherman chose Howard, Hooker's junior to replace McPherson. Hooker resigned, ending his field service.

39 Bragg's over-confidence in the strength of his defensive position may have contributed to his defeat.

40 Maj. Gen. Patrick R. Cleburne's stalwart defense of Bragg's right against Sherman and his stubborn rearguard defense while other Confederate units surrendered or fled in disorder saved Bragg's army from a worse disaster. In his strong defensive position at Ringgold he turned back Union efforts to cut off the Confederate retreat.

It did not appear to be in General Grant's plans to follow the enemy, and all detachments sent out to feel for them and shove them farther off were soon brought back and the movement made to relieve General Burnside at Knoxville.

On Sunday General Sherman started for Knoxville taking with him the 11th Corps, 4th Corps, General Davis'[41] division of the 14th Corps, and one division of his own Army. He has two of my batteries with him, Wheeler and Dilger. I have confidence that he will relieve General Burnside unless General Longstreet shall have defeated him before General Sherman can render assistance.

This short campaign has completely used up all our artillery horses, and I am doing all in my power to get mine in working condition again.

My conclusions in regard to General Grant are that in point of ability, as a General he is head and shoulders above any other General under whom I have served, not alone because he won this battle for I have been in battles which were won before. But from beginning to the end, the plan of this battle was the work of a master, a military engineer, and a genius; and the execution of the work, the fighting of the battle, was the work of a master in military science and grand tactics.[42]

General Grant evidently has first, unlimited confidence in himself and second in General Sherman. From all I have seen and learned, both are worthy of the confidence from the Army which he has in himself and in General Sherman.

Please forward this letter to S. C. as I cannot rewrite it.[43]

Headquarters
Artillery Brigade, 11 Corps
Bridgeport, Ala.
December 14, 1863

[To S. C. O.] We moved from Lookout Valley to this place in order to more easily feed the horses. It is difficult even now to supply the

---

41 Brig. Gen. J. C. Davis, commander of the Second Division, Fourteenth Corps.
42 Grant's Chattanooga Campaign had been as brilliantly planned and executed as the one at Vicksburg although he admitted he had been aided by Confederate President Davis's strategy to send Longstreet to Knoxville in an effort to separate the warring factions among the Confederate High Command. As Grant pointed out, Chattanooga was the key to the west and without it, Knoxville was worthless. The fall of Chattanooga was the turning point in the western theater. Grant, *op. cit.*, p. 96.
43 In December, Osborn and his batteries returned to winter quarters at Bridgeport.

Army at Chattanooga. I think we shall remain where we are until spring.

The Army has been successful in every particular, and the force which went north to drive General Longstreet from Knoxville will have returned to its old camp in a couple of days having fully accomplished its object.[44] I believe our campaign next summer will be active and successful, and I feel confident that in one year from now we shall have completed our work and the Confederacy will be subject matter for history. I like the President's message and think it very timely.[45] It is time too the enemy knew what to look for in the future.

I should have been glad to have taken Thanksgiving dinner with you, but General Bragg had us otherwise employed. The weather now is all we could wish, like early September with you.

*Headquarters
Artillery Brigade, 11 Corps
Bridgeport, Ala.
January 10, 1864*

[To S. C. O.] This is the coldest winter I have seen south, much colder than either of those I passed near Washington. The ground is and has been frozen several inches deep for several weeks. Two men froze to death a few nights ago at this place.

This is a mountainous and worthless country for any purpose except its mines, and none of them are now worked.

*Headquarters
Artillery Brigade, 11 Corps
Bridgeport, Ala.
February 2, 1864*

[To A. C. O.] I am kept busy by routine duty. I am a little confined as two of my staff officers are on leave of absence. I have applied for a leave of absence of a few days for myself and hope soon to visit you.

---

44 Sherman left for Knoxville on November 28th to assist Burnside. On November 29th, Burnside repulsed Longstreet's attack against Fort Sanders. After learning of Bragg's defeat and Sherman's approach, Longstreet withdrew into eastern Tennessee and Sherman returned to Chickamauga.

45 Osborn probably refers to Lincoln's annual message, read to Congress on December 9, 1863, and his Amnesty and Reconstruction Proclamation on December 8, 1863.

I have made application for an appointment to the position of contract surgeon for young Samuel L. Merrill who has been studying medicine with Dr. George N. Hubbard, of Carthage, New York. I think he will be appointed.

Headquarters
Artillery Brigade, 11 Corps
Bridgeport, Ala.
February 3, 1864

[To S. C. O.] You appear to be having a terrible winter in the north. It has also been severely cold here, but it is now pleasant and has been so for several days. We still remain in the valley of the Tennessee River, between the mountains but so close to them that a ten minutes ride takes us to the foot of the hills. Our camp is pleasant; still, I wish we were nearer a large city. Nashville is 150 and Louisville about 300 miles away, and these are the nearest cities where we can get anything which does not come from the Quartermaster's or Commissary Department of the Army.

This place now has a worldwide reputation because of its military importance, and that is all there is of it. It is a military depot. It never was a town and never will be.

You ask me how we live. I assure you very well. We have a good table and the food is well cooked. Indeed I believe this headquarters has the reputation of setting a good table. Of my staff there are three, myself making four. These officers are Lieutenants Freeman, Mickle, and Wickham—all bright, accomplished, and agreeable young men. As a general thing, however, we have other officers at the table. Our living is all well enough while in camp, but while on the marches it is sometimes a little rough.

I have no one with me now who was with me when I commanded the old battery. I wish I had. They were officers and men, the best soldiers I have ever seen.

You ask me how I amuse myself. I can hardly answer the question. A winter's camp is an Elysium of laziness, the sluggard's paradise, and a purgatory for an energetic man. I sleep and eat and read everything I can get hold of, and by the way that is not much. I watch the batteries and keep them up to their work and discipline so they may not be injured by too much idleness. I write letters whenever there is a call for writing them but keep up no social correspondence outside of the family. When my mood is that way, I call on other officers. At these headquarters we neither drink or play cards but when all else fails, I smoke.

You ask for a letter of gossip and I have written it.

Louisville, Ky.
March 13, 1864

[To S. C. O.] I have a little unpleasant news for you this time. A week ago today while on my way from Nashville to Bridgeport while passing through Stevenson, Ala., the boxcar I was in was thrown from the track and I thrown out of it and my left leg broken. The fracture is about two inches above the ankle. Both bones are broken square off, no other injury or even bruises of any kind. It is a simple fracture and is now doing exceedingly well.

I have nothing to fear or give myself uneasiness about. I have had the best of care from the moment of the accident. The bone was set at once by the surgeons of the 12th corps, three or four of them being present. The employees of the Sanitary Commission took care of me while I was at Stevenson. I telegraphed General Howard of the accident and he sent one of his headquarter's surgeons with orders to take care of me and bring me here. I arrived yesterday morning having been carried 350 miles without injury of any kind.

I found Dr. S. L. Merrill about six hours before the mishap on the train on his way to see me at Bridgeport. He was with me at the time of the accident and remained with me until now, but goes to the Army with the surgeon who brought me here. I am much pleased with Merrill. He will write you more fully.

I am alone responsible for not sending you word sooner, as I wished to know how serious the injury might be and where I should be left. I am now at the house of Mr. Matthews and will remain here where I shall have the best of care. I do not think it worthwhile for either mother or you to come here. The trip would be too hard for her and you cannot well leave home now, and I shall be well cared for. I have very little pain at present though I get very tired from lying square on my back as I am now compelled to do.

Louisville, Ky.
March 20, 1864

[To S. C. O.] My leg is doing very finely, in fact much better than I had even hoped it would. I am nearly without pain and lie much more comfortably than I did a few days ago. I shall necessarily be confined some time yet. There are no splints on the leg, but it lies in a wooden box with a little cotton on each side of it to keep the foot from tipping over, as in that case it might become permanently crooked. The surgeons all say it is doing remarkably well and that I will recover the full use of the leg.

General Grant passed through here yesterday going east. He will make his headquarters with the Army of the Potomac. There is a statement in the papers that the 11th Corps will go east.

Louisville, Ky.
March 20, 1864

[To A. C. O.] I am improving in about the same ratio as when you left me. The leg is comfortable and I rest with about the same ease as before. The Medical Director for this post was in just now and says it is doing well. He thinks I can begin to use the foot in about three weeks. That is he says so, but I think he says it for encouragement and not because he believes it.

Generals Grant and Sherman passed through here on their way to Washington last night.[46] General Sherman will return in three days and General Grant will make his headquarters with the Army of the Potomac.

Editors' Note: Osborn returned to active duty on July 28th as Chief of Artillery of the Army of the Tennessee and participated in the struggle for Atlanta that ended with Sherman's occupation of the city on September 2nd. The balance of his service for the remainder of the war is told in his journal and letters which were published as *The Fiery Trail* published in 1986 as the final sequel of his Civil War record.

---

46 Grant returned to Washington after meeting with Sherman prior to launching the spring campaign against Lee, as Commander-in-Chief of all Union armies, with his headquarters in the field with the Army of the Potomac. After Congress had renewed the grade of Lieutenant General, Lincoln nominated Grant on March 1st to the army's highest rank and the Senate confirmed the appointment on March 2, 1864. At long last, Lincoln had found a general who could win major victories. Chattanooga proved to be the turning point in the careers of four Union generals—Grant, Sherman, Thomas, and Sheridan—the four men who would lead Union forces to victory.

Appendix

Report of Maj. Thomas W. Osborn, Chief of Artillery. [From the *OR*, Series 1, Vol. 31, Part 2, Chapter 43, Pp. 384-386.]

Hdqrs. Arty., 11th Corps, Army of the Cumberland,
Bridgeport, Ala., January 5, 1864.

Colonel: I have the honor to report the part borne by the artillery of this command in the engagements of the 23d, 24th, and 25th November, near Chattanooga, and the march toward Knoxville, Tenn.

The batteries of this command are:

Second Division: I, First New York Artillery, Capt. M. Wiedrich; G, Fourth U.S. Artillery, Lieut. C. F. Merkle.

Third Division: I, First Ohio Artillery, Capt. H. Dilger; Thirteenth New York (Independent), Capt. W. Wheeler; K, First Ohio Artillery, Lieut. N. Sahm.

My instructions, as received from Major-General Howard, were to leave the batteries of Captain Wiedrich and Lieutenant Sahm in the valley to assist Major-General Hooker, if required, and to take a sufficient number of horses from these batteries to fully equip the remaining three batteries; to direct Captain Wheeler to report to General Brannan, chief of artillery of the Army at Chattanooga, for assignment to protect the troops of General Sherman in crossing the Tennessee River above the town. Captain Dilger and Lieutenant Merkle were to accompany the corps to Chattanooga. These dispositions were made as directed on the 22d.

On the afternoon of the 23d, by direction of General Howard, I placed the battery of Lieutenant Merkle on a slight eminence on the left of General Sheridan's division, and reported to General Sheridan for orders. I also placed Captain Dilger on the right of the same division. This division at the time was being moved forward with the main line of battle. A few shots were fired by Lieutenant Merkle this p.m.

On the morning of the 24th he was moved forward, taking position with the main line of battle, and occasionally, when circumstances appeared to require, fired a few shots, generally with good effect. On the 25th, he again opened about noon, clearing the ground for an advance of the division. A little later moved forward with the advanced infantry, and from the outset of the charge by which Mission Ridge was carried he did fine work, by assisting materially to clear the enemy from their trenches and disturbing their fire greatly while our troops were climbing the hill.

The position to which Captain Dilger had been assigned unfortunately did not admit of his taking an active part, his position being such as to cover a plain over which it was feared the enemy would attempt to reach our rear.

Early in the morning, on the 24th, Captain Wheeler took position, under the immediate direction of Major Cotter, near and a little below the crossing of General Sherman. He was only required to fire about 20 rounds at long range, the enemy not massing sufficiently near his position. Colonel Barnett, of the Ohio artillery, in command of all the artillery at this position, speaks of Captain Wheeler's practice and evident good judgment.

Captain Wiedrich, in command of the batteries in the valley, engaged his batteries in the advance of General Hooker at the capture of Lookout Mountain, his own battery remaining as when the corps left the valley, on the range of hills running parallel to and between Lookout and the valley below. Lieutenant Sahm's battery he placed on the crest between his position and the creek, and by this means gained an admirable cross-fire with batteries placed on the same range to their right. In the attack on the mountain they are reported to have done good service. Generals Hooker, Butterfield, and Osterhaus have spoken of their practice as excellent.

On the 26th, Lieutenant Sahm's battery was moved to Rossville with General Hooker's column and left at that point. On the same day Captain Dilger, Captain Wheeler, and Lieutenant Merkle reported to the corps then at Chickamauga Station. On the 27th, at Graysville, Captain Wheeler and Lieutenant Merkle were ordered to report to General Hooker at Ringgold. Both batteries again reported to the corps on the 28th, at Parker's Gap, not being engaged during this absence. A gun carriage of Captain Wheeler broke down on the march, and, being unable to repair the carriage, the captain sent the gun to his camp in the valley in a wagon. Captain Dilger accompanied the corps from Graysville to Red Clay on the 27th, and on the 28th returned to Parker's Gap.

Expecting the corps to move to Lookout Valley, the general directed me to move Lieutenant Merkle's battery at the head of the column, and, by reason of a separation at this moment, I did not participate in the trip to Knoxville. Having reached the valley, I brought the three batteries to their former camp and did what I could to again fit them for service.

Captain Dilger and Captain Wheeler accompanied the corps to Knoxville. Captain Wheeler reports having used his battery upon the enemy at the crossing of Hiwassee River, and again at the Tennessee River, opposite Loudon. I have received no report of Captain Dilger of this march. On the 20th December, the batteries returned to their old camp in the valley. It is a gratification to say that during these operations not one artillery officer or man was lost or injured, and everywhere officers and men did well. The artillery practice was everywhere good. The command lost very largely in horses.

When the corps moved from its camp on the 22d the horses were greatly reduced, both by the long passage from Virginia to this place and by starvation in the valley. I could then only horse three batteries indifferently. The roads over which we marched were very bad; much of the time we could get no forage either from the depots or in the country. The horses were continually giving out from exhaustion and want of food. Captain Wheeler and Captain Dilger report that they were unable to move with the column to and from Knoxville without impressing a considerable number of horses and mules in the country. Under the circumstances I think each battery did all that could be expected of it.

I regret the artillery of the corps could not have remained with the corps and fought in the principal engagement with it. It being, as it was, distributed through the army, it could gain little or no credit of its own, as all it may have earned would naturally be claimed by and accredited to the commanding officer of the troops with which it was serving during the engagement. The losses were confined to the loss of horses and ordnance property, a considerable amount of which was rendered unfit for further service.

I am, colonel, respectfully, your obedient servant,

THOS. WARD OSBORN,
Major, And Chief Of Artillery, Eleventh Corps.

Lieut. Col. T. A. Meysenburg,
Assistant Adjutant-General.

Bibliography

Primary Materials

Osborn, Thomas Ward. Unpublished letters and papers. Hamilton, NY: Colgate University Special Collections.

Documents

U.S. War Department. (1880-1901) *The War of the Rebellion: A Compilation of the Official Records of the Union and Confederate Armies*. 128 Vols. Washington, DC: U.S. Government Printing Office.

Newspapers

Mohawk Valley Register. Fort Plain, NY. (Fort Plain, NY Free Library, Matthewson Letters).

Carthage Republican. Carthage, NY.

Books

Alexander, E. P. (1977) *Military Memoirs of a Confederate*. Dayton, OH: Morningside Reprint of C. Scribner's 1907 Edition.

Bigelow, J. (1910) *The Campaign of Chancellorsville*. New Haven: Yale U. Press.

Connelly, T. L. (1979) *Civil War Tennessee: Battles and Leaders*. Knoxville: U. of TN Press. Published in cooperation with the TN Historical Commission.

Crumb, H. S. (Ed.) (1991) *The Eleventh Corps Artillery at Gettysburg: The Papers of Major Thomas Ward Osborn*. Hamilton, NY: Edmonston Publishing, Inc.

Faust, P. (Ed.) (1986) *Historical Times Illustrated Encyclopedia of the Civil War*. New York: Harper & Row.

Fox, W. F. (Ed.) (1902) *New York at Gettysburg*. 3 Vols. Albany, NY: Lyon Co.

Fox, W. F. (1904) *Slocum and His Men: A History of the Twelfth and Twentieth Corps*. New York State Monuments Commission. Albany, NY: Lyon Co.

Freeman, D. S. (1944) *Lee's Lieutenants*. Vol. 1. New York: Scribners.

Gallagher, G. (Ed.) (1989) *Fighting for the Confederacy*. (by E. P. Alexander) Chapel Hill, NC: U. of NC Press.

Grant, U. S. (1885) *Personal Memoirs of U. S. Grant*. 2 Vols. New York: C. L. Webster Co.

Hamlin, A. C. (1896) *Eleventh Corps: The Battle of Chancellorsville*. Bangor, ME: Privately printed.

Harwell, R & Racine, P. N. (Eds.) (1986) *The Fiery Trail: A Union Officer's Account of Sherman's Last Campaigns*. Knoxville: U. of TN Press.

Howard, O. O. (1907) *Autobiography*. 2 Vols. New York: Baker & Taylor.

Johnson, R. V. & Buel, C. C. (Eds.) (1956) *Battles and Leaders of the Civil War*. 4 Vols. New York: Castle Books Reprint of Century Co. 1884-1889 Edition.

Livermore, T. (1900) *Numbers and Losses in the Civil War in America 1861-65*. Boston & New York: Houghton Mifflin.

Long, E. B. with Long, B. (1971) *The Civil War Day by Day: An Almanac, 1861-1865*. New York: De Capo Press.

Luvaas, J. & Nelson, H. (1988) *U.S. Army War College Guide to the Battles of Chancellorsville and Fredericksburg*. Carlisle, PA: South Mountain Press.

McClellan, G. B. (1864) *Report on the Organization of the Army of the Potomac and of its Campaigns in Virginia and Maryland: July 26, 1861-November 7, 1862*. Washington, DC: U.S. Government Printing Office.

Naisawald, L. V. L. (1983) *Grape and Cannister: The Story of the Field Artillery in the Army of the Potomac, 1861-1865*. Washington, DC: Zenger Reprint of Oxford U. Press 1960 Edition.

Nevins, A. (Ed.) (1962) *A Diary of Battle: The Personal Journals of Colonel Charles S. Wainwright, 1861-1865*. New York: Harcourt Brace & World.

Phisterer, F. (1912) *New York in the War of the Rebellion, 1861-1865*. 3rd Ed. 5 Vols. Albany, NY: Lyon Co.

Sears, S. W. (1988) *George B. McClellan: The Young Napoleon*. New York: Ticknor & Fields.

Sears, S. W. (Ed.) (1989) *The Civil War Papers of George B. McClellan: Selected Correspondence, 1860-1865*. New York: Ticknor & Fields.

Sherman, W. T. (1891) *Personal Memoirs*. 2 Vols. New York: C. L. Webster Co.

Symonds, C. L. (1983) *A Battlefield Atlas of the Civil War*. Annapolis, MD: Nautical & Aviation Publishing Co. of America.

Warner, E. J. (1904) *Generals in Blue: Lives of the Union Commanders*. Baton Rouge: L. S. U. Press.

Index
Letters from the Field

Alexandria, VA, 71–72, 85, 163
Allen's Farm, Battle of, See Peach Orchard
Ames, Lt. A. N., 98
Amnesty & Reconstruction Proclamation, 183
Antietam, 88
Antietam, Battle of, 108
Aquia Creek, 11
Arkansas Post, 103
Arlington Heights, VA, 85
Army of Northern Virginia, 170
Army of the Cumberland, 163, 167–168
Army of the Potomac, 11–12, 16, 85, 87, 106–107, 123, 141, 186
Arnold, Lt. J., 137
Artillery Reserve, 140–143, 145

Bailey, Guilford D., 3, 5–8, 43
Baird, Brig. Gen. Absalom, 178
Banks, Maj. Gen. Nathaniel P., 42
Barry, Maj. Gen. William F., 8, 108
Bates, Capt. Thomas H., 43–44, 47–48
Battery A, 1st NY Light Artillery, 43
Battery A, 4th U.S. Artillery, 75
Battery B, 1st CT Artillery, 141
Battery B, 1st NJ Artillery, 125
Battery B, 1st NY Light Artillery, 8, 9, 64
Battery C, 4th U.S. Artillery, 75
Battery D, 1st NY Light Artillery, 2-9, 125, 137
Battery E, 1st NY Light Artillery, 33
Battery H, 1st NY Light Artillery, 6, 43
Battery H, 1st U.S. Artillery, 125, 137
Battery K, 4th U.S. Artillery, 97, 125, 137

Battery M, 1st CT Artillery, 141
Battery M, 1st NY Light Artillery, 33
Beauregard, Gen. Pierre G. T., 57
Beaver Dam Creek, 67
Belle Plain, VA, 98
Berlin, WV, 148
Berry, Maj. Gen. Hiram G., 107, 109, 113, 123, 125, 127–129, 137, 139
Birney, Brig. Gen. David, 131, 133
Boonsboro, MD, 145
Bottom's Bridge, 41, 53
Bragg, Maj. Gen. Braxton, 100, 169, 171–178, 180–181, 183
Brainard, Orville V., 35
Bramhall, Capt. Walter M., 14, 24, 26–28, 63, 85
Brandy Station, Battle of, 144
Bridgeport & Chattanooga RR, 169
Bridgeport, AL, 164–165, 167–169, 185
Brown's Ferry, 170
Buell, Maj. Gen. Don Carlos, 65
Bull Run, 71, 163
Bull Run, Battle of, 2
Burns, Brig. Gen. William W., 89–90, 93–94
Burnside, Maj. Gen. Ambrose E., 20, 65, 89–90, 94–95, 98, 104–105, 108, 172–173, 182
Butler, Maj. Gen. Benjamin F., 21

Camp Barry, 8
Campbell's Station, Battle of, 172
Carthage, NY, 184
Casey, Maj. Gen. Silas, 43–45
Catlett's Station, VA, 145
Centerville, VA, 88, 145
Chancellorsville, Battle of, 123-140
Chancellorsville House, 126, 133, 136, 139, 141
Chapin, Sgt. Darius, 69
Chattanooga, Battle of, 174-182
Chattanooga Creek, 178
Chickahominy River, 35–36, 41, 53,

INDEX

56, 62, 67–68, 78
Chickamauga Creek, 174–176
Chickamauga, Battle of, 166
Clark, Capt. A. Judson, 85, 125, 137
Coburn, Gov. Abner, 114–115
Colgate University, See Madison University
Conant, Cpl. Frederick W., 25, 35
Corinth, MS, 14
Couch, Maj. Gen. Darius N., 44–45
Craven house, 177
Crittenden, Maj. Gen. Thomas, 166
Cumberland Gap, 65
Custis Estate, 35

Dalton & Cleveland RR, 181
Davis, Brig. Gen. Jefferson C., 174, 182
de Russey, Capt. Gustavus A., 68
Derbey, Capt., 19
Dike, Harrison, 35
Dilger, Capt. Hubert, 144, 182
Dimmick, Lt. Justin E., 11, 125–127, 129, 134–135, 137
Duly, Lester, 35

Eakin, Lt. Chandler P., 24
East Tennessee, 173
Eleventh Corps, 114, 126, 128, 138, 143, 146, 162–165, 167, 169–170, 174, 178, 181–182, 186
Eleventh NY Independent Battery, 136
Elmira, NY, 4–7
Emancipation Proclamation, 105
Excelsior Brigade, 27

Fair Oaks, Battle of, 42-51
Fifteenth NY Independent Battery, 141
Fifth Corps, 111, 114, 162
Fifth NJ Infantry, 27
Fifth NY Independent Battery, 141
First Corps, 162
First CT Artillery, 141
First Division, 8th Corps, 125, 137
First NJ Artillery, 125
First U.S. Artillery, 125, 137

Fort Hindman, See Arkansas Post
Fort Magruder, VA, 24, 28, 32
Fort Taylor, VA, 85
Fort Wood, TN, 177, 179
Fortress Monroe, 12–15, 65, 70
Foster, Maj. Gen. John G., 101
Fourteenth Corps, 174, 182
Fourth Corps, 174, 182
Fourth NY Independent Battery, 73, 125–126, 131, 136
Fourth U.S. Artillery, 97, 125, 137
Franklin, Maj. Gen. William B., 53, 67, 73, 90, 92, 95–96, 104, 108
"Fred," Maj. Osborn's horse, 171
Fredericksburg, Battle of, 91-96, 138, 149
Fredericksburg, VA, 11–12, 104-105, 108, 113, 139
Freeman, Lt. George W., 137, 164, 184
Fremont, Maj. Gen. John C., 20

Gaines' Mill, Battle of, 56, 62, 67
Garrison, Emmanuel E., 25
Geary, Capt., 167
Geary, Maj. Gen. John W., 167, 169–170, 174, 177
Geneva, NY, 98
Gettysburg, Battle of, 146–147, 161, 179
Gordonsville, VA, 20
Gouverneur, NY, 4, 98
Grand Division, Center, 87, 90, 104
Grand Division, Left, 104
Grand Division, Right, 90–91, 97
Grant, Lt. Gen. Ulysses S., 103, 110, 169–170, 172–176, 178, 181–182, 186
Griffith, Brig. Gen. Richard, 75

Hagerstown, MD, 86
Hamlin, Col. A. C., 137
Hancock, Maj. Gen. Winfield S., 33–34
Harpers Ferry, WV, 145
Harrison's Landing, VA, 72
Hartwood Church, 125
Hays, Brig. Gen. William, 133
Hazzard, Capt. George W., 75

INDEX

Heintzelman, Maj. Gen. Samuel P., 32, 55–56, 72–78, 111–112
Hill, Lt. Gen. Ambrose P., 129, 138
Hill, Marvin, 35
Hooker, Maj. Gen. Joseph, 9, 11, 13, 15–16, 22, 24–28, 30, 32–35, 45–47, 50–51, 57, 61, 66, 68–69, 71–72, 74, 85, 87, 89–91, 95–98, 104, 106–113, 126, 131, 138–139, 141–142, 144–146, 160–161, 163–165, 168–169, 171–174, 176–181
Howard, Col. C. H., 148
Howard, Maj. Gen. O. O., 143–145, 164, 169, 173–174, 178, 181, 185
Hubbard, Dr. George N., 87, 184
Hunt, Brig. Gen. Henry J., 89, 111, 136, 143-144, 162

Jackson, MS, 148
Jackson, Lt. Gen. Thomas J. (Stonewall), 57, 65, 129, 138
James River, 12, 16, 42, 52, 57, 66, 74, 77
Jefferson County, NY, 2, 4
Johnston, Maj. Gen. Joseph E., 34–35

Kearney, Maj. Gen. Philip, 29, 32–33, 45, 47, 68, 72, 113
Keyes, Maj. Gen. Erasmus D., 43, 45–47
Kieffer, Maj. Luther, 3–8, 10
Knoxville, TN, 173, 182–183

Le Duc, Col. William G., 165
Lee, Gen. Robert E., 67, 71, 89, 111, 129, 144, 147–148, 162–163, 167, 179
Lewis County, NY, 4
Lincoln, Mrs. Mary Todd, 111
Lincoln, President Abraham, 105, 111, 138, 183
Liverpool Point, MD, 13–14
Longstreet, Lt. Gen. James, 167, 170, 172–173, 182–183
Lookout Creek, 174, 176–177
Lookout Mountain, 168–171, 173–175, 178

Lookout Valley, 167, 169, 171, 174, 182
Louisville, KY, 184

Madison (Colgate) University, 162
Malvern Cliff, 61, 63
Malvern Hill, 61, 63, 66, 131
Manassas, See Bull Run
Manassas Junction, 87
Marye's Heights, 94–95
Mason, Lt. Philip D., 24, 127
Matthews, Mr., 185
Matthewson, Lt. Angell, 98, 106
McCall, Brig. Gen. George A., 67
McClean, Lt. William T., 126–127
McClellan, Maj. Gen. George B., 11–13, 19–20, 25, 31–33, 35, 45, 48, 54–57, 62, 65–68, 85–86, 88, 93, 106
McCook, Maj. Gen. Alexander M., 166
McCurtis, Capt., M., 34
McDonald, Lt., 8
McDowell, Maj. Gen. Irvin, 20, 42
Meade, Maj. Gen. George G., 147, 161
Meagher, Brig. Gen. Thomas F., 76
Memphis & Charleston RR, 169
Merrill, Dr. Samuel L., 184–185
Merrimac (CSS Virginia), 14–15
Mickle, Lt., 184
Mink, Lt. Charles E., 6
Mission Valley, 174, 177
Missionary Ridge, TN, 171, 174–178, 180
Mississippi River, 100
Mohawk Valley Register, 98, 106
Monitor, 14–15
Morell, Brig. Gen. George W., 61, 67
Morgan, Brig. Gen. John H., 149
Mosby, John S., 148
Mott, Brig. Gen. Gershom, 125
"Mud March", 105
Mullen, Joseph, 3
Munger, Pvt. Oren, 161
Murfreesboro, Battle of, 100
Murfreesboro, 165

INDEX

Naglee, Brig. Gen. Henry, 13
Napoleon Guns, 12-pound, 71
Nashville & Chattanooga RR, 166
Nashville, TN, 164, 166, 184–185
New Jersey Brigade (Mott's), 134
New Kent Courthouse, VA, 25, 32, 35
New Orleans, 21
New York City, 109
Newton, Brig. Gen. John, 125
Ninth Corps, 90, 98
Ninth Independent NY Battery, 24
Norfolk, VA, 14–15
North Wilna, NY, 2, 5

Oak Grove, Engagement of, 55, 61
Ocquacon River, 88
Osborn, Amelia Van Deursen, 5
Osterhaus, Brig. Gen. Peter J., 174
Oswego, NY, 98

Palmer, Capt., 52
Pamunkey River, 35
Parker, Gov. Joel, 114
Parrott Guns, 10-pounder, 125
Parrott Guns, 20-pounder, 141
Patterson, Brig. Gen. Francis E., 88
Patterson, Maj. Gen. Robert, 88
Peach Orchard (Battle of Allen's Farm), 61, 73
Pettit, Capt. Rufus D., 8–9, 64, 75
Pittsburg Landing, See Shiloh
Pope, Maj. Gen. John, 65, 70, 72, 85
Port Hudson, Battle of, 147
Porter, Maj. Gen. Fitz-John, 53, 56, 62, 67–68, 70, 106
Potomac River, 88, 148
Puttkammer, Capt. Albert A. von, 136

Raccoon Mountain, 169
Railroad Bridge, 53
Railroad Merrimac, 75
Randolph, Capt. George E., 136
Rapidan River, 163
Rappahannock River, 90, 104, 125, 144, 163

Rappahannock Station, VA, 113
Red Clay, GA, 173, 181
Reserve Artillery, 162
Reynolds, Maj. Gen. John F., 125
Rhode Island Artillery, 145
Richardson, Lt. J. L., 98
Richardson, Maj. Gen. Israel B., 47–48
Richmond, VA, 36–37, 43, 66–68, 72, 111, 113
Rifled Guns, 3-inch, 141
Ringgold, GA, 181
Roll of Honor, 162
Rosecrans, Maj. Gen. William S., 100–101, 110, 163–164, 166
Rossville, GA, 181
Rumsey, Lt. William, 43
Russell, NY, 69

Sackets Harbor, NY, 86–87
Saint Lawrence County, NY, 4
Savage Station, VA, 61, 72, 74, 78, 134
Savage Station, Battle of, 72-78, 149
Sawyer, Azariah H., 2–3
School of Lt. Artillery Instruction, 7
Second Brigade, Volunteer Division, 141
Second Corps, 111, 162
Second Division, 107
Sedgwick, Maj. Gen. John, 125, 139
Seeley, Lt. Francis W., 125, 131, 134–135
Seven Pines, 61
Seven Pines, Battle of, 42–51
Seward, Sect. of State William H., 114–115
Sheridan, Maj. Gen. Philip H., 178, 180–181
Sherman, Maj. Gen. William T., 169–180, 182, 186
Shiloh, Battle of, 14, 21
Sickles, Maj. Gen. Daniel E., 27–28, 45–46, 50, 52, 69, 89, 96, 98, 131, 138
Sigel, Maj. Gen. Franz, 104
Sixth Corps, 111, 162
Sixty-fourth NY Volunteer Infantry, 5

INDEX

Smith, Capt. James E., 24, 29, 33, 75, 85
Smith, Maj. Gen. William F. ("Baldy"), 73–74, 78
South Mountain, Battlefield of, 146
Spratt, Capt. Joseph H., 3–6, 43–44, 46
Squire, Capt., 131
Stafford Court House, VA, 145
Stanton, Sect. of War Edwin M., 34
Starbuck, James F., 2, 7, 86
Stevenson, AL, 165, 185
Stolper, Lt. Augustus, 8, 29
Stone's River, Battle of, See Murfreesboro
Stoneman, Maj. Gen. George, 111–112
Stringer's Ridge, 175
Sumner, Maj. Gen. Edwin V., 32–34, 46–48, 57, 61, 68, 72–78, 91–93, 95, 98, 104, 108, 134
Sykes, Brig. Gen. George, 61, 63

Tennessee River, 166, 184
Tenth NY Heavy Artillery, 107–110
Third Corps, 68, 72–74, 77, 85–86, 90, 96, 98, 107, 111, 125, 143, 162
Thirtieth NY Independent Battery, 141
Thirty-fifth NY Infantry, 139
Thirty-second NY Independent Battery, 141
Thomas, Maj. Gen. George H., 165–168, 170–171, 174–176, 178–180
Tompkins, Maj. John A., 145
Turner, Lt. Col. Henry E., 6
Twelfth Corps, 114, 131, 134, 162–165, 167, 169, 174, 185
Twelve pounders, light, 125
Twenty-ninth NY Independent Battery, 141

Tyler, Brig. Gen. Robert O., 63, 142–143, 145

United States Ford, 125

Van Valkenburg, Brig. Gen. R. B., 5–6
Van Valkenburg, Maj. David, 6, 43
Vicksburg, MS, 100
Vicksburg, Battle of, 147

Wainwright, Col. Charles S., 6, 9–10, 23–24, 85, 97, 110
War Department, 109
Warrentown, VA, 148
Washington, DC, 62, 70–71, 108–109, 111, 161–162
Watertown, NY, 2–5
Wauhatchie, TN, 167
Webber, Capt. Charles H., 24, 30
Weeks, Mary, 5
West Point, NY, 3, 6
West Point, VA, 34
Western Virginia, 144
Wheeler, Capt. Charles C., 33
Wheeler, Capt. William C., 182
White House Plantation, 177
White House, VA, 35, 125
White Oak Swamp, 41–42, 73, 77
Wickham, Lt., 184
Willcox, Brig. Gen. Orlando B., 99
Williamsburg Road, 51, 73, 75–76
Williamsburg, Battle of, 21–35
Williamsburg, VA, 50, 97, 108, 113
Winslow, Capt. George B., 4–8, 10, 29, 48, 54, 70, 73, 86, 98, 125–127, 134, 139–140
Wood, Pvt. George, 35
Wood, Maj. Gen. Thomas, 180
Wool, Maj. Gen. John E., 42

York River, 15–16
Yorktown, VA, 14–16, 19, 21–22, 26–27, 30, 32–33, 53–54, 71

*The text of this book is set in 10 point
New Century Schoolbook type face;
the title page, cover, and dust jacket are in Palatino.
A Glatfelter neutral pH paper has been used to assure
the future permanence of the book,
and the binding is a vermin proof, moisture resistant,
impregnated Arrestox B cloth
made by Industrial Coatings Group, Inc. of Tennessee.
The printing and binding was done by McNaughton & Gunn, Inc.
Composition and design are by Edmonston Publishing, Inc.
Jacket design is by Ellen Walker.*

Also available from Edmonston Publishing, Inc.

Edmonston, W. E. Jr. (Ed.) *Unfurl the Flags.* (1989)

Fuller, Charles A. *Personal Recollections of the War of 1861.* (Reprint) (1990)

Crumb, H. S. (Ed.) *The Eleventh Corps Artillery at Gettysburg: The Papers of Major Thomas Ward Osborn.* (1991)

Mills, George A. *History of the 16th North Carolina Regiment in the Civil War.* (Reprint) (1992)